"*Leadership Lessons of White House Fellows* takes a close look at the young Americans who have participated in this program and at their interesting and absorbing stories and insights."
—*The Honorable Elaine L. Chao, former United States Secretary
of Labor, President and CEO of United Way of America,
Director of the Peace Corps*

"The lessons I learned as a White House Fellow have informed my leadership principles and influenced me deeply throughout my career. In this powerful and insightful book, Garcia shows readers how to use these same lessons within their lives."
—*Marshall Carter, Former Chairman and CEO,
State Street Bank and Trust; Senior Fellow, Harvard University's
John F. Kennedy School of Government*

"This is a reflective and compelling account of how a remarkable program shaped the lives of many of America's best leaders – and continues to shape the leaders that we'll need in our future."
—*Clayton M. Christensen, Robert & Jane Cizik Professor
of Business Administration, Harvard Business School;
bestselling author of* Innovator's Prescription, Disrupting Class,
and The Innovator's Dilemma

"This book is full of illuminating leadership lessons that teach and inspire."
—*Roger B. Porter, IBM Professor of Business
and Government, Harvard University*

"Garcia has done a tremendous service by writing this book. There is absolutely no better training ground for the next generation of leaders than the White House Fellows Program."
—*Myron E. Ullman, III, Chairman and CEO
of J.C. Penney and Chairman of the National Retail Federation*

"Charlie Garcia's book recounts the stories of Americans who have given their lives to public service, and explains in their own words the "how" that made them effective servant leaders. Read, learn, enjoy and be inspired."
—*Major General Bernard Loeffke (U.S. Army, ret.),
former Commanding General Army South.*

"The White House Fellowship catapults the lives and careers of every person lucky enough to go through it. This book gives you a glimpse of how and why—and shares key leadership lessons for the future."
—*Kinney Zalesne, coauthor,* Microtrends: The Small Forces
Behind Tomorrow's Big Changes

"A must read for anyone interested in leadership development."
—*Garrey Carruthers, Ph.D., Governor*
of New Mexico 1987–1990, Vice President
and Dean, New Mexico State University

"A great read, with fascinating White House Fellow stories about the power of leadership."
—*Susan Stautberg, President of Partnercom,*
Cofounder Women Corporate Directors
and The Belizean Grove

"With this clear, focused and honest book, Charles Garcia shares the secrets of successful leaders, rooted in service to country and community. Now, all Americans can be inspired to serve and to lead."
—*Jami Floyd, Anchor, Court TV*

"Inspiring, thoughtful, and engaging—a real winner! This ambitious work is an invaluable resource for all who want to understand what the call to leadership entails."
—*Diane C. Yu, Chief of Staff and Deputy*
to the President, New York University;
Immediate Past President, White House
Fellows Foundation and Association

"This is a great read about leaders, leadership, and making a difference."
—*Vice Admiral Ann E. Rondeau,*
the highest-ranking woman in the
United States Navy

"My experience as a White House Fellow was unique and unforgettable in that it involved me in the affairs of yesterday, today, and tomorrow with the opportunity to learn and contribute to each."
—*Dr. George H. Heilmeier, Kyoto Prize*
Laureate (2005); Chairman Emeritus,
Telecordia Technologies Inc., formerly Bellcore,
serving as CEO from 1991 to 1996.

"Garcia's work underscores the White House Fellows program's success in creating a dedicated cadre of national leadership for today and the future."
—*Dana G. Mead, Former Chair & CEO,*
Tenneco; Former Chair, Business Roundtable;
Chair of the MIT Corporation; and 25-year member
of the WHF Presidential Commission

LEADERSHIP LESSONS OF THE WHITE HOUSE FELLOWS

★ ★ ★ ★ ★ ★ ★ ★ ★

LEARN HOW TO INSPIRE OTHERS, ACHIEVE GREATNESS, AND FIND SUCCESS IN ANY ORGANIZATION

★ ★ ★ ★ ★ ★ ★ ★ ★

CHARLES P. GARCIA

New York   Chicago   San Francisco   Lisbon   London   Madrid   Mexico City
Milan   New Delhi   San Juan   Seoul   Singapore   Sydney   Toronto

The **McGraw·Hill** Companies

1 2 3 4 5 6 7 8 9 0   DOC/DOC   0 1 0 9

ISBN: 978-0-07-159848-4
MHID: 0-07-159848-0

This publication is designed to provide accurate and authoritative information in regard to the subject matter covered. It is sold with the understanding that the publisher is not engaged in rendering legal, accounting, or other professional service. If legal advice or other expert assistance is required, the services of a competent professional person should be sought.

—From a Declaration of Principles Jointly Adopted
by a Committee of the American Bar Association and
a Committee of Publishers and Associations

McGraw-Hill books are available at special quantity discounts to use as premiums and sales promotions, or for use in corporate training programs. To contact a representative, please visit the Contact Us pages at www.mhprofessional.com.

This book is printed on acid-free paper.

For Cristina

CONTENTS

CONTENTS

PREFACE

Imagine an awestruck young African American man entering the Oval Office for the first time to meet the president of the United States. The year was 1965, and that young man was Ron Lee, one of 15 Americans selected for a groundbreaking yearlong leadership development program called the White House Fellowships.

After shaking Lee's hand and inviting him to take a seat, President Lyndon Johnson asked him with whom he would like to work during his Fellowship year in Washington. Lee gave his answer without a moment's hesitation: he wanted to work with Larry O'Brien. A legendary force in Democratic politics, O'Brien had been the organizational genius behind John F. Kennedy's two successful U.S. Senate races in Massachusetts in the 1950s and also his 1960 campaign for the presidency. He had orchestrated Lyndon Johnson's landslide victory in 1964, and as President Johnson's congressional liaison, he had served as the architect of the Great Society legislation designed to eliminate racial injustice and poverty in America. Everyone in Washington was aware of O'Brien's influence. Since Lee believed the Great Society legislation was the most important thing happening in the country at the time, he couldn't imagine being matched with a more outstanding mentor than Larry O'Brien.

Upon hearing Lee's choice, the president picked up the phone, summoned O'Brien to the Oval Office and introduced him to his eager new apprentice. The trajectory of Ron Lee's life changed forever. With guidance from his skillful and caring mentor, Lee began a whirlwind career journey that took him just three years later beyond the limits of his imagination and led him to become one of the highest-ranking African Americans in the United States government. Lee's determination to level the playing field for others will inspire any leader hoping to build a winning team.

Consider also one of Lee's classmates—an underprivileged 24-year-old cub reporter from Georgia named Tommy Johnson, who wanted nothing more during his Fellowship year than to work alongside White House Press Secretary Bill Moyers. To Johnson's amazement, his request was granted. His ensuing experience in leadership at the highest level of government under the tutelage of a proficient mentor like Moyers provided Johnson with a strong dose of the confidence and expertise he needed to launch his career. When the president and first lady left Washington in 1969 and returned to their Texas ranch, they took Tommy with them to help run their family business, and to help the former president write his memoirs. In the years that followed, Tommy Johnson continued his climb toward the pinnacle of his profession, ultimately rising to the level of publisher of the *Los Angeles Times* and later becoming president of CNN. But Johnson's professional triumphs were nearly overshadowed by a personal life in shambles. His workaholic tendencies deprived his family of a loving husband and father, and he began to suffer from severe bouts of depression. His candid assessment of how he overcame those challenges offers invaluable guidance to anyone who wants to be a great leader without sacrificing his or her health, or more importantly, his or her family.

Next, picture an IBM executive, a young woman named Jane Cahill Pfeiffer who, as a White House Fellow in 1966, was mentored by Robert Weaver—the country's first African American Cabinet secretary who was chosen by Lyndon Johnson to lead the newly created U.S. Department of Housing and Urban Development. At the end of her Fellowship year, Pfeiffer was personally recruited by legendary IBM chief executive Tom Watson Jr. to become his executive assistant. In 1978, Jane became the most powerful female executive in America when the National Broadcasting Company (NBC) picked her as its chairman of the board, and also as a director of RCA, the network's parent company before General Electric bought it. Within weeks of her arrival at NBC, an internal scandal came to light involving expense-account fraud and kickbacks among field managers. She acted swiftly and aggressively, bringing in outside counsel and auditors and leading to criminal charges being filed against almost a dozen executives. She then began a major corporate reorganization, ruffling many egos, which ultimately led to her being fired. Imagine also what it was like for Francis Harvey, a Fellow from the class of 1977–1978 who was mentored by Secretary of Defense Harold Brown, who nearly thirty years later in 2007 was dealt a similar blow as the one delivered to Pfeiffer when, as Secretary of the Army, he reached a critical impasse with his political superiors over the appropriate level of funding to sustain the war readiness of his soldiers. Harvey made the tough decision not to compromise, placing his reputation and the Army he led at risk. Like Pfeiffer, he too was abruptly forced to resign, allegedly for his handling of incidents at the Walter Read Medical Center, but in reality, it was for standing firm on the Army budget. Their determination to do the right thing—even if it meant losing their dream jobs—will undoubtedly encourage aspiring leaders to hold fast to their principles and maintain their honor at all costs.

Consider as well a young man named Colin Powell, who, as a White House Fellow in 1972–1973, was mentored by Fred Malek, President Nixon's former head of personnel and deputy director of the Office of Management and Budget. Powell credits this leadership program as the turning point of his career, laying the foundation for his later assignments working for three presidents as National Security Advisor, Chairman of the Joint Chiefs of Staff, and Secretary of State. Imagine too, a young Fellow named Louis O'Neill, who was mentored by then–Secretary of State Powell in 2005 and who became Powell's special assistant for Russian affairs. As a nice perk, O'Neill, a former captain of the Stanford University cycling team, spent most weekends mountain-biking with President George W. Bush. Just one year after leaving his Fellowship, O'Neill became one of the nation's youngest ambassadors, serving as head of the Mission to Moldova, and later went on to work as a headquarters manager for Senator Barack Obama's presidential campaign. Powell's legendary team-building techniques and the insights O'Neill gained by working and playing in the company of some of the world's most powerful leaders will inspire anyone seeking to bring out the best in themselves and those around them.

Now imagine all of these extraordinary leaders—plus two hundred more— sharing their wisdom and remarkable leadership expertise directly with you. What an enlightening experience that would be for anyone hoping to become a more effective leader.

Someone once told me that I should write the book I'd most like to read, and the result is this volume: *Leadership Lessons of the White House Fellows*. By writing it, I hoped to uncover and share the leadership lessons the Fellows have learned from their many mentors—lessons that have laid the foundation for many of them to assume some of the most important leadership positions in American society. Having served as a White House Fellow myself, I knew there was a gold mine of information out there. I just needed to figure out how to effectively tap it and compile it in such a way that any aspiring leader would benefit from it.

I first called upon alum Jack LeCuyer, the executive director of the White House Fellows Foundation and Association, for help locating former Fellows. He not only provided me with the most up-to-date contact information available, he took the initiative to communicate individually with many of the alumni to personally encourage their participation in the project. I then met with Janet Eissenstat, the current director of the White House Fellows program, who was an invaluable resource on the more recent alumni. Next, I created an eight-question survey for the Fellows to complete. Among other things, I asked them to name their White House Fellows mentor, or "principal," and to tell me about the most profound lesson they learned from that person. I also asked them to describe some of the qualities they think are important for a leader to possess, as well as one specific tried-and-true technique they use to inspire people to follow them. And I asked them to disclose the most challenging leadership experience they have ever faced and tell me how they resolved it and what they learned from it. I e-mailed this questionnaire to each Fellow, along with a request for a date and time to conduct an interview. In short order the questionnaires started rolling back to me, chock full of wit, wisdom, and priceless anecdotes.

In the meantime, I began piecing together the history of the program. I wanted to discover why President Lyndon Johnson created the White House Fellowships in 1964. I received a treasure trove of information and related documents from Tom Carr, the founding director of the White House Fellowship, who ran the program for its first five years. I also scoured the Library of Congress and LBJ's Presidential Library for documents and recordings I hoped would bring the program's earliest days to light. My research was rewarded with papers and tape recordings that proved what I had long suspected—that Lyndon and Lady Bird Johnson had more than just a superficial interest in bringing young people into the highest levels of the executive branch. Indeed, the Johnsons, along with LBJ's Republican friend John Gardner, were active partners in developing this nonpartisan program, which has stood for more than four decades as a rare and enduring bridge of trust, camaraderie and collaboration between America's opposing political parties.

The most time-consuming yet enjoyable portion of my research was personally interviewing more than 200 former White House Fellows. With their completed questionnaires in front of me, I encouraged them to expand on their answers to my core questions. The result was over five thousand pages of notes and transcripts filled with entertaining and insightful stories from the administrations of every president from LBJ through George W. Bush. The stories I collected were each distinctive, but they all had one thing in common—they were inspiring. Some tales were lighthearted—one that immediately springs to mind from a now distinguished federal appellate judge involves a bowl of soup, four bird's heads, and a dinner table full of talkative Vietnamese dignitaries; some were poignant, such as a former Fellow's recollection of watching President Johnson's reaction to Dr. Martin Luther King's assassination; and some were downright serious, as in the story of a computer programming whiz who was called upon during the first week of his Fellowship to develop cyber security measures for the country in the immediate aftermath of the 9/11 terrorist attacks.

My interview subjects also revealed lessons learned in their professional and personal lives after the Fellowship. Since former Fellows work in so many different fields—including business and finance, media, the military, the faith community, government, law, the arts, education and the nonprofit sector—there was great variety in the stories they told. My sincerest regret is that space constraints prevented me from including all of their leadership lessons in this book. In fact, I was only able to use anecdotes from half the sources I interviewed. To do my small part to strengthen this leadership program, I am gifting all the royalties from sales of this book to the White House Fellows Foundation, which provides financial support each year to the Fellows education programs.

One point I want to emphasize is that no one becomes a world-class golfer just by reading a book on golf—so too with leadership. Successful leaders develop their skills most effectively through practice, perseverance, and guidance from caring mentors. While I believe that studying these leadership lessons will certainly help you become a better leader, there's just no substitute for getting out there, taking charge, and receiving some hard knocks along the way. Whether you're leading a family, a local community group, a military unit, a sales team, a sports franchise, or a Fortune 500 company, my hope is that you'll turn to these leadership lessons for guidance whenever you need a dose of inspiration.

Many of the Fellows I interviewed experienced great triumphs in their careers following their year in Washington, but some have suffered glaring setbacks. Several made deep personal and professional sacrifices for what they believed was right. But all of them say they learned and grew from every experience they had, whether it was positive or negative. Reading their stories can help aspiring leaders learn and grow as well. The White House Fellows understand—and I hope you will come to recognize too— that leadership is not heralded by a sudden bolt of lightning and a great thunderclap from on high. It's certainly not the natural outcome of spending a remarkable year in Washington, D.C. Rather, genuine leadership is measured by the individual moral choices one makes every day. I believe the anecdotes in the following pages clearly illustrate that truth and will also shed light, not only on the benefits of authentic leadership, but also the costs.

At this time in our nation's history, as we face enormous political and economic challenges due to overwhelming failures by leaders at all levels in public and private enterprise, the time has come for statesmanlike leadership in every sector of our great society. I sincerely hope this book will serve as an encouraging guide to all who aspire to offer the capable, bold leadership our country—and indeed, our world—so desperately needs right now. If it does, then Lyndon Johnson's vision of a genuinely free society populated by zestful, knowledgable, and active participants will be one step closer to reality.

Charles P. Garcia
Boca Raton, Florida

PART I

THE PROGRAM

CHAPTER 1

OPENING THE DOOR TO THE WHITE HOUSE

A genuinely free society cannot be a spectator society. Freedom, in its deepest sense, requires participation—full, zestful, knowledgeable participation. Toward that end, I have today established a new program entitled the White House Fellows.

—President Lyndon Baines Johnson,
October 3, 1964

BOURBON AND BRANCH WATER

For a young man, Air Force Major John Pustay already had accomplished a lot. The New Jersey native had served as a military officer in South Korea and Japan, earned a doctorate, published a book on counterinsurgency warfare, and taught at the U.S. Air Force Academy. Although only one military officer had made it into the first class of fifteen White House Fellows in 1965, he decided to apply for the prestigious program. After a grueling selection process, he was chosen in 1966 and assigned to work for Secretary of State Dean Rusk.

Pustay knew that as a Fellow he would be given access to people and places in government that are generally off limits to everyone but the best-positioned Washington insiders, but nothing had prepared him for the experience he was about to have. In his first month as a Fellow, Secretary Rusk sent him to the Oval Office to take notes for him at an impromptu meeting between President Lyndon Johnson and some of his most trusted foreign policy advisors. The Vietnam War was in full swing, and the topics of the meeting were the American response to an insurrection within South Vietnam's leadership and target selection for the bombing of North Vietnam as part of Operation Rolling Thunder.

Pustay recalled the small group huddled around the president: Secretary of Defense Robert McNamara, National Security Advisor McGeorge Bundy, Director of Central Intelligence Richard Helms, and General Earle Wheeler, the chairman of the Joint Chiefs of Staff. The young major listened intently and took copious notes so that he could give Secretary Rusk a proper briefing on the important meeting. "So everybody leaves, and I am the junior guy, so I am going to be the last guy out," Pustay recalled. "And as I'm leaving, the president taps me on the shoulder and he says, 'Would you like to have a bourbon and branch water?' I did not know what the heck branch water was, but if the commander in chief asks you to have bourbon and branch water, you probably ought to do it."

The president summoned a steward, who quickly produced a bottle of bourbon and a pitcher of clear liquid. Pustay soon discovered—much to his relief—that branch water is just a southern term for fresh water. The two men settled onto the sofa in the Oval Office, Pustay sipping his bourbon, the president his scotch and soda, while engaging in small talk for most of an hour. During a lull in the conversation, Pustay swirled the amber liquid in his glass and marveled at the fact that he actually was sitting in the Oval Office sharing a drink with the president of the United States. He knew that being a White House Fellow had its benefits, but this was beyond his wildest dream—the folks back in New Jersey would never believe it! He smiled to himself and took another sip, enjoying the whiskey's rich flavor and smoky aroma, and he was about to congratulate the president on his fine taste in bourbon when he looked up to see Johnson's eyes welling with tears. "Mr. President," Pustay said. "I didn't realize, perhaps, the gravity of the situation we discussed in that meeting and the decisions that you had to make there."

"No, that's not it," Johnson said in his soft drawl. "I am very sad right now because this is still Jack Kennedy's house. Jack had charm—he was witty and handsome. And here I am, just a poor Texas schoolteacher, a dirt farmer. Since we got back from Dallas, the only one who has ever accepted me here at the White House is Lady Bird."

Pustay sat with President Johnson, reflecting on the private thoughts of the man who dominated public life with the historic passage of sweeping Great Society legislation aimed at eliminating poverty and racial injustice. President Johnson continued to talk about some of the burdens of that great office. Starting to feel self-conscious because he was taking up too much of the president's valuable time, Pustay said, "Sir, I think it's probably time for me to leave."

"Yeah, young man," Johnson said. "You know, thanks for listening."

That experience taught Pustay early on that even the most powerful leaders are human and that at the core, it is emotion that drives human behavior. He has recalled that lesson often throughout his distinguished military career. It undoubtedly helped guide him as he rose to the rank of three-star general, served as the lead advisor to the chairman of the Joint Chiefs of Staff, and led the National Defense University as its president. Forty-two years later, Pustay counts his experience as a White House Fellow—especially that extraordinary hour as President Johnson's confidant over a glass of bourbon and branch water—as one of his most cherished memories.

President Johnson had opened the door to the White House with the new Fellowship program. Whether or not he intended it, he also had opened a window for Fellows to witness firsthand how the nation's top leaders personally cope with the burdens of immense responsibility, impossible expectations, and brutal public criticism, a side of their essential humanity the general public rarely gets to see.

A "RHODES SCHOLARSHIP" FOR PUBLIC SERVICE

Each year since 1965, the White House Fellows program has granted exclusive access to the Oval Office and other Washington power chambers to some of the nation's most promising young leaders. Similar to the Rhodes Scholarship competition in which thirty-two of the nation's brightest college graduates are selected each year to study in Oxford, England, the White House Fellowships are offered to a handful of young Americans from all walks of life, who spend a year working at the highest levels of government, learning the process of leading a nation. Out of the thousands of applications submitted for Fellowships each year, fewer than twenty outstanding people—mostly in their late twenties and early thirties—are chosen to work in the executive branch with cabinet secretaries, the vice president, and senior White House officials. Indeed, nearly forty Rhodes Scholars over the years have gone on to become White House Fellows. The formal purpose of the White House Fellows program is "to provide gifted and highly motivated young Americans with some first-hand experience in the process of governing the Nation and a sense of personal involvement in the leadership of society." What's really special is the access to the people, places, and procedures that are at the heart of governing the world's most prosperous and powerful nation.

During his Fellowship year in the Office of Management and Budget, former Secretary of State Colin Powell [White House Fellow (WHF) 72–73] recalled the opinion of the Office of Management and Budget (OMB) public relations director who thought the Fellowships gave young people too much access to the down-and-dirty inner workings of government. "It's like letting little children watch the sex act," he told Powell. "Now, there's nothing wrong with sex, but there is something immoral about having children watch it, until they know what they are watching."[1] Indeed, Powell has said that the program was "the turning point" in his career and gave him "instant entrée to people one did not ordinarily encounter at Fort Devens or Chu Lai."

In addition to Colin Powell, the White House Fellows alumni include former CNN president Tom Johnson, historian and Pulitzer Prize–winning author Doris Kearns Goodwin, CNN senior medical correspondent Dr. Sanjay Gupta, U.S. Senator Sam Brownback, retired U.S. Army General Wesley Clark, former Senator Tim Wirth, New York Stock Exchange Euronext Deputy Chairman Marshall Carter, Court TV Anchor Jami Floyd, Secretary of Labor Elaine Chao, Heisman Trophy winner and retired Army Brigadier General Pete Dawkins, U.S. Court of Appeals Judges Margaret McKeown and Deanell Reece Tacha, Baptist Pastor Suzan Johnson Cook, former dean of Wharton and president of the University of Delaware Pat Harker, Honolulu Mayor Mufi Hannemann, JC Penney CEO Mike Ullman, former New Mexico Governor Garrey Carruthers, Stanford Business School Dean Robert Joss, former Secretary of Housing and Urban Development Henry Cisneros, Dallas Mayor Tom Leppart,

---

[1] Colin L. Powell with Joseph E. Persico, *My American Journey* (New York: Random House), p. 173.

former Tenneco CEO and MIT Corporation Chairman Dana Mead, and Michelle Peluso, CEO of Travelocity, among others. I am proud to count myself among their ranks.

MR. GARCIA GOES TO WASHINGTON

When I was twenty-three years old, I saw an advertisement for the White House Fellowship program in *BusinessWeek* magazine and was intrigued by it. In a fit of youthful optimism, I requested information about the program. However, when the brochure arrived and I scanned the pictures and read the backgrounds of the current class listed in the back of the booklet, my optimism was crushed. There was no way I could apply for a White House Fellowship; it was totally out of my league. I set the brochure aside but never stopped dreaming about what it might be like to be a White House Fellow.

A few years later I was assigned to work for Army General John Galvin, commander of the U.S. Southern Command in the Republic of Panama, and he asked me to write an in-depth analysis of Cuba's efforts to destabilize Latin America. After an extensive yearlong study during which I traveled throughout the region gathering data and evidence, I completed the 200-page report. Galvin gave an abbreviated declassified version of it to his friend Mort Zuckerman, owner and editor in chief of *U.S. News & World Report*. Zuckerman was intrigued and wanted to learn more, and so he visited us in the Republic of Panama, where I gave him a slide presentation highlighting the conclusions of my research. Zuckerman published a summary of my work in his magazine in a cover story titled "Drugs, Terror and Politics: The Deadly New Alliance." Coincidentally, Zuckerman was part of a regional panel that chose the finalists for the White House Fellows program from the Boston area. He suggested that I apply for the program and graciously offered to write a recommendation letter for me on the basis of the publication of my research in his magazine. General Galvin offered to write a recommendation letter too, and he also dashed off handwritten notes to Major General Bernard Loeffke (WHF 70–71) and Colonel Jack LeCuyer (WHF 77–78), two former Fellows in his command who he believed could offer me valuable guidance.

I called General Loeffke's office to make an appointment to discuss my desire to become a White House Fellow. I spoke with his aide, who checked and said the general would decide whether to help me the next day, but only if I agreed to meet him at 0500 hours (five o'clock in the morning) to go on a two-mile run carrying an M14 rifle with the rest of his battalion. This was a signature Burn Loeffke request.

Before I met the general, I thought I'd do a little research to learn what I could about him. I discovered that he was a West Point graduate from the class of 1957 and that he had an undergraduate degree in engineering, a master's degree in Russian, and a doctorate in political science and that he spoke fluent Russian, Chinese, French, Spanish, and Portuguese. As a White House Fellow, he served on Henry Kissinger's National Security Council staff, and in the mid-1970s he was chief of the military mission in the Peoples Republic of China and later served as the U.S. Army attaché in the former Soviet Union during the Brezhnev era.

He was in combat in Vietnam, serving in the 82nd Airborne Division, Special Forces, and as an advisor to a Vietnamese parachute battalion, earning two Purple Hearts for wounds in combat, four Silver Stars, and five Bronze Stars for his daring under fire, which included running through enemy fire during an ambush to retrieve a badly wounded soldier and hoisting him on his back to save him. An airborne ranger, he was the first Westerner to jump with a regular Chinese communist parachute unit. He later served as chief of staff of the 18th Airborne Corps at Fort Bragg, North Carolina. He was a champion swimmer at West Point. He competed in a military decathlon in Russia and ran a full-length marathon in Communist China.

I sure tossed around that night. How would I possibly keep up with this guy?

Somehow I managed the run. It was even fun, though I was exhausted. I met the general in his office the next day, and the meeting went extremely well. Loeffke was inspiring and seemed to take great pleasure in mentoring a young officer. He was kind enough to spend an hour with me, pointing out the ins and outs of the application process, the pros and cons of the program, what to expect, what not to expect, and the best way to approach the interview process if I advanced to the regional or national panels.

Encouraged by everyone's support and faith in me, I made the leap and applied. At age twenty-seven, after what seemed like an endless gauntlet of interviews and tests, I was selected to be a White House Fellow. I was headed to Washington to serve during the transition between the administrations of Presidents Ronald Reagan and George H. W. Bush.

My mother was a seventh grade science teacher in the public schools for twenty-two years, and she ingrained in me the idea that the root cause of many of the nation's fundamental social problems was a crumbling educational system in desperate need of reform. Secretary of Education William Bennett was a brash education reformer who was determined to raise student achievement, and so I decided that working with him would be a great assignment. My wish was granted, but unfortunately, shortly before I arrived in Washington, Bennett resigned to write and lecture. I quickly was reassigned to the State Department, where Deputy Secretary John Whitehead gave me a home and asked me to work on global strategies to help stem the tide of illicit narcotics entering the country. Whitehead had been the chairman of Goldman Sachs, and he was a great mentor and a wonderful leader. But when President George H. W. Bush took office in January 1989, he appointed William Bennett to a cabinet post as the first director of the National Office of Drug Control Policy, a position that came to be known as the drug czar. Bennett would be responsible for coordinating twenty-three federal agencies fighting the war on drugs, and I just had to get in on that!

I went to my interview with Bill Bennett armed with facts, figures, and advice on how to win the newly declared War on Drugs. But when I walked into the room, he didn't ask to see my data or hear my recommendations. Instead, he looked me over from head to toe and said, "Charlie, you look like you can run fast. Do you have good hands?"

"Excuse me, sir?" I replied, dumbstruck.

"I'm talking about football, son." Bennett grinned. "We have a game every Sunday. We're playing Jack Kemp's team this weekend, and I need a wide receiver. Can you play or not?"

Recovering quickly, I volunteered, "I'm your man—quicker than a jackrabbit and good hands to boot."

That was music to his ears, and to my amazement, he hired me on the spot to join his team. What an opportunity! Not only did he design a special program to attack the drug culture and violence that permeated the nation's capital in 1989—even the mayor was indicted—he also drove the first comprehensive national strategy composed of a balanced array of demand-reduction and supply-reduction actions. I was proud to do my part, and my experience as a White House Fellow changed my life and opened great opportunities.

PELOTON ONE: PEDALING WITH THE PRESIDENT

During my Fellowship year I worked hard, and yes, I got to play football with quite a few White House insiders. I have lots of stories to tell about the amazing year I spent in Washington, but it turns out that every Fellow has stories to tell. Take Louis O'Neill (WHF 04–05) and Travis Matheson (WHF 07–08) for example. Now, these guys have stories.

At least twice each year during his two terms in office, President George W. Bush met with each White House Fellows class. "One of my favorite activities as president is to meet with the White House Fellows," Bush said. "I love to sit down with the Fellows and answer their questions. It's an inspiring experience for me."[2] In fact, President Bush enjoyed his association with the Fellows so much that he invited a few to join him in one of his favorite pastimes: mountain biking. The first Fellow invited along for the ride was O'Neill, who at that time was serving as a special assistant to Secretary of State Colin Powell.

"At the end of one of our meetings with the president, we were all chatting, and he mentioned he was going to ride his bike that weekend. He asked if anyone rode, and somebody suggested he talk to me because I was captain of Stanford's cycling team," O'Neill recalled. "And he said, 'Oh, really? Well, you're coming with me.'" So it was that O'Neill became part of President Bush's riding group, Peloton One. He rode with the president for over an hour at a time most weekends, nearly fifty times in all. O'Neill was surprised at the president's athleticism—and his mischievous nature. "We rode in a pack, and he was always in front pushing the pace, and he would routinely outrun some of the invitees and also some of the Secret Service guys who were half his age. He took such pleasure in leaving people behind. It was so much fun," O'Neill said. Occasionally, the president would stop the ride and organize everyone into a trail-clearing crew, handing out rakes, clippers, and cutters so that they could create a new path for the next weekend's ride.

Another Fellow who rode with the president most weekends during his year in Washington was Travis Matheson, a lieutenant with the Washington State Patrol and a triathlete. "There were probably eight or ten of us

---

[2] George W. Bush, remarks, White House Fellowship Fortieth Anniversary Gala Celebration (Washington D.C., 2005).

one day, and about an hour into the ride we came to an area where they had talked about putting in a new trail. So we all, including the president, went to work. It was fun," Matheson recalled. "Some people were staking out the trail, and a couple of others were pulling roots, and a couple of the people were sweeping leaves and removing small trees and brush. The president seemed to really enjoy the exercise and camaraderie. I think he believes that exercise is very important to creating a healthy mind and sound body."

For Matheson and O'Neill, biking through forests, up and down hills, and across small rivers with the president was an exhilarating and beautiful experience. "It humanizes the man," O'Neill said. "You see up close how much weight is on his shoulders, and I often think how wonderful it was that he shared his time with us that way." Apparently, the president treasured the riding experience just as much as the Fellows did. While giving a speech at the White House Fellows fortieth anniversary celebration in 2005, Bush broke from his scripted remarks after spotting O'Neill in the audience and spoke off the cuff about cycling with "Sweet Lou" and the other White House Fellows. "Lou had been a captain of the Stanford biking team, and he felt like he was strong enough to ride with a fifty-nine-year-old, and it turns out he *was* strong enough," President Bush joked. "I really enjoy it. I get a chance to see the caliber and quality of the Fellows." O'Neill's last ride with the president came in 2006, just before he left Washington after being named ambassador and head of mission in Moldova by the Organization for Security and Co-operation in Europe. At thirty-eight, he was one of that organization's youngest ambassadors. After leaving that post in 2008, he went to work as a headquarters manager for Senator Barack Obama's presidential campaign. In every Fellowship class since O'Neill's, President Bush found at least one willing and able cyclist to join him on his weekend rides.

Being a White House Fellow certainly has its privileges, and one of the most extraordinary is the remarkable level of access one gains to some of the world's most powerful people. Often, as in the case of Lou O'Neill and Travis Matheson with President Bush, that access extends beyond the bounds of work. Indeed, some Fellows have become like family to cabinet members, White House staffers, and even presidents. At the end of their year in Washington, Fellows typically leave with a deeper perspective on government and the people who govern.

CHAPTER 2

A FOUNDATION FOR FELLOWSHIP

Our Founding Fathers all came from villages or the countryside or from what would now be regarded as very small cities. All of them had the opportunity, as youths, to see at first hand the process of governing. Today young people of comparable ability grow up in a huge, complex, noisy society, and almost none get a close-up view of government. The White House Fellows program is one attempt to deal with that unfortunate fact. Each year a selection of the most promising young men and women in America are given the opportunity to see and participate in the process of governing at the highest levels. As the years go by they have become a growing reservoir of exceptional individuals prepared to serve their country.
—FORMER SECRETARY OF HEALTH, EDUCATION,
AND WELFARE JOHN W. GARDNER

THE POWER OF MENTORSHIP

In 1964, there was a core group of people in and around President Johnson's administration who had the insight to recommend reserving a place for the nation's youth to work directly for officials at the highest levels of government. It wasn't an obvious need: Cabinet officers were busy, and bringing in, well, neophytes to work on serious national issues certainly entailed some risk. But whether you call it destiny, providence, coincidence, or even divine intervention, several key people arrived at the same general idea at virtually the same time.

At the head of this foresighted band was President Johnson himself. Johnson had an intense desire to work with young people, to share his wisdom and open doors for them the same way others had done for him. Johnson's first job in politics—he previously had been a teacher and administrator at a school for poor Mexican children in Texas—was as an assistant to Congressman Richard Kleberg. In Washington, Johnson and his new bride, Lady Bird, did their best to fit into the fast-paced political scene, and since Kleberg spent much of his time out of the office, it was up to Johnson to hold down the fort. It was a huge responsibility for such a young man. He was not yet thirty years old, but his energy and ambition quickly garnered attention, and in 1935 he was tapped as state director for the Texas branch of the National Youth Administration. The purpose of the NYA was to provide people between the ages of sixteen and twenty-five with counseling, recreation, education, and job opportunities. Getting such an ambitious program off to a successful start was another feather in Johnson's cap and would help inform his opinion about tapping the energy, idealism, and enthusiasm of young people working in government to make the nation a better place.

In 1937 he won his first election, a congressional seat representing his district in central Texas. Shortly after the election, President Franklin D. Roosevelt was passing through the Lone Star State on his train and invited the young congressman-elect along for the ride. President Roosevelt later predicted that Johnson would become "the first southern president" since the Civil War.[3] When it came time for committee appointments, Johnson reaped the benefits of that train ride when the president and another mentor, House Majority Leader Sam Rayburn, helped him land an appointment to the Naval Affairs Committee. When he was elected to the Senate in 1948, yet another mentor, Georgia Senator Richard Russell, helped him get his next plum assignment, this time an appointment to the powerful Armed Services Committee, which Russell chaired. Throughout Johnson's political career, he appreciated the leg up he'd received from elder statesmen who believed in him. He also understood that young people could make a difference, especially if they had support from the kinds of mentors he had been blessed to have.

---

[3] William J. vanden Heuvel, "Franklin Delano Roosevelt and Lyndon Baines Johnson: Architects of a Nation" (address at the LBJ Presidential Library, March 14, 2000). Available from www.feri.org/news/news_detail.cfm?QID=4568.

Before winning over thirty Emmy Awards for producing many of public television's groundbreaking series, Bill Moyers served as a top aide during Lyndon Johnson's unsuccessful bid for the 1960 Democratic presidential nomination and then became the liaison between the vice presidential candidate and the nominee, Senator John F. Kennedy. Moyers was one of the organizers of the Peace Corps during the Kennedy administration. Then, after Johnson was sworn in as president after Kennedy's assassination, Moyers became a special assistant to Johnson and later served as his White House press secretary. "LBJ had a record from the beginning of his public life of bringing young men into his circle, granting them his confidence, expecting high performance from them, and treating them as equals with others around him," Moyers said. "He had been the beneficiary of such patronage and felt instinctively that he owed it to others. He also was impressed that the White House Fellows program would be a program he could launch—it wasn't a hangover from the Kennedy agenda—and he liked being associated with moderate Republicans like David Rockefeller and John Gardner," said Moyers.

AN OBLIGATION TO SUCCEED

Although twenty-four-year-old Tom Johnson was not kin to the first family, he became a kind of surrogate son to President Johnson and was treated like a brother by his daughters Lynda and Luci. Johnson (WHF 65–66), who later became publisher of the *LA Times* and president of CNN, was in the first class of White House Fellows in 1965, and he knows what a difference a caring mentor can make.

Johnson began working as a sports stringer at the *Macon Telegraph* in Macon, Georgia, when he was in the ninth grade. The son of a disabled jack-of-all-trades and a grocery store clerk, "Tommy" worked at the newspaper throughout his high school years and caught the attention and captured the hearts of not only the crusty editors in the newsroom but also Peyton Anderson, the kindly publisher in the front office. Impressed by his dedication, ambition, and ability, Anderson offered to pay Johnson's tuition to the University of Georgia, but there was a catch: Johnson not only would have to earn good grades, he would come back to Macon each weekend throughout the school year and during his summer vacation to work at the *Telegraph*. That sounded like a swell deal and a win-win situation to Johnson, who considered the newspaper staff a second family and the

Telegraph offices a home away from home. He gratefully accepted Anderson's offer and kept up his end of the bargain by earning his bachelor's degree in journalism while maintaining his commitment to the paper. While other boys his age were out cruising on Friday and Saturday nights, Johnson was hard at work in the newsroom, cheerfully repaying his debt to his mentor. Anderson had so much faith in Johnson that he also paid the young man's tuition to Harvard Business School.

It was at the end of his graduate studies at Harvard in 1964 that Johnson applied for the inaugural class of the White House Fellows program. He was selected, and although he felt obligated to return to Macon to work for the paper, Anderson told him not to give it a second thought: How could he turn down a chance to work at the White House for a year? Johnson and his new wife, Edwina, moved to Washington for what they thought would be an interesting twelve months in the nation's capital. Since he was a journalist, Johnson was assigned to work in the White House Press Office with Press Secretary Bill Moyers. "The president felt that the Fellows should have the opportunity not just to be observers during their year but to be *participants* in the process. I'll never forget my first meeting with him on my very first day on the Fellowship," Johnson recalled. "Bill Moyers took me in to meet the president, and Lyndon Johnson said to me, 'Tom, we are going to treat you just like a full-time member of our staff.' And he did."

Tom and Edwina became close friends with President Johnson and Lady Bird, and it became clear to them that the president and the first lady were deeply committed to the Fellowship program. "President Johnson said the Fellows and their wives reminded him of a young Lady Bird and Lyndon Johnson coming to Washington as New Dealers—idealistic, wanting to make a difference, needing mentors, needing friends, and perhaps even feeling alone. Mrs. Johnson spoke to me about this too. She embraced the Fellows and their wives. She made all the spouses feel welcome." The president became so attached to Johnson that at the end of his Fellowship year, LBJ asked him to stay and serve as assistant press secretary. Again, Johnson was torn between a new opportunity and his obligation to return to Macon and work for Anderson at the *Telegraph*.

It was then that the president intervened and wrote a letter to Anderson asking if he might release Tom Johnson from that obligation, because without Anderson's blessing the young man would not stay in Washington. The president wrote, "I have told Tom that I would like for him to stay on if he could do so without breaching your confidence and faith in him. I know him well enough now to know that his sense of loyalty to you and his profound appreciation for your help in his life are overriding. He is torn between knowing that I need him and his desire to honor your confidence. I wanted you to know this, and also to say that if you feel you can spare Tom Johnson, his country and his President need him."[4]

In a letter to his loyal protégé, Anderson wrote, "We are all mighty proud of you, Tommy, and especially your high regard for an obligation. In this case, though, I don't feel you can ignore the opportunity you have been offered. There can be but one answer to an appeal such as the President made in his letter . . . you should have no hesitancy in staying on there."[5] Johnson accepted LBJ's offer and continued working directly for him in one capacity or another until January 22, 1973, when he phoned to interrupt Walter Cronkite's live *CBS Evening News* broadcast to announce President Johnson's death. Even today he remains a consultant to the Johnson family, serving as chair of the Lyndon Baines Johnson Foundation.

ESPECIALLY YOU HARVARDS . . .

During her interviews for the White House Fellows program, Doris Kearns Goodwin (WHF 67–68) informed the commissioners that although she supported the Johnson administration's efforts to promote civil rights, she was absolutely opposed to the Vietnam War. She was selected for a Fellowship anyway. She first met President Johnson at a special ceremony for the newly appointed Fellows in a ballroom at the White House, where he asked her to dance. After talking with the energetic, fascinating, and brilliant young woman—she was only twenty-four years old at the time—Johnson picked her to be one of the White House Fellows assigned to the Office of the President. However, there was something the president did not know. A month before, Goodwin had cowritten an article for the *New Republic* proposing that a new political party be developed from a partnership formed by minorities, women, and poor people. Without her knowledge, the magazine editors titled the article "How to Remove LBJ in 1968." The press had a field day when the article came out, and Goodwin

---

[4] Lyndon B. Johnson, letter to Peyton Anderson, July 28, 1966.

[5] Peyton Anderson, letter to W. Thomas Johnson, Jr., August 1, 1966.

was mortified, to say the least. "I had heard of the President's reaction to earlier, more trivial public embarrassments," Goodwin wrote. "I could easily imagine his punishing, or even canceling, the entire White House Fellow program for its error in selecting me."[6]

Goodwin was correct in her assumption that the president would not be pleased. Johnson's personal secretary, Marie Fehmer Chiarodo, witnessed his reaction to the *New Republic* article. "He had some very graphic language, and I'm not going to repeat what he said," Chiarodo recalled. "But he used all of the four-letter words that he knew and some of the several-syllable phrases that he used. He wondered why those selectors didn't know that this woman had this article coming out, and he said this was his White House, and here someone had been selected that really made him feel like an idiot. He thought he ought to have something to say about why these Fellows were selected. I remember sort of a red-faced feeling, as if we didn't do our homework, which is always very bad."

In spite of Johnson's embarrassment, Goodwin received word that the president still wanted her to be a Fellow—just not in *his* office—and she was reassigned to the Department of Labor. It wasn't long, though, before he invited her to work for him at the White House, telling her, "I've always liked teaching. I should have been a teacher, and I want to practice on you. I want to do everything I can to make the young people of America, especially you Harvards, understand what this political system is all about." Chiarodo—who was one of the select few to accompany Lyndon Johnson on his flight from Dallas to Washington after John F. Kennedy's assassination—said that the president viewed Goodwin as a challenge to his ability to persuade. "Not only was [she] an eastern establishment nonbeliever, but [she] was a *female* eastern establishment nonbeliever, and that was before females were supposed to be very smart," Chiarodo explained. "So this, in a way, was another challenge to him, and he set about to eruade her and to understand her and what made her think this way."[7]

---

[6] Doris Kearns Goodwin, *Lyndon Johnson and the American Dream* (New York: St. Martin's Press), Foreword.

[7] Transcript, Marie Fehmer Chiarodo, Oral History Interview III, August 16, 1972, by Michael L. Gillette, pp. 15–17, LBJ Library. Online: http://www.lbjlib.utexas.edu/johnson/archives.hom/oralhistory.hom/Chiarodo/Chiarodo3.pdf (accessed June 22, 2008).

Goodwin moved into an office just down the hall from the president's, and over the next six years she was LBJ's willing student both inside and outside the White House. When it came time for him to leave the presidency and return to his Texas ranch, he asked her to help form the team that would work full-time writing his memoirs, telling his story so that people might understand. He also wanted her to help establish his presidential library and the LBJ School of Public Affairs at the University of Texas in Austin. Goodwin said yes, and she later wrote her own book in 1976, *Lyndon Johnson and the American Dream*, which was a *New York Times* bestseller that launched her career as a world-renowned presidential historian. "I think I was so aware of the privilege of having this man, for some reason, having chosen me to talk to. He talked to me about his mother, his father, his dreams, his sadnesses," Goodwin explained. "And I realized that it was just a pretty lucky thing in some ways that he had chosen me to be there in those last years, and use that information for that first book on Lyndon Johnson. I think from then on, it made me want to understand the private side of the public figures, because I'd had that connection with this first one I ever knew."[8]

Goodwin taught history at Harvard and won the Pulitzer Prize for history in 1995 for *No Ordinary Time*, her biography of Franklin and Eleanor Roosevelt. Her latest book is the 2005 bestseller *Team of Rivals: The Political Genius of Abraham Lincoln*, which Steven Spielberg is turning into a movie scheduled for release in 2009.

A BILLIONAIRE GOES TO THE WHITE HOUSE

After selling his Silicon Valley company SnapTrack to Qualcomm Inc. for $1 billion in March 2000, the entrepreneur Steven L. Poizner (WHF 01–02) could have retired and lived a life of luxury and leisure. However, the forty-four-year-old electrical engineer whose company created global positioning technology, which identifies the location of cell phone users in an emergency, could not imagine sitting on the sidelines. After all, he still had lots of energy and great ideas. "I was concerned about California's economy, its education system, and its aging infrastructure, and I didn't want to sit around and just complain about the Golden State going south,"

---

[8] Doris Kearns Goodwin, interview, Academy of Achievement, June 28, 1996.

Poizner said. "So I decided to switch careers and retire from the private sector so I could focus on public sector service."

Poizner had no illusions—he knew he had a great deal to learn—and so he started looking for a leadership training program to help him make the transition from the boardroom to the public sector. His search led him to the White House Fellows program, where he found a home at the National Security Council's Office of Transnational Threats under Richard A. Clarke, the national coordinator for counterterrorism. "I was pretty senior in the business world," Poizner recalled. "But I was definitely still on the learning curve when it came to applying my leadership skills to the public sector." All Poizner's skills and knowledge would be put to the test just one week after he started his Fellowship, when terrorists attacked the United States on September 11. The focus of Poizner's Fellowship year changed in a split second, and he was tapped to work on a host of homeland security issues related to cybersecurity. Toward the end of this time in Washington, he was even able to make a presentation to President Bush on a highly sensitive project he had completed, and the president adopted all his recommendations.

When his Fellowship ended, Poizner passed on his newfound knowledge of the federal system by volunteering to teach American government to at-risk twelfth graders in a San Jose high school for a year. He was named "Rookie Teacher of the Year" for his efforts. He also credits the White House Fellows program with giving him the experience and skills necessary to handle his newest job: In 2006 Poizner was elected insurance commissioner of California, where he manages a team of 1,300 people and oversees the state's $130 billion insurance industry. "The White House Fellows program isn't just seminars and lectures but hands-on, in-the-trenches work," he said. "It was a fantastic experience." Poizner is one of only two Republicans elected recently to statewide office in California. On September 15, 2008, he joined the race for governor of California to replace the other Republican—his good friend Governor Arnold Schwarzenegger— who is barred by term limits from running again after his second term ends in 2010.

The White House Fellows program began with a good idea—to choose a handful of outstanding young leaders like Tom Johnson, Doris Kearns Goodwin, and Steve Poizner and bring them to Washington, D.C., to work at the highest levels of the executive branch. The hope of the founders was to give young people a sense of personal involvement in the leadership of America, a vision of greatness for the country, and, most important, a sense of responsibility for bringing that greatness to reality.

PROGRAM ORIGINS

In mid-July 1964, the Republican National Convention met in San Francisco to choose a candidate to face Johnson in the November general election. Senator Barry Goldwater, a staunch Arizona conservative, emerged victorious after a bitter fight against moderate rival Nelson Rockefeller of New York, a battle that left the party scarred and deeply divided. Goldwater came out of the convention swinging, challenging President Johnson's liberal programs. On college campuses across the country, young Americans began joining Youth for Goldwater organizations and rallying around what they saw as Goldwater's platform of nonconformity.

Exactly one week after the gavel came down to close the Republican Convention, John W. Gardner, president of the Carnegie Corporation and a Republican, sent a memo to President Johnson's special consultant Eric Goldman, outlining what he called a "National Service Plan" for Johnson's consideration.

A year after Gardner was born in California in 1912 his father died, and his mother remarried several times during his childhood. One of her husbands was a gold prospector who thrilled his young stepson with exciting tales of the gold rush. "In each, the theme was constant—riches left untapped," Gardner recalled.[9] Educated at Stanford and the University of California at Berkeley, Gardner earned a Ph.D. in psychology and taught at a women's college in Connecticut. He later worked in the Federal Communications Commission's Foreign Intelligence Broadcast Service, where he analyzed enemy propaganda, and served in the Marine Corps during World War II. In 1945, he was hired by the Carnegie Corporation, where he helped establish model United Nations programs as well as programs piloting the use of television in the classroom. He was also instrumental in setting up a Russian Research Center at Harvard, which was the first center of its kind. In 1961, Gardner published his first major book, *Excellence*, arguing that the United States must strive for both excellence and equality

---

[9] "Can the Great Society Be Built and Managed?" *Time,* January 20, 1967, p. 5.

at every level of society. The book caught the attention of President Kennedy, and Gardner not only became more involved in federal efforts to improve education but also edited a volume of JFK's speeches and position papers. Gardner followed that volume with his second major book, *Self-Renewal.* Just as the United States was about to begin a period of profound change in its society, culture, and politics, Gardner argued that change—both personal and societal—is a great source of renewal and should be embraced. For his work and writings on leadership he received the Presidential Medal of Freedom in 1964.

Gardner had written a very similar memorandum in 1957 but, finding no groundswell of support, had put it back in his desk drawer. He dusted off the memo and sent it to Goldman. Gardner's memorandum gave the rationale for a "Presidential Corps," and in it he suggested that "a small organization would be formed to select one hundred of the ablest and most highly motivated young men and women in the nation for a fifteen-month period of service with the government." He suggested that the president serve as the honorary chairman of this organization and that a group of individuals from the highest reaches of society be recruited to select the young people. Selection would be predicated on "intelligence, character, special talents and general promise, and the standards would be so high that this would be as impressive an honor as a young person could win." Gardner recommended that the age range be twenty-one to thirty-one and that the candidates be required to have earned a four-year degree. He proposed that they be paid a decent but not excessive salary and that married candidates be provided with family allowances. Academic credit might be allowed, he added, and perhaps the program could grant credit toward military service.

Gardner wanted each person to be given a meaningful work assignment in Washington, writing that "the whole success of the plan would depend, of course, on the educational value of these assignments. If the individual were assigned to meaningless routine, the experience would be fruitless." Gardner suggested that the work assignments closely adhere to each candidate's current work or education. For example, young men involved in ROTC would be sent to work for the armed forces or an accountant would go to the Office of Management and Budget. The only requirement was that the candidate be exposed to government processes. To keep the group cohesive, Gardner suggested that the young people be brought together for weekly seminars that exposed them to the "big picture" issues of governing, and he proposed holding a ten-day retreat during which the class would discuss leadership principles. He envisioned panels in which the participants would not only identify challenges to the country in the coming years but also hash out ways to meet those issues head on. He recommended that a few of the participants be invited to continue their work for a second term, perhaps in the overseas offices of their current agencies.

Finally, he suggested that if some of the candidates chose to stay on in Washington at the end of their service period, they should be allowed to apply that time toward civil service seniority. Gardner justified his plan by stating that "if the sparsely settled American colonies of the late eighteenth century could produce Washington, Jefferson, Adams, Monroe, Madison, Hamilton, Franklin, and others of superlative talent, breadth, and statesmanship, should we not be able to produce ten times, or fifty times, that number? Where are they? We have few. Surely the raw material is still there . . . the program described here should be so designed and so administered as to give these superbly qualified young people precisely those experiences. Then, whether or not they stayed on in government, they would constitute a natural resource."

Through his Presidential Corps program, John Gardner, like his stepfather, was mining for untapped resources. Now he waited to see if the president thought he'd struck gold.

THE PLAN COMES TOGETHER

Born in Washington in 1915, Eric F. Goldman earned a Ph.D. in history from Johns Hopkins University at age twenty-two. He was a history professor at Princeton when President Johnson, newly sworn in, asked him to come to the White House to serve as his "idea man." Goldman was a gatekeeper of sorts, always on the lookout for promising proposals that would further the president's agenda. Upon receiving Gardner's proposal for the national service program, Goldman sent him a letter that called the plan "very welcome indeed," noting that "by coincidence, it fits in very much with something toward which I was fumbling and it also fits in with a desire which Mrs. Johnson expressed to me." Goldman assured Gardner that he had sent the plan to Lady Bird for her input. However, Goldman later wrote that he was not impressed with Gardner's plan because he feared it would create a new crop of "government internees," of which there were already vast numbers in Washington. However, since he knew that both the president and Lady Bird had a great desire to bring talented young people into federal government service and because he had such deep respect for Gardner, he set aside his reservations and prepared to send the plan to the president and first lady.[10]

Shortly after receiving the Gardner missive, Goldman also heard from William C. Friday, the young president of the University of North Carolina. Friday was concerned about the support Goldwater was drumming up on college campuses, and he suggested that the president consider reaching out to student leaders with a White House invitation. "I decided to put together the possibilities prompted by the Friday and Gardner communications: a plan quite different from Gardner's national service Presidential Corps but having some of its overtones, to be announced at a White House college student meeting," Goldman wrote. "The combination might further the long-range purposes shared by Gardner and me—and I was sure by Friday too—and it might possibly build greater understanding between President Johnson and the younger age group during the election and for future years of his administration."

In a memo to the president on September 15, 1964, Goldman outlined Friday's concerns, writing that the young university president "was bothered by the crusading enthusiasm for Goldwater that he sees among a minority of the young people. But he is not thinking entirely in terms of the campaign. He argues—as do quite a few people in contact with the younger people—that a sizeable part of this population does not feel as great a sense of rapport with the Administration as do other age groups, regardless of whether the young people intend to vote for you or not. Friday believes—and I agree with him—that the most practical way to get at the younger group is through the college leaders . . . they can be invited without criticism as to why this or that organization was not invited." Goldman closed his proposal by noting that no other president had ever summoned such an assortment of college leaders to the White House before. He then attached an abbreviated version of Gardner's letter outlining his vision for the program and suggested that if the number of

---

[10] Eric F. Goldman, *The Tragedy of Lyndon Johnson* (New York: Dell, 1968), p. 284.

candidates was reduced significantly, Gardner might be persuaded to fund a three-year pilot of the program through the Carnegie Foundation.

Goldman received the memo back with "an enthusiastic go-ahead from President Johnson and with notations by both him and Mrs. Johnson." President Johnson decided that the work assignments would not be in agencies as Gardner had suggested but in the highest reaches of the federal government. The total number of Fellows would decrease from 100 to 15—one for each of the ten cabinet officers, one for the vice president, and four in the Office of the President. The first lady indicated that she liked the name *White House Fellows,* and so it was chosen. The program would be announced at a special event for student leaders that was to be held, at the president's request, on October 3, 1964—only two weeks away.

Goldman was correct in guessing that the Carnegie Foundation would fund a pilot of the program: At Gardner's behest, the Carnegie board approved a $225,000 grant for the White House Fellows program. From the campaign trail, President Johnson appointed a bipartisan Commission on White House Fellowships and chose a Republican, David Rockefeller, as chairman. David Rockefeller was the younger brother of New York's governor and former Republican presidential candidate Nelson Rockefeller. Goldman wrote that "the presidential approvals of the names came back from the campaign jet over a radio-telephone which was acting up in a storm. The words were so garbled that it took me several minutes to make sure whether David Rockefeller, as chairman, was being okayed or berated. He was okay, bounteously so."

At that time, Rockefeller was president of Chase Manhattan Bank, chairman of the Museum of Modern Art, a founder and chairman of the Council of the Americas, and president and chairman of the Executive Committee of the Harvard College Board of Overseers, to name a few of the positions he held back then. He was exceedingly busy but felt obligated to accept President Johnson's appointment. "I was sitting in my office at the bank, and I was told that President Johnson wanted to speak to me. He was on Air Force One," Rockefeller said. "I haven't been asked that often by presidents to do things. I guess I felt a request was a command, and so I agreed to serve as the first chairman of what became the White House Fellows Commission." Rockefeller wrote in a 2008 letter, "I have never regretted that decision. The White House Fellows program has been an exceptional success. Based upon my experience with the first few classes of Fellows and meeting many others who have been selected over the past four decades, I think we have achieved all of the goals originally envisioned by President Johnson. More than 625 Fellows have worked in Washington and then moved on to distinguished careers that have benefitted our country immeasurably."[11]

As a group, the president's appointees reflected his total commitment to ensuring the program's diversity and nonpartisan spirit. He tapped liberal *New York Times* editor John Oakes as well as Stanford University Graduate School of Business dean and businessman Ernest C. Arbuckle. He chose Senator Margaret Chase Smith, whose name had been submitted at that summer's Republican convention as a nominee to run against him in the upcoming election, and U.S. Education Commissioner Francis Keppel, who was responsible for enforcing the Civil Rights Act of 1964 in the nation's public schools. University of North Carolina President William Friday, Chancellor of the University of Texas Harry Ransom, and O. Meredith Wilson, president of the University of Minnesota, brought unique academic perspectives from different regions of the country. Other important perspectives were brought by African-American civil rights pioneer and U. S. Circuit Court Judge William Hastie and James Carey, president of the Electrical, Radio and Machine Workers Union of America, then known as "Labor's Boy Wonder." Rounding out the commission were Civil Service Commission Chairman John Macy and Johnson's Republican friend and program cocreator John Gardner. Clearly, President Johnson wanted his White House Fellows to be selected by as esteemed and bipartisan a committee as he could muster.

Invitations signed by the president were sent to campuses across the country, inviting them to send a representative to the White House because the president of the United States "would like to get to know them and their thinking." According to the invitation, the evening would begin with a reception with the first lady and remarks by the president and progress to talks by Secretary of Defense Robert McNamara, Secretary of Labor Willard Wirtz, and Ambassador Adlai Stevenson. Afterward, the guests would enjoy a buffet dinner and entertainment hosted by the Johnsons' daughter Lynda.

---

[11] David Rockefeller letter to the White House Fellows, 24 October 2008, files of the White House Fellows Program, Washington D.C.

The RSVPs poured in, and on October 3, 1964, President Johnson signed Executive Order 11183 establishing the President's Commission on White House Fellows. Later that afternoon, he addressed 250 of the nation's best and brightest college leaders and unveiled the program, telling them that "a genuinely free society cannot be a spectator society. Freedom, in its deepest sense, requires participation—full, zestful, knowledgeable participation. Toward that end, I have today established a new program entitled the White House Fellows."

LAYING THE FOUNDATION

On October 4, 1964, the Office of the White House Press Secretary authorized a release of the news that the president had established the White House Fellows program and was inviting bright young Americans to apply for the privilege of spending a year working in Washington. In a classic example of why it's wise to be careful what you wish for, the White House quickly was inundated with an avalanche of inquiries about the program. Within days of Johnson's announcement to the assembled student leaders, over 8,000 starry-eyed young people wrote, called, or sent telegrams requesting details about the Fellowships.

Not bad for a program that didn't even have an office, a budget, or a staff. The time had come to find a proper director for the White House Fellows, one with just the right mix of youthful exuberance and discipline to step in and bring the project up to speed in a hurry. John Macy, chairman of the Civil Service Commission and a member of the first White House Fellows Commission, tapped an energetic young official at the Civil Service Commission's Office of Career Development, Tom Carr, to develop the fledgling program until a permanent director could be named. Thirty-five years old, Carr was a graduate of the Citadel and George Washington University and a decorated Korean War veteran.

"Within days my office was piled high with mailbags containing perhaps 8,000 inquiries about a program that didn't even exist," Carr recalled. "The Civil Service Commission sent over a stenographer and my former secretary, Elois Wade, a remarkable woman who became my assistant. If we needed an excuse to get busy, we tripped over it every time we turned around!"

On November 15, 1964, Johnson received a call from David Rockefeller, who wanted to brief him on the first meeting of the President's

Commission on White House Fellows. President Johnson secretly recorded that call, as he did many of his telephone conversations. During the four-minute call, Rockefeller told the president, "I want to just tell you a couple of things that we did and make sure that they were in keeping with your ideas on the subject." The commission had decided to extend the application deadline by one month, to January 15, with the hopes that it would give university presidents more time to rally quality applicants. Rockefeller also told the president that the commission had decided to set the program for one year rather than fifteen months, since most people operate on an annual basis. Therefore, the first class of White House Fellows would commence on September 1. "Does it disturb you to see that?" Rockefeller asked the president, who replied that it did not trouble him at all; he trusted Rockefeller and the commission to do the right thing for the program. The president approved all of Rockefeller's suggestions. Johnson stayed involved in the program's formulation from the very beginning.

Carr and his bare-bones staff managed to answer each of the thousands of letters and telegrams within a matter of weeks, and by the time the Rockefeller Commission came together two months after the event with student leaders, Carr had developed plans for everything from the program's rigorous selection procedure to job assignments and a continuing education component. The commission adopted all of Carr's plans without revision. They also hired him on the spot to become founding director of the White House Fellows Program, a post he manned with distinction for the next five years.

A few states and some countries have implemented many of Carr's selection methods for their own versions of the White House Fellows program. In 2004, former Governor Jeb Bush, who was a yearly guest at the Fellows off-the-record lunches, decided to replicate the program at the state level by establishing the Gubernatorial Fellows program in Florida. Each year, the Florida program provides hands-on public service experience to as many as twelve exceptional graduate and undergraduate students who are selected to perform high-level work in the governor's administration. The Fellows move to the state capital for their term, earn a small salary for their work, and have their tuition waived in exchange for their year of service. Gubernatorial Fellows also meet weekly as a group to participate in a lecture series as well as additional government activities, such as press conferences and budget and policy briefings. "I modeled the White House

Fellows program and created an exciting opportunity for young people in Florida who want to develop leadership skills and real job experience that will carry through to future employment and life situations," former Governor Bush said. Honolulu Mayor Mufi Hannemann (WHF 83–84) has established a similar program in Hawaii. Richard Greco (WHF 02–03) was sent to Afghanistan by former Secretary of Defense Donald Rumsfeld to assist in setting up a comparable program there. And Burn Loeffke (WHF 70–71) has been advising the Chinese government on setting up a Great Wall Fellows Program that is modeled on the White House Fellows.

AN ISSUE OF PATERNITY

During a speech at the White House Fellows' Fortieth Anniversary Celebration in October 2005, Colin Powell said, "John Gardner was the spirit of the White House Fellows program, but not just the initiating spirit—he stayed with it for all those years. He put his heart and his soul and his love and his energy into this program until he was no longer with us . . . this is John Gardner's program and it always will be."

Although Gardner has been widely credited for creating the White House Fellows program, in the early days some members of President Johnson's staff were uncomfortable with that and felt that the president should receive recognition too. After all, it was a team effort if there ever was one, and a bipartisan team effort to boot.

Bill Moyers understood that. When delivering John Gardner's eulogy at his memorial service on April 17, 2002, Moyers had this to say: "They were the right two at the right time. Johnson—impetuous, imperious, impatient; Gardner—reflective, righteous, resolute. Both were radical middle-of-the-roaders who believed in widening the road into a broad boulevard of opportunity so more people could travel it. One memorable summer evening, we sat on the south lawn of the White House—the six of us: LBJ and Lady Bird, John and Aida Gardner, Judith and me, both of us barely thirty. I just listened that evening, listened to one man who understood power and politics and another who understood the process and programs. Equality was no stranger to their political discourse, and it was clear to me both intended a fair and just America. Lyndon Johnson knew how to create opportunity; John Gardner how to fulfill it."

In the case of the White House Fellows, it's a testament to President Johnson's leadership that he was willing to let all the credit fall to his

Republican friend John Gardner. Johnson apparently didn't worry about credit; he had accomplished his goal. He had opened the door to the White House so that the nation's best and brightest young men and women could go to Washington and work with mentors to tackle the nation's biggest challenges, just as he and Lady Bird had done thirty-five years before.[12] Two great Americans, Lyndon Johnson and John Gardner, in a true bipartisan spirit, came together to establish through a public-private partnership the first leadership and public service program of its kind in the nation.

---

[12] Shortly after President Johnson's death, Lady Bird Johnson wrote the White House Fellows, "You should know that Lyndon had such great pride in the accomplishments of this program and for the individuals it has produced. The program was, for him, a chance for exceptionally talented young people to experience some of the same satisfactions and personal growth which were afforded a young congressional secretary more than 30 years before." March 1, 1973 Letter to the White House Fellows.

CHAPTER 3

CONNECTIONS: A LIFETIME OF FELLOWSHIP

The White House Fellows program has a truly remarkable network around the country. When I need anything—from a doctor to a car repair person in some other area of the United States, I immediately consult my White House Fellows Directory and receive the best advice in town. Yet another benefit is the sheer personal reward of having friends around the country and the globe with very diverse professional callings, backgrounds, and interest areas. All of them have enriched my life, and whenever I get together with former Fellows, I am challenged, entertained, and educated.

—Judge Deanell Tacha, U.S. Court of Appeals for the
Tenth Circuit (WHF 71–72)

THEY'LL NEVER ROAM ALONE

When Michelle Peluso and Jeff Glueck met during their White House Fellowships in 1998–1999, they hit it off from the start. Both came from business consulting backgrounds, both had won scholarships to Oxford, and each wanted to do something entrepreneurial someday. When their Fellows class had trouble making arrangements for a last-minute trip to New Orleans for the Jazz Fest, Glueck and Peluso started brainstorming. "We were organizing this trip at the last minute, and we wondered why someone didn't make it easy to schedule flights and line up hotels and cars at the same time so you didn't have to book one and then find out you can't get one of the other pieces," Glueck said. "That was one of the genesis moments for what became Site59, which stood for the site where you went at the fifty-ninth minute to make your travel arrangements." At the end of their Fellowship year, Peluso, then twenty-eight, and Glueck, thirty, moved to New York and started Site59 with funding from Peluso's former employer, the Boston Consulting Group. In spite of launching in March 2000—the same month the dot-com bubble burst, followed by the 9/11 terrorist attacks eighteen months later, which sent the travel industry into a tailspin—Peluso, Glueck, and their four partners had grown Site59 into a profitable venture within two years. "We actually had awful timing several times, but we made it through," Glueck said. "We were probably the ten thousandth travel site, but we solved a problem that no one had really thought about before, and we broke the great technology." That technology and the team's brilliant management skills caught the attention of Travelocity, which bought Site59 for $43 million in 2002. Peluso now serves as CEO and president of Travelocity, and Glueck is its chief marketing officer; all that is due in large part to the relationship they forged and the bright idea they had during their year as White House Fellows.

STAR POWER

Since the first Fellows arrived in Washington in 1965, the program has served as a conduit for connections between Fellows past and present as well as their principals and others they have met along the way. Working alongside Washington's elite has benefits that extend well beyond the Fellowship year, as nearly every Fellow has learned. For example, if you had told Dr. Sanjay Gupta (WHF 97–98) that within a few years of completing his Fellowship he would become a television star, a bestselling author, and a household name, he would have flashed that dazzling smile and told you—with his best bedside manner, of course—that you were totally out of your mind. But today Gupta *is* a star and a household name thanks to a connection he made when he was a White House Fellow.

At a Fellowship function, Gupta met former Fellow Tom Johnson (WHF 65–66), who was chief executive officer of CNN at that time. "He really cared deeply about health issues, and when he found out I was a doctor, we started talking," Gupta said. "He was very interested in bringing health news to the global network. It was a great discussion. But it didn't make sense to me then—I didn't quite understand what it would mean." What it meant was that four years later, when it came time to expand his network's medical coverage, Johnson remembered the young neurosurgeon and former Fellow and recruited him to serve as CNN's chief medical correspondent. "He clearly had a huge impact on my life professionally, but personally Tom is very close to my family—he's like a grandfather to my daughters," Gupta said. "We spend time together talking about life and the world, and I can't say enough about how that particular relationship has affected my life."

Gupta recalled others he met during his Fellowship year who have gone on to become lifelong friends. Ted Sorenson, who had been President Kennedy's special counsel and main speechwriter, spoke to Gupta's class during a lunch seminar, and Gupta approached him afterward and told him how much he admired his body of work. Sorenson invited Gupta to call him to arrange a lunch date. "I thought, Yeah, right, like he's going to have time to have lunch with me," Gupta recalled. "But I called him, and he did have lunch with me, and we have remained friends. And U.S. Senator Bill Frist came to talk to us too. He had been a heart surgeon who became Senate majority leader, and I was fascinated by that. So I called his office—he didn't know me at all—and said I was a White House Fellow. Within an hour his office called back and said, 'Send him up.' You could call people that you really wanted to meet, and they would return your call and meet with you. That's the power of the Fellows program."

U.S. Labor Secretary Elaine Chao (WHF 83–84) shares Gupta's belief that the White House Fellows program opens doors. "People are extraordinarily accommodating and accessible . . . if I wanted to learn about any topic, there would be people inside the government and outside who would be more than willing to come and give me a tutorial right away, whenever I called," Chao said. "This was a tremendous privilege." Chao credits one of those people, senator and two-time cabinet secretary Elizabeth Dole, with giving her a boost in her career, saying, "Senator Dole appointed many young women to leadership positions, and I am one of them. I've met so many others whose personal examples of leadership have taught me a lot about how to strive to be an inspiring, motivational, and effective leader."

ON GOOD ADVICE FROM FELLOW FELLOWS

During his Fellowship, Sam Brownback (WHF 90–91) was assigned to the Office of the U.S. Trade Representative. At the conclusion of his year in Washington, he returned to his previous position as Kansas's secretary of agriculture. But only three years after completing his Fellowship, Brownback revisited Washington, D.C., with a new title: U.S. representative from the Second Congressional District of Kansas. Brownback credits his White House Fellowship with helping him gain a quick and firm footing on Capitol Hill after his election. "In 1994, I was part of the biggest class of freshmen in the U.S. Congress since 1974, when Tim Wirth (WHF 68–69) and seventy-four other Democrats came to Washington in the aftermath of Watergate," Brownback explained.

"Before we took office, I asked several people in Washington for advice, including Paul Gigot (WHF 86–87), who was editorial page editor of the *Wall Street Journal.* The advice was to act quickly because our power would be strongest immediately following our election. But this was also the time when our knowledge level was generally the weakest. However, I got out of the blocks fast because the Fellows program had already given me an idea of how Washington works. I already had relationships, and I already had insight and a sense of how to push the system." His early accomplishments as a member of Congress launched his successful bid in 1996 for the U.S. Senate seat vacated by Bob Dole, who had resigned to focus on his presidential campaign. When Brownback ran for president in 2008, he again called upon lessons learned during his Fellowship year. "It gave me the big world picture. Meeting with so many intriguing people—it just gave me a view of how the world works, so when I was running for president I had some notion of how the whole system pulls together—or pulls apart. It was a fabulous experience."

A STEALTHY FELLOWSHIP CONNECTION

Few people have had a greater impact on the modern era than electrical engineer extraordinaire George Heilmeier (WHF 70–71). At RCA Laboratories in the 1960s, he developed the first liquid-crystal displays (LCDs) for use in computers, watches, calculators, and instrumentation, an innovation that earned him the prestigious Kyoto Prize, the Japanese equivalent of the Nobel Prize. If you own a laptop computer or a flat-screen television, you can thank Heilmeier for creating the display. If you use a digital camera, modem, or cell or cordless phone, you can thank Heilmeier too. It was during his tenure at Texas Instruments that the stage was set for the development of the digital-signal processor, the backbone of those electronic wonders.

Heilmeier had such an impressive year as a White House Fellow in the Department of Defense that at the close of his Fellowship year, he was appointed assistant director of defense research and engineering, which made him responsible for all of the Defense Department's electronics programs. Then, in the mid-1970s, he was named director of the Defense Advanced Research Projects Agency, better known as DARPA, where he led a team that was striving to stay one step ahead of the Russians and other threats both real and perceived. On Heilmeier's watch, DARPA researchers worked to perfect a way of tracking submerged Russian nuclear submarines, and he and his team hatched a plan to build an airplane with the ability to fly undetected by enemy radar.

However, he encountered roadblocks in building his "invisible aircraft." "I thought this airplane program was going to go down the tubes because we were ready to build and we needed help only the Air Force could give, and we weren't getting it," Heilmeier said. "So here is where White House Fellows connections count. There was a former Fellow who was an Air Force officer working in General David Jones's office. General Jones was the Air Force chief of staff. So I called the Fellow on the phone and said I needed to see the chief, and he said, 'Okay, I'll get you on the schedule,' and he did." Heilmeier kept the appointment, briefed the general on his plan to build the cutting-edge plane, and received the support that previously had been denied. By 1977, he had helped produce two aircraft that served as prototypes for the Air Force's F-117A Nighthawk and other "stealth" aircraft. During Operation Desert Storm in the early 1990s, F-117A's flew over a thousand sorties over Iraq and hit 1,600 significant targets. The F-117A was the only U.S. or allied fighter aircraft to score direct hits in downtown Baghdad. In 2003, twelve Nighthawks returned to Iraq, where they flew more than a hundred combat sorties. The Air Force retired the historic fleet in April 2008.

THE ULTIMATE IN FELLOWSHIP

William Kilberg (WHF 69–70) is a senior partner with the law firm Gibson, Dunn & Crutcher LLP in Washington, D.C., where he specializes in labor and employment law. As a White House Fellow he worked as a special assistant to Labor Secretary George Shultz and only three years later became the youngest person ever appointed to a subcabinet post in the federal government when he was confirmed as Solicitor of the Department of Labor. In 1982, President Reagan appointed him to the Commission on White House Fellows. Over the years, Kilberg has established quite a network of Fellows, but there's one particular relationship from that year that he cherishes most of all. "I met my wife, Bobbie Greene, who was also a Fellow my year," Kilberg explained. "We have been married for thirty-eight years and have five children and four grandchildren. When we got engaged on June 12, 1970, at the White House, George Shultz, who was then director of the Office of Management and Budget, declared that 'this is carrying fellowship just a bit too far.'" In all, eleven other couples have been associated with the White House Fellows program.

THE FELLOWSHIP NETWORK

After the terrorist attacks on September 11, 2001, Massachusetts Governor Jane Swift appointed a special advisory task force to evaluate security measures at Boston's Logan International Airport, which was where two of the four hijacked airplanes originated that day. The task force was asked to review security operations at the Massachusetts Port Authority (Massport), which ran Logan and other nearby airfields as well as the Port of Boston and Tobin Bridge. Governor Swift appointed Marshall "Marsh" Carter (WHF 75–76) to head the commission. Carter had been chairman and CEO of State Street Bank and Trust Company, but at the time of his appointment he was a senior fellow and adjunct lecturer at Harvard University's Kennedy School of Government (he is now deputy chairman of New York Stock Exchange Euronext). Carter quickly came to the conclusion that Massport's management structure needed a major renovation, and his first recommendation to Governor Swift was that the new leader of Massport be a true CEO and not a political appointee, as had been the case.

Governor Swift concurred, and Craig Coy (WHF 83–84) was tapped as Massport's new CEO. Coy had graduated from the U.S. Coast Guard Academy, served in the Coast Guard for more than twenty years, graduated from Harvard Business School with an MBA, and worked as deputy director for counterterrorism at the National Security Council. He seemed tailor-made for the job.

However, overhauling Massport at its darkest hour was still a tall order. "My most challenging experience as a leader was going in as CEO of Massport after 9/11 to face an organization completely beaten down by events, under severe financial pressure, and lacking any sense of mission or direction," Coy said. "I used all the lessons I learned as a White House Fellow and more. I called upon trusted mentors and local White House Fellows alumni who could help. Richard de Neufville (WHF 65–66) and Priscilla Douglas (WHF 81–82) both enthusiastically answered my call for help. And Marsh Carter served as a valuable behind-the-scenes advisor who offered to run 'public interference' on controversial issues, which would take the heat off me. That's what friends and White House Fellows colleagues do!" Carter had nothing but praise for Coy's efforts, saying with pride that "Craig did a great job and stabilized the place, then got way ahead of the Homeland Security people and made Logan a model for the rest of the country." Coy left his post at Massport in 2006 to take a position as president and COO of L-3 Communications Homeland Security Group.

SUCCESS BY ASSOCIATION

When John Shephard, Jr. (WHF 88–89), was a Fellow, he heard a speech that would change his life. "John Gardner told us we should be bold, reassess our career paths from time to time, and consider 'the road not taken,'" Shephard recalled. When the Cold War ended, he decided to take Gardner's advice and be bold, leaving a successful army career to pursue his childhood dream of becoming a novelist. But after two years of writing and with no book deal on the horizon, the bills had begun to mount and a new baby was on the way. He then polished his résumé and hit the streets looking for a job with a decent salary. "Within a month I was hired by two White House Fellow alumni who were CEO and COO of one of America's largest corporations," Shephard said. "They gave me my start in business because they liked my background and had had great success hiring other White House Fellows. I was given a boost by the reputations of those Fellows who had gone before!"

Shephard worked hard at his new job in one of the company's operating divisions, which spun off into a new public company. Within a few years, Shephard became financially independent, and he credits the White House Fellows program for making it possible. "I've been invited onto boards or received consulting work either directly or indirectly due to rec-ommendations from White House Fellow alumni I have known," he said. "Above all, I have made a lot of dear friends through the program and the alumni network and forged friendships that I hope will last a lifetime. That's what counts the most. Among other interests, now I'm working on a new novel. I'm hoping one day some of them will buy it and maybe even read it. I can still dream."

TOSSING A PEBBLE INTO THE GOVERNMENT POND

The White House Fellowship experience had a profound effect on my career. In 1972, Frank Carlucci selected me to serve my Fellowship year at the Office of Management and Budget. Seven years later, he asked me to be his senior military assistant when he became Deputy Secretary of Defense. Six years later, he asked me to be his deputy when he became National Security Advisor. Ten months later, I replaced Frank when he became Secretary of Defense. What I learned about govern-ment as a White House Fellow was the key to the opportunities that came my way. I know of no other program that provides such a learn-ing experience."[13]

COLIN POWELL (WHF 72–73),
FORMER JOINT CHIEFS OF STAFF CHAIRMAN,
NATIONAL SECURITY ADVISOR, AND SECRETARY OF STATE

Former Secretary of State Colin Powell (WHF 72–73) has called the day he received orders from Infantry Branch to apply for a White House Fellowship "the turning point" in his life. He had never heard of the pro-gram and was absolutely not interested in applying. "The major made clear that Infantry Branch was not asking me. It was ordering me," Powell wrote.[14] Therefore, he applied and was selected. Although the story of Powell's ascension from army officer, to White House Fellow, to general, to national security advisor, to secretary of state is well documented, per-haps what is not clear is the ripple effect Powell's Fellowship had on the lives of other Fellows. Take Mitchell Reiss (WHF 88–89). Powell chose

---

[13] White House Fellowship brochure, 1994–1995, p. 4.
[14] Colin L. Powell with Joseph E. Persico, *My American Journey* (New York: Random House), p. 161.

Reiss above all the other Fellows that year to be his special assistant at the National Security Council. Reiss recalls that "General Powell wasn't sure what I'd be able to do for him, but he said if I kept my mouth shut and my eyes and ears open I would probably learn a lot. That was good advice, because one of the things he did for me was invite me to the senior staff meetings every morning, where I had a chance to observe firsthand how a very skillful leader handled senior staff, and substantively how he handled policy issues and how he saw his role as protecting and promoting the president and the country's interest," said Reiss. "I spent a lot of time on the arms-control side, which was my primary interest at the time, and I also focused on Asia, the Middle East, and the Soviet Union—I had free run of anything I wanted to see."

Indeed, after Reiss completed his Fellowship and became a consultant to several governmental agencies and departments as well as chief negotiator and general counsel of the Korean Peninsula Energy Development Organization, Powell tapped him in 2003 to be policy planning director at the State Department. At his swearing-in ceremony, Powell said, "Back in 1988, a dashing young national security advisor had the foresight to choose Mitchell from an impressive crop of White House Fellows as his special assistant. It's so gratifying to confirm my own wisdom. It was clear to me then that Mitchell had the dedication, the brains and the judgment to be effective. By effective, I don't just mean in the bureaucratic sense. I mean how he knows how to get things done that matter to real people. I wasn't the first in government and I certainly won't be the last to recognize Mitchell's many talents and put them to good use."[15]

Then there is the case of Robert "Bud" McFarlane (WHF 71–72), who was President Ronald Reagan's national security advisor from 1983 to 1985. I asked Bud if he would have risen to this position on his own if he had not been a Fellow. "No, I never would have," he replied. "I was a known quantity, and that was only true because I was a White House Fellow and my office was physically right next door to Al Haig and Henry Kissinger, so I had to bump into them every day. In short, the Fellowship put me in a position to establish relationships that were key to my advancement."

---

[15] Colin Powell, remarks at Mitchell Reiss's swearing-in ceremony, October 30, 2003.

EVERYONE WINS

The Fellowship network is far-reaching and powerful, and it has the potential to change not only the Fellows' lives but also the world. E. Kinney Zalesne (WHF 95–96) was working as an assistant district attorney in Philadelphia when she was selected as a White House Fellow. An honors graduate of Yale and Harvard Law School, Zalesne served her Fellowship in Vice President Al Gore's office under the guidance of her principal, Chief Domestic Policy Advisor Greg Simon. The Internet was new technology in the mid-1990s, and the Clinton administration was concerned that Internet availability could become a civil rights issue: A digital divide could emerge in which only people of means would have access to information and people with lower incomes would be left out of the loop. President Clinton and Vice President Gore made it a high priority to wire all of the nation's schools and libraries and make sure that low-income schools had access to hardware, software, teacher training, and the infrastructure necessary to bring in the new technology.

One of the people tasked with making that happen was Kinney Zalesne, whose main focus during her Fellowship year was educational technology. "The office of the vice president was like a beehive, with lots of people crowded into a small space, all caught up in the excitement of their work," Zalesne said. "One of the things I did was write an executive order that streamlined the donation of excess federal computers to schools. Basically we had vast numbers of computers that were being turned over every year from government agencies, and we streamlined a process where they could be recycled, refurbished, and given to schools and educational nonprofits."

Presidents typically issue executive orders to direct and guide agencies and departments in the executive branch; these are complicated documents that are legally binding and carry the same weight as a law passed by Congress. Zalesne drafted the complex order to establish the surplus computer donation program, and President Clinton signed it at a special ceremony. At the conclusion of her Fellowship year, Zalesne went on to become president and executive vice president of two national social-change organizations—College Summit and Hillel—and also served as counsel to Attorney General Janet Reno. Along with coauthor Mark Penn, she wrote the 2007 bestseller *Microtrends: The Small Forces Behind Tomorrow's Big Changes.*

Zalesne's desk in the vice president's office next would be occupied by Elisabeth Stock (WHF 96–97), who stepped in to implement the program mandated by Zalesne's executive order. Stock pulled together a small team and launched the Computers for Learning program, which began the worthy task of redirecting thousands of surplus government computers to the neediest American schools. Stock wanted to take the concept to the next level, and so upon leaving Washington at the end of her Fellowship year, she started a program that would get donated computers not just into schools but into the homes of low-income families so that kids—and their parents—could have a computer loaded with educational software accessible to them every single day. For direction, Stock reached out to Gaynor McCown (WHF 93–94), who worked for three years after her Fellowship as a senior education policy maker in the Clinton administration before returning to New York City to work as senior vice president for educational and workforce development for the New York City Partnership and Chamber of Commerce. At the partnership, she focused on increasing the private sector's role in public education. She also led the first pay-for-performance system in the New York City public schools. McCown linked Stock with the right people, and in 1999 Stock launched Computers for Youth, which operates in New York, Philadelphia, and Atlanta and has provided approximately 15,000 families with refurbished computers full of educational software.

Stock hopes Fellows will continue to reach out to one another, not only to provide a leg up in business or government but also to work together to have a positive impact on the nation. "Everyone is supposed to follow their heart. So some people decide what they really want to do is be in business—to make lots of money for themselves and their investors," she said. "There are other people who go out and do nonprofit work and change the world; others will say I want to go into government and change the world that way. But the thing is, all of us need each other. Even those people who have gone off to make lots of money, they then want to use their money to improve the world too, and they just don't necessarily want to be doing the work at the ground level since that's not where their leverage is. There are others of us who do want to be on the ground and can make a profound difference there. If we could all just join forces and band together—imagine what kind of world we would have."

PART II

THE LESSONS

CHAPTER 4

LEADERS KNOW THERE'S MORE TO LIFE THAN WORK

In preparing to write this book, I interviewed 220 former White House Fellows and asked each of them to name the most important traits that great leaders possess. Just as I expected, integrity, vision, judgment, stamina, and the ability to inspire and communicate effectively were among the characteristics cited most often as leadership essentials. However, I was struck by how many told me that the greatest leaders insist on establishing a proper balance between their work and their lives outside the office. One such source was presidential historian, Pulitzer Prize–winning author, and NBC news analyst Doris Kearns Goodwin (WHF 67–68).

When her telephone rang at 6 a.m. on that bitterly cold January morning in 1973, Goodwin knew exactly who would be on the other end of the line. Former president Lyndon Baines Johnson had wakened her often for early-morning chats since leaving the White House for his Texas ranch. His dependence on Goodwin to assist him with his memoirs had deepened, and over the years the young woman had become his trusted confidante.

"He was speaking very softly when he called that morning, and he sounded incredibly sad," Goodwin recalled. "He had read Sandburg's biography of President Lincoln, which made him think about how *he* was going to be remembered, and he was afraid that ordinary people in the future would forget him. I tried to cheer him up by promising to put a question about him on every exam I gave at Harvard for the duration of my teaching career so everyone would remember him. Well, he kind of cut me off abruptly, which was odd, and demanded that I listen to what he was telling me. He told me to get married, have children, and spend time with them. He talked about how he should have spent more time with his family, because that's a different and more worthy kind of posterity than the public one that he had been seeking throughout his entire political career. That would be our last conversation, because he died of a heart attack two days later—but what a wonderful thing to leave me with."

Lyndon Johnson's wise words would come back to Goodwin years later when she was offered a chance to be considered for head of the Peace Corps during President Jimmy Carter's administration. Since his death, she had followed LBJ's advice—had gotten married and had children—and at the time she was writing a book about the Kennedys. "I'm not sure I would have gotten that job anyway, but there was no way that I could have taken it," Goodwin explained. "I had a family—two young children—and that job would have eliminated any possibility of balance because I would have been traveling all the time. So I did not try for it. Lyndon Johnson's advice also helped me not just in that moment but later on when I decided to take a longer time to write these books so I could be home with the kids. I decided that it didn't matter to the world if the books came out in five years versus ten years, but I like to believe that it mattered to the kids that I could be home when they were little and also when they came home from school. And I think seeing Lyndon Johnson so desolate in his later years did have an impact on my trying to strike a greater balance in my own life."

Goodwin believes that although it's natural to think career achievement will bring happiness, those who live the richest lives manage to achieve a healthy balance of work, love, and play. "To commit yourself to just one of those spheres without the others is to leave open an older age filled with sadness, because once the work is gone, you have nothing left—no hobbies, no sports," Goodwin said. "Your family may love you, but they are not in the center of your life as they might have been had you paid attention to them all the way through. And I always argue that the ability to relax and replenish your energy is absolutely essential."

Goodwin recalled how Abraham Lincoln set aside his worries by attending the theater over a hundred times during the Civil War and how Franklin Roosevelt diverted his attention from the immense burden of leading the nation through World War II by hosting a cocktail hour every evening in the White House. "The rule was that you couldn't talk about the war. You could only gossip about people or discuss the books you'd read or the movies you'd seen, so for a few precious hours he could forget that the war was raging," Goodwin said. "And then when Churchill would come, the two of them would stay up talking, smoking, and drinking until 2 a.m., and at one point Roosevelt's wife, Eleanor, came in to see them and said, 'Isn't it time for you two little boys to go to bed?' Roosevelt also relaxed by playing poker. John F. Kennedy would go to Hyannis Port and sail and play touch football. All those men knew that there was more to life beyond the pressures they were under, and it made them more effective leaders."

One Fellow who nearly learned that lesson too late was my White House Fellows classmate John Shephard, Jr. (WHF 88–89). It was September 2003, and Shephard was senior vice president of operations of Northrop Grumman Newport News, a 550-acre shipyard full of nuclear-powered aircraft carriers and submarines. The Virginia coast was in the path of Hurricane Isabel, the Atlantic's most deadly and destructive storm that year, and Shephard was responsible for securing the shipyard and its several billion dollars' worth of naval vessels, buildings, cranes, docks, and equipment. The hurricane was churning just offshore and heading straight for Newport News, but the storm preparations were coming together nicely at the shipyard, and so Shephard left for a brief time to help his wife secure their home. He was carrying a potted tree into his garage when he suddenly felt a sharp pain in his head. "It felt like a knife through the top of my head, the worst headache I'd ever had or could imagine. I got nauseous and went in the bathroom to vomit. I thought maybe it was some kind of migraine," Shephard recalled. "My wife insisted I go to the emergency room at the hospital, but I shrugged it off, saying I had to go run the shipyard and guide our emergency crews through the storm. No way was I going to be a wimp and bail out on my people over a bad headache."

Shephard returned to the shipyard and for the next thirty hours steered his team through the storm, whose eye passed directly over the huge complex of ships and facilities. The crushing pain in his head had not subsided, but he kept his agony to himself. Once the storm had passed, he supervised the effort to restore the shipyard's operating capacity. Although the hurricane inflicted serious damage to the area, the shipyard came out well.

No one was injured, and no navy vessels were harmed. Shephard's home and family survived intact too, although many homes nearby were ruined. He spent the next few days jockeying back and forth between the shipyard and his neighborhood, where he helped people clear downed limbs and other debris. "My headache was constant and no better," Shephard said. "I knew something more serious than a migraine had occurred, but my doctor's office was closed, all phones and power were out, and my only option was the emergency room, which I figured had better things to do than dealing with a dude with a wicked headache." Shephard pressed on, and the shipyard reopened just six days after the storm. It was only then that he agreed to go to the emergency room. The attending doctor determined after a battery of tests that Shephard had suffered a subarachnoid hemorrhage in his brain, an event that often results in paralysis or death. He was admitted to the intensive care unit and then spent two weeks undergoing a series of procedures designed to save his life and prevent a future occurrence.

"Lesson number one: As leaders, we tend to think we are indispensable, but we aren't. As DeGaulle said, 'the graveyards are full of indispensable men.' We are actually more indispensable *to our families*, but we tend to forget their needs when we play at being Superman on the job," Shephard explained. "The shipyard did well through the storm mostly because of good advance preparation and excellent work by our on-site emergency teams. The leadership I provided on site during and after Isabel could have been provided by someone else. It takes a little trust and humility to admit that. If I had collapsed at the shipyard—a real risk in retrospect—it would have interfered unnecessarily with the important job at hand. As it was, I didn't burden my people by mentioning my situation, and by the grace of God the hemorrhage neither killed me nor kept me from doing the job. But my surgeon pulled no punches, saying how dumb it was to wait to seek help when my body was clearly sending a signal. If I'd died, it would have been a blow to my family, and my fiftieth birthday would've been a major dud. Lesson number two: If you feel a knife through the top of your head, go see a doctor." This certainly points to the need for regular visits to the doctor for full physical checkups. More important, leaders understand the value of regular exercise and a healthy lifestyle, which serves as an antidote to the high levels of stress in one's professional life.

Thankfully, everything came out okay for Shephard. but it took a personal tragedy for former Fellow William "Bill" Drummond (WHF 76–77) to realize the importance of work-life balance. Drummond started his journalism career at the *Louisville* (Kentucky) *Courier-Journal.* He then worked his way up the ladder at the *L.A. Times*, progressing from staff writer to assistant metropolitan editor to bureau chief of New Delhi and Jerusalem before being appointed to a White House Fellowship by President Gerald Ford. He was assigned to work in the State Department, but when Jimmy Carter was inaugurated in January 1977, Drummond was tapped to be an associate White House press secretary. After his Fellowship, he returned to the *L.A. Times* and then accepted an offer to become the first editor of National Public Radio's *Morning Edition.* In 1983, he left NPR to become a journalism professor at the University of California at Berkeley, where he remains today. Throughout his impressive careers in journalism and teaching, Drummond was a self-described workaholic—that is, until the day in 1997 when his wife of fifteen years, Faith, was diagnosed with breast cancer. Suddenly nothing at the office mattered anymore.

"She was getting chemotherapy, and she was in such pain. I felt utterly helpless—like a fifth wheel. I desperately wanted to help her, so I took it upon myself to enroll in a massage therapy course, and I got certified as an acupressure therapist. Acupressure helped her so much, and I liked it so much that I enrolled in another course on emotional balance," Drummond said. "So when she was dying, we used this guided therapy and revisited all the places we had been when we were the most happy. Faith and I had visited Mexico often. Our favorite place was the Pueblo Bonito resort in Mazatlan, on the western coast of Mexico. We had bought a time share there not long after the resort opened in 1984. We often took long strolls along the beach. We knew all the contours along a one-mile route south of the resort. It wasn't hard for us to remember that place. We could see the water glistening on the beach. It helped both of us to do that, and I believe in the power of it. Then I looked at all my colleagues, and their family lives were in such chaos, so I decided we must do something to show people that there's another way. At U.C. Berkeley we started a course called "Emotional Balance for Journalists," which shows the students that there's a mind-body connection and gives them some techniques that will not only prolong their working lives but also their lives as human beings. There's an old saying that on one's deathbed, you never hear somebody say, 'I wish I spent more time at the office.' It's an article of faith these days that stress kills and destroys. But in the news business we tend to accept stress as the cost of doing business. I reject that. I try to help students gain an inner calm. It begins with some simple concepts, good diet, rest, and exercise. I am a firm believer in the healing powers of touch. In my introductory journalism writing and reporting class, one class meeting per week takes place at the gym. We spend two hours in meditation, bodywork, and guided imagery."

If Drummond's class had been available when Tom Johnson (WHF 65–66) was studying journalism back in the 1960s, he might have taken the curriculum to heart and spared himself and his family a considerable amount of suffering later on. Beginning with his first job at a daily newspaper when he was only a teen, Johnson held incredibly stressful positions throughout his career and put tremendous pressure on himself not just to succeed but to excel. From the *Macon Telegraph,* to Harvard Business School, to the White House, to the LBJ family business, and then to the publisher's desk at the *Dallas Times Herald,* for decades Johnson pushed onward, driven by an ambition that totally consumed him. Although he adored his wife, Edwina, and his children, Wyatt and Christa, he made work his top priority until at last he reached a pinnacle: In 1980 he was named publisher of the prestigious *L.A. Times.* As was his pattern, Johnson threw himself totally into that job too, much to the frustration of Christa, who at the wise old age of nine scolded him for missing yet another of her soccer games, saying, "Don't forget you're a daddy, too!"

Johnson realized that his workaholic nature had caused him to lose his compass, but he didn't know how to go about getting his sense of direction back. He had invested all of his self-worth in his career journey and job title. Then, one day in 1989, that investment turned sour. Despite the posting of the highest earnings, circulation, and revenues that year in the paper's entire history, the family that owned the Times Mirror Company wanted a less liberal paper, and Johnson was ordered to fire the editor of the editorial pages, Tony Day. Johnson refused and was fired summarily. It was the first time he ever had "failed" at a job, and he was devastated.

"Stripped of my position as publisher, I convinced myself that I was a failure, and my self-worth crashed. I plunged into very deep depression. It was like a trapdoor suddenly opened beneath me. I fell so swiftly down, down, down into a dark, deep blackness—almost a very deep well with no light visible above me," Johnson explained. "My wife, Edwina, was the first to try to rescue me, taking me to UCLA Medical to see a psychiatrist."

The psychiatrist determined that Johnson displayed many of the common symptoms of chronic depression: He felt hopeless, worthless, adrift, and hurt. He did not want to get out of bed in the morning, and preferred to withdraw into a darkened room where he would be left alone. He snapped angrily at his wife and experienced an almost total loss of libido. The doctor prescribed a series of antidepressants—including lithium and Prozac—that left Johnson feeling like a zombie. Nothing moved him. He began having thoughts of suicide. "I had rationalized that Edwina and my two children would be better off without an angry, verbally abusive failure of a father—that my departure from their lives actually would be better for them," Johnson admitted. "But I did not kill myself because it would have destroyed my eighty-year-old mother in Georgia. I was her only child and the greatest pride of her life. She thought I was the finest son in the whole world."

Family, friends, and colleagues rushed to Johnson's side to offer support and encouragement. From across the country came a series of new job opportunities that in normal circumstances would have made him spring to action in a heartbeat. Don Graham, his mother Katharine Graham, and *New York Times* publisher Punch Sulzberger offered Johnson a job as publisher of the *International Herald Tribune*. Knight-Ridder Chairman Alvah Chapman, President Jim Batten, and Vice Chairman Lee Hills also offered him several jobs, including publisher of the *Philadelphia Inquirer*. His friend Joe Allbritton suggested that he take a senior leadership role in his media and banking company. Although Johnson did not leap instantly out of bed, he gradually began to notice all the goodness and love that surrounded him. "What pulled me back from the brink was the belief—even in the darkest days—that maybe, just maybe, I could escape from the grip of depression and find my way out. The job offers reassured me that I was still respected in my profession," Johnson said. "Then Ted Turner offered me the presidency of CNN in August 1990. The excitement of running a global news organization, of returning to my home state of Georgia, and of getting out of Times Mirror compelled me to accept Ted's offer."

With a renewed sense of hope, Johnson began seeing Dr. Charles Nemeroff, chairman of psychiatry at the Emory University School of Medicine. Dr. Nemeroff prescribed the medication Effexor, which Johnson described as a "miracle drug" that helped return him to his old self. "I still have occasional bouts of depression, but they are not as deep or as lengthy as those I experienced in the late 1980s," Johnson said. "I speak openly about this to show that even severely depressed people can escape from depression with the right professional help. Depression is an illness, not some sickness that can't be discussed openly and honestly. We must do more about the stigma, and I intend to do my part."

If Johnson had known when he was starting his career what he knows today, he would have done many things differently. "I would have balanced my work with play. I would have been as wonderful a father as I think I am now as a grandfather. I would have loved Edwina more, laughed more, and enjoyed the splendid world outside an office. And I would have been a far better balanced person—not the uptight, disciplined workaholic that I was."

In short, he might have been more like White House Fellow cocreator John Gardner.

Of all the great leaders I've ever met, Gardner offered perhaps the best illustration of how to live a balanced life. I met him during my Fellowship year, and I learned that this great man who had accomplished so much in his professional life—as an advisor to presidents and a cabinet secretary, an author, and a founder of a citizen's lobbying organization, among other things—was not a workaholic who burned the midnight oil, chained to his desk in a downtown office six or seven days a week. On the contrary, John Gardner knocked off at a reasonable hour each weekday afternoon and went home to his family. Although he typically took a briefcase full of papers home with him, he worked and wrote his books at a desk he had placed in the middle of the busiest part of his house, with the hustle and bustle of family life going on all around him.

"His desk was, by choice, always placed and exposed to the full noise, commotion, interruptions, and ups and downs of family activity in which he participated fully. The policy was never a closed door, and we took advantage of it," recalled Gardner's daughter Francesca. "In his last few years . . . I asked him about this, and he said an interesting thing. He said, 'I made a great point of never closing my door so that the scramble of infancy and childhood just went on around me. I learned to tune it out when I had to, but it always kept me in very close touch. I knew every little waver in my family's psyche because I lived with it, and that's valuable. That's family life.'"

Howard N. Nemerovski (WHF 65–66) served as the first White House Fellow assigned to work with John Gardner during his tenure as secretary of health, education, and welfare. Nemerovski recalled how Gardner focused on family life and on a wide variety of lifelong friendships yet at the same time managed to achieve great success in his career. "He never showed any interest in his personal advancement, and of course, he had achieved as much prominence and success as anyone could want," Nemerovski said. "Other people who had cabinet posts might say, 'Well, what's my next career move, and who is going to paint the portrait of me that's going to go up on the wall?' John never thought that way. He took me to the State of the Union message in 1966. During the drive over to the Capitol, he told me that President Kennedy had offered him the job of assistant secretary of state for international affairs. John said he rejected that offer of a prestigious post because he didn't want to leave his family and didn't want to leave his then-current position at Carnegie. He believed there were many other opportunities to accomplish valuable things without sacrificing time with his family."

Gardner's ego was such that he did not worry about reaching the next rung on his career ladder, and he never resorted to power-tripping devices such as scheduling meetings to begin at seven at night just to prove his importance. "He was not a person who was addicted to the symbolism of power," Nemerovski recalled. "John's plate was full of challenges as he accomplished so many things that benefited society, but he consistently balanced his time among work, quiet periods of reflection, family, and friends. He was a different kind of man, totally different from anybody I observed in that town."

Indeed, Gardner was a beloved mentor and role model to many, Nemerovski included. "John's generosity to his many friends was remarkable. For example, he encouraged Stanford University to offer the position of dean of the business school to a longtime close friend. Not knowing that Gardner was responsible for the offer, the friend, who was established as CEO of a major international corporation, sought Gardner's concurrence in his tentative decision to remain in his comfortable and prestigious position among America's corporate elite. Gardner offered a simple refutation that I have repeated to my friends in similar quandaries many times over the past forty years. He simply said, 'Everyone needs repotting every twenty years or so!'"

Gardner's generosity to friends led to an unlikely but memorable surmise. On a gray overcast day in 2002, Nemerovski attended Gardner's memorial service at the Stanford Memorial Chapel. The officiant called for a moment of silent reflection about John Gardner. "Shortly after the organ music began, the sun burst through the thick layer of clouds, shone through the stained-glass window, and suddenly a marvelous bright multicolored aura lit up the Memorial Chapel," Nemerovski recalled. "Some of us talked about it after the ceremony, and we joked that God probably knew that John would have liked his friends to have some cheer on that gray day, so He ordered the sun to shine through a break in the clouds."

Reflecting further on that memorial service, Nemerovski recalled another vital aspect of Gardner's complex yet straightforward philosophy. "John's generosity was balanced by a conviction that there is no free lunch and that all of us have duties to others if we are to have a civil society. Therefore, it was fitting and moving that the front page of the memorial service program contained a frequent saying of John's: 'Liberty and duty, freedom and responsibility. That's the deal.' And that's the essence of John Gardner."

Somehow Gardner instinctively knew that if he was going to live a happy life, he'd have to achieve some sort of equilibrium among all his competing interests. That instinct helped him attain great personal and professional success, and he passed his wisdom on, either directly or indirectly, to hundreds of young people through his association with the White House Fellows program. I think he would have been particularly pleased to hear the story of how Mimi Ghez (WHF 00–01) achieved greater balance in her life by developing a spiritual foundation during her Fellowship. Ghez's mother is Catholic, and her father is Jewish. As a compromise, they pledged to not "impose" their religions on their children. Thus, Ghez grew up with very little exposure to any religion. However, as time went by, she noticed that many of the country's greatest leaders were influenced strongly by religion. Dr. Martin Luther King and Malcolm X were the two who most intrigued her.

When Ghez became a White House Fellow, she was surrounded for the first time by people who discussed religion and talked about the varieties of services they attended. She became especially close to one classmate whose values and character she had come to admire over the course of the year. "Of all the people in the class, he struck me as the most upstanding and the person with the most natural charisma and people-person skills—the only person who made it a policy not to gossip about others," Ghez said. "In one private conversation, we were discussing how we rank different aspects of life—community, relationships, etcetera. He told me he always put God first, even above his wife, whom he loves very much. I found that both shocking and intriguing, because I knew how much he loved her. We also discussed how the Bible has been understood as a series of leadership allegories and that his understanding of the Bible in this context, and his love of God, helps guide his way to better relationships with others, including his wife, coworkers, and subordinates."

Ghez's classmate invited her to attend services with his family, and finally, during the last week of the Fellowship, she did. Because of that experience and the support of other White House Fellows classmates, Ghez began to believe in God. She now attends services regularly. "I share this personal anecdote because I know, like my fellow Fellow knew, that my faith is helping me become a better person, friend, and leader," Ghez said. "When all is said and done, the most significant thing I got out of the White House Fellowship Program is faith. I will always be grateful for that, and I know my life is better and more balanced as a result of it."

Always remember that great leaders have deep reserves of physical, spiritual, and emotional energy and that that energy usually is fueled by a strong and supportive relationship with the people they love, regular exercise, a healthy lifestyle, and setting aside time for reflection. For instance, I try to exercise at least three times a week and stay fit by following a healthy lifestyle. In terms of balance, I work very hard to devote quality time to the three most important aspects of my life. First come the people I love—my family and all my close friends. Second are all the activities that make me come alive as a man and that I'm deeply passionate about— my professional life, my community involvement, and my many hobbies. And finally, above all else is my spiritual life—my faith and belief in God. I'm happiest and most effective when I achieve the right balance among these three critical components.

Of course everyone has his or her own priorities and beliefs, and you must determine yours. When you know what is truly most important for you, develop a plan to devote the quality time each deserves. The balance you achieve will help create the inner strength necessary to make you a much more effective leader.

CHAPTER 5

LEADERS FOCUS ON THE MISSION

"The mission is what you exist for, and everything is secondary to the mission," explained former Secretary of State Colin Powell (WHF 72–73). "The mission is what will take people up the hill. . . . The mission has to be driven down through every level of the organization so everybody understands what we are trying to accomplish and is committed to its accomplishment. The mission has to be clear. It has to be straightforward. It has to be understandable. But above all, it has to be achievable, and it has to be something that will cause people to believe so that they will *want* to follow you and not just *have* to follow you."[16]

When he was selected to be in the first class of White House Fellows in 1965, Tom Veblen was a thirty-five-year-old corporate vice president at Cargill Inc., where he had worked for the previous six years managing Cargill's soybean business in Norfolk, Virginia. He was a high achiever and a savvy businessman accustomed to jumping in and getting things done, but he was slightly out of his element in Washington D.C.; he knew he had to learn the ropes first. His first week as a Fellow in the Department of the Interior was spent reading reams of documents about the department's activities and becoming acquainted with the staff and the office routine. He quickly decided he liked the atmosphere. The people were down to earth

---

[16] Colin L. Powell, remarks, "2003 Leadership Lecture: Why Leadership Matters in the Department of State," October 28, 2003.

and friendly and responded to his questions in a professional, direct way. However, there was one question that neither the paperwork nor the staff could answer and that Veblen was determined to understand: What was the mission of the Department of the Interior?

After several days, Veblen was sent to meet Interior Secretary Stewart Udall to get acquainted and discuss the young Fellow's assignment. Udall was a lawyer who had served in the U.S. House of Representatives from his home state of Arizona before President Kennedy named him Secretary of the Interior. In that role he became one of the country's most fervent conservationists, pushing through many of the environmental laws that sprang from President Johnson's Great Society legislation, including the Clean Water Restoration Act, the Wilderness Act, the National Trails System, and the Endangered Species Preservation Act, to name a few. When young Veblen appeared at his office door in September 1965, Udall skipped the pleasantries and went right to the heart of the matter.

"Well, it's good to have you with us. I hear you're ready to go to work. What have you learned so far?"

"As a matter of fact, lots," Veblen replied. "The variety and breadth of things going on in the department is amazing. My week of reading has given me a pretty good sense of the programs, but I must admit that I'm somewhat frustrated. I have yet to come across a simple, straightforward statement of Interior's mission. Nobody has been able to tell me. That suggests that either this place is adrift or I haven't figured out yet the right questions to ask."

Stewart stared at Veblen for a moment and then laughed.

"You know what, that's just about what I said to President Kennedy when he asked me to take this job," Udall said. "And then President Kennedy said to me, 'Stew, come over here and take a look at this map showing the national parks. What a great country. We have a national park system second to none. The problem is, the parks are all out in the West and the people are all in the East. Your mission, should you agree to be Secretary of Interior, is to figure out how to put parks where the people are.' And that, Tom, is Interior's mission! So, now that you know the mission, what would you like to do around here?"

With that simple and clear mission communicated from his boss, everything clicked for Veblen, who enthusiastically responded, "I want to work on the things that most concern you. The tougher they are, the better I'll like it. And of course that means I should be working right here in your office."

"Fair enough," Udall replied. "I need a third assistant, and you're it. You'll work out of my office and lend a hand wherever we both agree it will be useful. I have several things that need doing, and one of them is to figure out how we can create a national park for the performing arts at Wolf Trap Farm. I don't understand why we can't get that done, and I'd like you to take a crack at it. My assistant Orren Beaty will be glad to answer any questions you have about how we go about things around here. Come and see me when you run out of things to do or need my help. Have a great weekend."

And with that Udall headed for the door, where he paused, turned, and with a big grin said, "Oh, by the way, we work Saturdays here."

Beaty explained to Veblen that Wolf Trap was just outside Washington, between downtown and the newly completed Dulles International Airport. The lovely property was owned by Catherine Filene Shouse, a wealthy widow who in the early 1960s declared her wish to create a national center for the performing arts on the property and to have it administered by the National Parks Service. Udall was in favor of that—it fit his department's mission to bring parks to where the people are—and encouraged the Parks Service to pursue the opportunity and develop a plan for making it happen. However, the ensuing negotiations came to a screeching halt when Mrs. Shouse said she would donate the farm to the government only if she could maintain full control over the new park's policies and operation. The Park Service offered to give Mrs. Shouse an advisory role and nothing more, and so she withdrew her offer.

Mrs. Shouse proceeded to bring whatever political pressure she could muster to bear on the Park Service. It didn't work. In fact, her attempt to pressure the Park Service backfired. George Hartzog, the Park Service's director, called Udall to ask him to tell Mrs. Shouse that his people no longer would accept her, or for that matter her attorney's or her architect's, phone calls. Hartzog said, "Not on your life." Mrs. Shouse then called to ask Stewart to intervene. He demurred, telling her that the problem was Congress and that there was, in his opinion, no chance of passing the legislation required for the government to accept her donation. An impasse was declared, and the Wolf Trap Farm Performing Arts Park was deep-sixed.

"My first impulse was to deep-six the idea myself," Veblen recalled. "Then I got to thinking. The idea was a good one; in fact, it might even be classified as a nifty one. Maybe the Park Service was overreacting." But Veblen soon learned that Mrs. Shouse was not the only roadblock to establishing a performing arts center at Wolf Trap Farm. "I went to see Director Hartzog, who came across as a solid citizen, and after some preliminaries, he gave me the full story," Veblen recalled. The national park system was woefully underfunded, with a budget that couldn't even sustain the country's existing facilities, let alone any new ones. Even if he could get Mrs. Shouse to relinquish control of Wolf Trap, there was no way Congress and the Budget Bureau would approve new expenditures while the Parks Service was unable to meet its present obligations. How could the service justify taking on a money sump like Wolf Trap when the rest of the system was falling apart?

"The Wolf Trap Park problem was a complex one. For certain, nothing would happen until the property had been deeded to the government, and the deeding couldn't happen until Congress authorized it," Veblen explained. "Congress wouldn't authorize it unless the Park Service and the Budget Bureau approved, a senator sponsored it, and the appropriate committees of both houses concurred on the legislation. Mrs. Shouse wouldn't donate if she couldn't control the artistic elements. The Park Service insisted on total control: If they owned it, they would manage it, period. Talk about a 'catch-22!'"

Veblen was almost ready to throw in the towel, but President Kennedy's words kept ringing in his ears: Figure out how to put parks where the people are. And then the light dawned. If he could make the Park Service's performing arts element self-supporting, the preservation element of the project could be fully justified. The newly passed Outdoor Recreation Act authorized the secretary of the interior to accept provisional donations of land to facilitate the development of local, state, and regional parks. Why not have Mrs. Shouse deed Wolf Trap Farm to the Secretary of the Interior? Then Congress could authorize the establishment of a park to be facilitated by transfer of the deeded land to the Park Service rather than to a state entity. A foundation endowed by Mrs. Shouse could be established to construct the performance venues and support Wolf Trap's future performances. The Park Service would plan the park's physical facility and manage it; the foundation would plan, pay for, and manage the performances; and Mrs. Shouse would chair the foundation and serve on a park advisory board.

Interest in Veblen's plan grew. A Virginia senator agreed to sponsor the legislation, and the chairs of the appropriate congressional committees bought into the plan too because the park would be self-supporting. Mrs. Shouse heeded her advisors and signed the necessary transfer documents. "We were stretching things a bit, and some winks and nods were required to justify the transfers of property and money, but by midspring everyone was fully on board and the legislation was drafted. But we decided to forgo petitioning the budget director for his approval before introducing the legislation because we felt this would be a major stumbling block," Veblen explained.

"The budget director first learned of the bill when it was introduced into Congress, and within hours the proverbial stuff hit the proverbial fan," Veblen said. "Three people—an Interior Department lawyer, Beaty, and I—were identified as the culprits and our session with the budget director was a bit tense, but in the end he decided there were bigger fish to fry—or skewer—and he sent us back to Interior properly chastised. He then called Stewart Udall to tell him 'never again,' which prompted Udall to call Orren and me into his office, where he said, 'I told the budget director that one Wolf Trap Farm Park is enough. Well done.'" Veblen's year as a Fellow ended in August 1966 with the legislation to establish the park still pending. Two months later the legislation passed both houses and was signed by the president. Two and a half years after that, Mrs. Shouse and Stewart Udall ceremonially broke ground for construction of the park's pavilion. Mrs. Shouse continued to stay involved in all phases of the development of the center, contributing her time and financial resources to bring the performing arts venue to life.

Today, forty years after its creation, Wolf Trap National Park for the Performing Arts still welcomes visitors to opera, ballet, jazz, the theater, and all other forms of the performing arts and remains the only American national park devoted to live performing arts.[17] It is a great example of how private interests and the federal government can work together, and it also stands as testament to a young White House Fellow's fierce determination

---

[17] Eve and Millar Carr, *The Wolf Trap Story* (Wolf Trap Associates, 1977).

to stay true to his department's mission and get the job done and his principal's ability to stand back and trust him to do it. The White House Fellows' first program director, Tom Carr, said, "Great followers not only solve their boss's problems, but they also keep a close eye on their boss's boss's problems. The president wanted Interior, as its mission, to bring parks closer to people, and Veblen instinctively dove into getting that done. He didn't sit on the sidelines 'learning about government.' He sought and got a grant of authority from his boss and struck out on his own to help carry out the department's mission."

Veblen would return to his business career with Cargill and a decade later would found two nationally prominent agribusiness consulting firms—Food System Associates, Inc., and Enterprise Consulting, Inc.—whose mission was to provide business leaders with the help they need to identify and focus on their core mission and grow their businesses in an increasingly harsh global business environment. Convener of The Superior Business Firm Roundtable, Veblen recently authored *The Way of Business: An Inquiry into Meaning and Superiority*, whose mission is to provide American business practitioners and the general public with insight into the role of business in society.

To be a great leader, you have to be intensely focused on the core mission of your organization: know it, understand it, and live it. It's the filter that lets in what you want to be spending your energy on and keeps out unnecessary tasks that waste your valuable time. Anyone who has been in the military will tell you that one of the first things you learn in boot camp is that the mission is everything. Without it, people are left to flounder and ultimately to fail.

Never forget that what counts in the end is results. The organization must perform and achieve its mission; otherwise the organization is rudderless, its people lost. Make sure everyone in your organization can answer these questions: Who are we? What do we do? Whom do we serve? At the end of the day, the mission is the true North Star that guides every action you take.

CHAPTER 6

LEADERS HAVE A LASERLIKE FOCUS ON THEIR PEOPLE

I think many people believe that the U.S. military is an autocratic, Pattonesque system in which leaders simply bark orders without regard for their subordinates' opinions or feelings. However, as I interviewed White House Fellows for this book, a pattern began to emerge that challenges that belief. In one interview after another, former White House Fellows who had been in the military or had worked alongside principals who had been in the military said time and again that the greatest leaders are those who focus on the needs of their people in a thoughtful and compassionate way.

Thus, it's no accident that the stories included in this chapter all have a military slant. I wanted to send the clear message that if there is room for kindness and consideration in the military, where people's lives are at stake, there ought to be room for kindness and consideration in the boardroom, the locker room, the classroom, and the office.

One who absorbed and practiced that lesson in all those settings is Pete Dawkins (WHF 73–74). Throughout his lifetime, Dawkins has amassed one of the most impressive lists of leadership credentials I have ever seen. From the time he was a young boy, he was determined to be a winner. When he was eleven years old, Dawkins was diagnosed with polio, a disease that often left its victims paralyzed. In the 1940s and 1950s, before Jonas

Salk introduced his lifesaving polio vaccine in 1955, the highly contagious and occasionally fatal disease was a frightening epidemic in the United States. Determined to survive, Dawkins underwent months of grueling physical therapy to regain the use of his limbs, and he beat the disease. From that victorious moment onward, Dawkins was unstoppable in his pursuit of personal excellence, rising to meet one extraordinary challenge after another.

After defeating polio, Dawkins won a scholarship to Cranbrook Kingswood Schools, a prestigious private school outside Detroit. He excelled academically and also on the playing field as captain of the baseball team and one of the league's leading quarterbacks.

Dawkins turned down the chance to attend Yale University, opting instead for the U.S. Military Academy at West Point. There he played halfback and was captain of the football team, assistant captain of the hockey team, brigade commander, and class president and was in the top 5 percent of his class academically. His achievements were so outstanding and his future held such immense promise that he was profiled in *Life* and *Reader's Digest*. In 1958, Dawkins won two of college football's most prestigious awards—the Heisman Trophy and the Maxwell Award—putting him in the same company with gridiron greats such as Tony Dorsett, Marcus Allen, Vinnie Testaverde, Roger Staubach, and Paul Hornung. Upon graduating with honors from West Point, he attended Oxford University on a Rhodes Scholarship.

After earning a degree in philosophy, politics, and economics from Oxford, Dawkins completed Infantry School and Ranger School and assumed duty with the 82nd Airborne Division, where he commanded a rifle company. He served as senior advisor to the Vietnamese 1st Airborne Battalion in Vietnam. He won two Bronze Stars for valor and was a battalion commander in Korea, a brigade commander at Fort Ord, and the division chief of staff in the 101st Airborne Division. He taught at West Point and was selected to be a White House Fellow, serving as military assistant to Deputy Secretary of Defense Bill Clements. During his Fellowship, Dawkins worked on a task force responsible for converting the army to an all-volunteer force in the aftermath of the Vietnam War. After serving twenty-four years in the Army, Dawkins retired as a brigadier general and launched his career in the private sector with a partnership at Lehman Brothers, a global investment banking company. He then served as vice chair of Bain and Company, a business and strategy consulting firm; CEO for Primerica, a financial services company; and CEO of Diversified Distribution Services for The Travelers Group before becoming vice chairman of Citigroup. Dawkins also earned a master of public administration degree and a doctorate from Princeton.

Through those incredible achievements, Pete Dawkins has gleaned an immense body of knowledge about what it takes to be a successful leader. However, there is one simple thing that he says has been the key to his leadership success: He keeps a laserlike focus on his people. Whether he was leading an airborne company parachuting into enemy territory, a corporate board trying to widen the company's profit margin, or a football team striving for a perfect record, his people always occupied the center of his attention. "People skills are simple but essential. In any team or organization, people need to believe that their leader knows them, understands them, and cares about them," Dawkins explained. "That doesn't mean that you're their buddy; it doesn't mean that you aren't tough. I don't think people want their leader to be their buddy—they want to *respect* their leader. Of course you have to have skill competence; you have to know what you're doing. But you also have to have people competence."

Dawkins says that to have people competence is simply to have regard for the individuals who are part of your team or organization. He knows the names of all the secretaries and clerks in his office and greets them warmly whenever he sees them. He knows the names of all the people who clean his offices at night. "The folks who work closely with me, I know if they're married, unmarried, who their kids are, if they've had an accident or been sick, what they do for fun," said Dawkins. "You don't learn those things as a mechanical checklist; you just do it naturally. In doing so, you build a reservoir of trust and regard where people understand that you care about them not just because of what they can do for you or for the organization but because they are human beings. That is much more powerful than people seem to regard it."

Mitchell Reiss (WHF 88–89) shares Dawkins's view that a leader's focus on his or her people is an incredibly powerful tool. He learned that valuable lesson during his White House Fellowship from his principal, the National Security Advisor and former Secretary of State and former White House Fellow Colin Powell. "Two weeks after I started my Fellowship there was a picnic over the weekend for the National Security Council staff and their families. We got there promptly, but General Powell was already there helping set up, helping cook the burgers and hot dogs, and personally greeting every single person, not just on the staff but their families," Reiss recalled. "He came over to me and knew not only my name but introduced himself to my wife, Elisabeth, and thanked her for allowing me to work the hours that I worked at the NSC. He told her she should feel that she is part of the NSC family as well. That very brief but very personal interaction with Powell had an extraordinary impact on her. After he left, she turned to me and said, 'You better do a good job for that man. If you need to stay late at work, I will never complain.' That's the sort of transformative impact that leadership can have, and I was able to see it up close and personal with Colin Powell. This lesson was invaluable when I later worked at the State Department, where I tried to replicate this sense of teamwork and compassion."

Powell's team members knew they were valued because he personally showed them they were.

U.S. Army Colonel Sharon Richie-Melvan (WHF 82–83) also had a principal who genuinely appreciated his staff and never missed an opportunity to prove it. Melvan was an army nurse, a major at the time of her White House Fellowship. Her principal was Richard Williamson, Sssistant to the President for Intergovernmental Affairs, whose office was responsible for assisting the nation's governors, mayors, and county commissioners in their interactions with the federal government. Despite working with some of the finest military leaders in the world during her long army career, Melvan said that Williamson was one of the best leaders she ever knew. "I learned so much by watching the way he and the other staff members interacted, whether we were working alone or in teams. He solicited input from everybody because he valued the input," she said. "We worked hard each day and stayed late most nights. But every Friday at five o'clock, the deputy pulled out the chips, dip, beer, and wine, which were all supplied by Rich, and we locked the doors, put our feet up, and just sat for about an hour or so and chatted about what happened during the week. That was every Friday. Rich respected, valued, and supported each member of the team, and he taught me to do the same."

Although Melvan was affected strongly by watching Williamson's day-to-day dealings with his staff, she said it was what he did one afternoon during her Fellowship that showed her more than anything else how focused he was on his people. Melvan was at work in the Interagency

Affairs Office when she received a telephone call with the happy news that she had just been selected for early promotion to lieutenant colonel. Melvan was shocked. She did not know she was being considered for promotion. When she hung up the phone, one of the secretaries sitting nearby asked her if everything was okay. "I told her what had just happened, and she looked kind of glazed, so I just walked back to my desk and worked the rest of the day thinking that these civilian people didn't have any idea what a big deal this was to me. I was excited about the promotion, but I didn't tell anybody else," Melvan said. "At four o'clock that day Rich called me over to do some work. He said, 'Now bring your notes on this and that,' and I went across the hall to the big conference room. The whole staff was in there, and they had champagne and roses for me, and they had a big American flag tacked up on the wall. One of my coworkers had a big helmet on his head, like he was Patton, and he put me in a chair in front of the flag and did a little skit about why I was going to be promoted. Rich knew; he had known weeks before that I had been selected but he didn't tell, and he arranged for the party so everyone could share in a celebration with me. I just thought that was wonderful."

Years later as chief nurse at three of the nation's leading army hospitals, Melvan put into practice what she learned from her White House Fellows principal. She personally met with every new nurse reporting for duty at her facility and asked them all about their personal and professional goals. She made daily rounds to make sure they had everything they needed to do their jobs and followed up to ensure that they were achieving their goals. She sent personal letters to staff selected for promotion and to those celebrating birthdays, anniversaries, and births. "The bottom line was they knew they could always call me to help them if they needed it," Melvan said. "At their exit briefings when they were changing duty stations, many staff members shared that they knew I cared about them and that I made a difference in their lives."

Just as Colonel Melvan learned significant leadership lessons from a civilian she met during her White House Fellowship, so did U.S. Army Colonel John Tien WHF (98–99). Tien, a former Rhodes Scholar and West Point graduate who was a major at the time of his Fellowship, was assigned to work with Deputy U.S. Trade Representative Ambassador Susan Esserman. Esserman allowed Tien to help her prepare for and attend her meetings with foreign trade representatives, and he witnessed firsthand how dedicated she was to establishing a personal relationship with those on the other side of the table. Before meeting with a foreign trade representative, Esserman would write a note thanking that person for agreeing to meet with her. She also would call the representative in the days before the meeting to say how much she was looking forward to getting together with him or her and to break down a bit of the formality that often accompanies such high-level gatherings. Finally, Esserman would do her homework, not only studying the negotiation points but also learning about what made that person—and the people in his or her country—tick. "From Ambassador Esserman, I learned the importance of establishing a personal relationship with a foreign policy counterpart first and then establishing the professional relationship after that," Tien explained.

Ten years later, Tien and a thousand of his soldiers were sent to Tal Afar, Iraq, to secure and stabilize the city, and he channeled Esserman's easygoing approach when dealing with his Iraqi counterpart, Mayor Najim Abdullah Al Jabouri. After almost a year in Tal Afar living fifty yards from Mayor Najim's office in the center of the city, enduring mortar and suicide bomber attacks together, and spending many late-night hours talking about local and global policy, the two became lifelong friends and trusting colleagues. "Iraq may or may not succeed as a country, but between my soldiers, Mayor Najim, and me, we helped transform Tal Afar from a battle-weary combat zone into an independent city," Tien said. "On October 18, 2006, 100 percent of the U.S. forces left Tal Afar and I personally handed the 'keys' back to Mayor Najim and the Iraqi Army, and the city has remained stable and secure ever since. I owe an incredible debt to Ambassador Esserman, who taught me how to be a true global citizen."

Tien learned another valuable lesson during his Fellowship year from Deputy U.S. Trade Representative Ambassador Richard Fisher, who is now the president and CEO of the Federal Reserve Bank in Dallas. The list of Fisher's accomplishments is impressive: He graduated from the U.S. Naval Academy, Harvard, and Stanford and studied Latin American politics at Oxford. He was an investment banker and the CEO of a capital management funds company and served as assistant to the secretary of the treasury during the Carter administration. In his role as deputy U.S. trade representative, Fisher managed the implementation of the North American

Free Trade Agreement and oversaw other agreements with partners in Asia, Latin America, and Canada. However, in spite of all these lofty positions and the complex knowledge Fisher possessed, it was a very simple, basic message from the Ambassador that changed Tien's outlook on leadership forever.

It was April 1999, and Tien and Fisher had traveled to Houston so that Fisher could give a major policy speech at Rice University for an event hosted by former Secretary of State James Baker. The pair was to return to Washington the following day. Fisher had scheduled a meeting with Texas Governor Mark White to take place after the speech, and the governor's assistant suggested a private lunch in one of Houston's exclusive government buildings. Fisher countered with an alternative site: a small Mexican restaurant near Rice University. "I asked him why he wanted to eat there instead of one of the government buildings," Tien recalled. "And he said, 'So it will be easier for you to sit at the table too, John. I don't want you to be left out.' Well, those were the best tortillas and Texas politics I ever experienced!" After lunch, Fisher received a call from his office instructing him to return to Washington immediately: He was needed early the next morning for an important meeting about China's trade status. The Houston police escorted Fisher and Tien to the airport, and Tien was sent to the ticket counter to change their tickets for the next flight out.

"The ticket agent told me that she had one first-class seat left and that the ambassador could have it at the government coach rate, and he could be back in D.C. by dinner," Tien explained. "I got him the ticket and told him I would catch the original flight back the next day. He said to me, 'John, you missed enough nights with your family during your time in the Army.' He then personally went up to the ticket counter and exchanged his first-class seat for two side-by-side coach seats on a later flight. We ate dinner together, sat next to each other talking about my time in Operation Desert Storm, and got in around 8 p.m. Washington time. On that day in April 1999, I spent the night with my family and the day with a true leader. Although I have never been as high-ranking as Ambassador Fisher, I have had similar relationships with subordinates—especially in terms of age spread and position—and I have always tried to do what he taught me that day, which is this: You must always treat those in your organization as human beings first and subordinates second."

While Tien learned about positive leadership traits from Ambassadors Esserman and Fisher, some White House Fellows unfortunately learn from their principals what *not* to do. Air Force Major John Pustay (WHF 66–67) was assigned to serve as U.S. Secretary of State Dean Rusk's military assistant during his Fellowship year. Rusk had been around the White House for years, serving as secretary of state for both President Kennedy and President Johnson. He had come from a poor southern farm family and was a hard worker who put himself through school and eventually became a Rhodes Scholar, a lawyer, and a decorated military man. However, from Pustay's viewpoint, Rusk's leadership skills were seriously flawed.

"Rusk wasn't pompous or anything, but he didn't spend much time with people in the building. I never got a feeling that he was in touch with his people," Pustay recalled. "He did his homework. I think he did the reading and all that sort of stuff, but I'm not sure that he was a person that exhibited true leadership in terms of leaving a footprint throughout the organization, which is very important to me. So later in my career, one of the major hallmarks of any command or directorship that I had was to have that footprint that permeated the whole outfit."

For example, when Pustay was a commander at a large Air Force training center that included a hospital as well as extensive maintenance and training wings, he would visit different areas of the complex at all hours of the day and night with the express purpose of chatting with the people working there. "I would go to the hospital psychiatric ward and talk to the residents. I would end up back in the kitchen connected to one of the ten dining rooms we had, and I would talk to the cooks," Pustay said. "It was so important to me to have everybody know who I was and to have them know that I was interested in what they were all about."

Pustay's technique of making himself available to everyone in his command had a positive impact on his entire outfit. Everyone from the clerk on the midnight shift to the second in command knew he or she could rely on their leader to be there for them and to listen to their complaints and suggestions, day or night. Pustay had built—and was intent on maintaining—a communication bridge between himself and his subordinates, one that would bind them through every conceivable trial and tribulation. His unique footprint became an enduring, respected, and necessary element of the organization and was largely responsible for its ongoing success.

Great leaders such as General Pustay (WHF 66–67) and General Bernard Loeffke (WHF 70–71) understand that when people feel valued and supported, they're naturally more productive and committed to their work. Years after leaving his White House Fellowship, Loeffke was named Commanding General of U.S. Army South. There, he regularly asked his staff to "name names," but not for the usual purpose of detecting and chewing out slackers. Loeffke instead wanted to know who was doing good work so that he could offer a word of thanks. The way he expressed that gratitude was through handwritten thank-you letters.

"I didn't want to know who screwed up. I didn't want to hear anything negative because I'd always hear that anyway. I wanted to know who helped my staff the most as they set about achieving their short- and long-term goals," Loeffke explained. "And I recorded the names of people I personally saw doing something right. For example, I would go into the range and see a sergeant who was doing truly good work, one of the best ranges I've seen, so I would get his name. My aide would get the right addresses for me, and every night I would sit down and write a minimum of five handwritten notes to the people who helped my staff or to those I had seen doing good work, thanking them for a job well done. Everyone needs recognition."

No organization is better than the people who run it. If you want to be a great leader, put people first. This lesson is so simple, it's easy to overlook. Why is it that most managers identify their business by the product it produces or the service it provides? The fact is that you are in the people business—the business of hiring, training, and managing people to deliver the product or service you provide. If the people are the engine of your success, to be a great leader you need to attend to your people with a laserlike focus.

CHAPTER 7

LEADERS ROOT OUT PREJUDICE IN THEMSELVES AND OTHERS

It was 1975, and even though the Civil Rights Act of 1964 had been in effect for eleven years, racism was still far too prevalent in American society. Cliff Stanley (WHF 88–89), an African American, had been in the Marine Corps for five years and had risen to the rank of captain at that time. Although he worked long hours teaching at the U.S. Naval Academy, he made sure he set aside time to be with his wife, Roz, their baby daughter, Angie, and his close-knit extended family.

Around five o'clock on Sunday afternoon April 13, 1975, Stanley and his family were returning to Annapolis from a quiet family dinner at his brother's home in Wheaton, Maryland. Stanley was driving his car with Roz beside him in the front seat and his mother and father holding Angie in the back. Leading the way in his own car about a block ahead was Stanley's uncle Connie. The Stanleys chatted away as their little caravan headed into Washington, D.C., down Georgia Avenue and south on University Boulevard, when suddenly the windshield shattered. "I put the car in park, and Roz just leaned over on me—she said she was okay. My dad and I saw my uncle's car stopped ahead, and we jumped out and ran to him and found that my uncle had been shot in the chest and stomach. He was dead," Stanley said. "There was just this incredible disbelief in what we were seeing. And we looked back at our car, and there were medics there, and they had Roz out. It was then we realized that she'd been hit, too—she didn't even know it; she hadn't felt it. Then people were saying, 'Get down; get down!'"

There was a sniper, and he was still in the area.

Police surrounded the gunman, who was armed with a .45 caliber pistol and a satchel filled with ammunition. When he refused to put down his gun, the officers shot and killed him. All told, the sniper killed two and injured five innocent African Americans who were walking or driving through the neighborhood that afternoon, including one young man strolling home from work with a bag of groceries in his arms. Roz Stanley would never walk again—she was paralyzed by the gunshot—and she and her family would have to adjust to the fact that she would spend the rest of her life in a wheelchair.

The Marine Corps gave Stanley plenty of time off and helped the young couple move into a wheelchair-accessible home on the Naval Academy campus so that Stanley could always be close to home. The corps even offered to release him from his obligation at Annapolis if he wanted to leave, but he chose to stay even though he had experienced discrimination there. "The Marine Corps wasn't perfect, but nothing is. There was bias there just like everyplace else. For example, there were fewer than a hundred black officers out of 21,000 officers in the Marine Corps, and not one black general or even a full colonel," Stanley explained. "I was dealing with stereotypical thinking, but it was just a function of the times. I knew if I wanted to be promoted, I'd have to work five times as hard as the other guys, so I put all my efforts into working hard. I just didn't want to waste energy dealing with the issue of race. But I love the Marine Corps. They treated us with great compassion, and things change—that's one of the most beautiful parts about American society."

Things have changed, but there's still much room for improvement: Recent statistics are only slightly better than they were back in Stanley's day. An Associated Press article from July 2008 reported that only 5.6 percent of all general officers or admirals in the U.S. military are black.[18] It is

---

[18] Lolita C. Baldor, "After 60 Years, Black Officers Rare," *Associated Press Impact*, July 23, 2008.

startling that sixty years after President Harry Truman integrated the military, senior-grade black officers are still such a rarity.

Stanley credited his faith with carrying him through the bias he faced his entire career and the tragedy that befell his family in 1975. "Through all this our faith was strong, our marriage got stronger, and we have a very fine daughter. After that happened with Roz being shot and my uncle being killed right in front of me, I thought, shoot, *this* is my life, right here. There are more important things than what someone else thinks of me, particularly if they're biased. I literally went off into the stratosphere in terms of my perspective. I have a lot of things to be thankful for, and I know that even the hardships in my life have been a blessing for me."

Stanley became the U.S. Marine Corps' first-ever African-American regimental commander and was one of the corps' highest-ranking African Americans when he retired in 2002 as a two-star general, and he had earned those stars through a fierce determination to triumph over adversity. Over the years he became a caring mentor to hundreds—especially African Americans—both enlisted and officers. He knew that those young people would have a tough time finding high-ranking role models of their own race, and so he reached out to them, counseling them and supporting them in their jobs and their personal lives. Throughout his career, he was sensitive to discrimination and ensured that wherever he went there was a level playing field and that everyone was judged on the basis of competence and character. Stanley turned down a third star to pursue his lifelong interest in higher education when he became executive vice president at the University of Pennsylvania, where he received a doctorate in education through his thesis, "The Importance of Character Development in Colleges and Universities." In 2004, he became the chief executive officer of Scholarship America, which has distributed nearly $2 billion to more than 1.5 million students so that they can go to college.

Indeed, leaders are always ready to lend a hand to others, especially those most in need of a lift. A sure sign that a true leader is in charge is when everyone in that workplace knows he or she will get a fair shake. One man who specialized in dealing out fair shakes was Secretary of Transportation John A. Volpe. The son of Italian immigrants, Volpe had launched his own construction business before beginning his political career and being elected governor of Massachusetts in 1960. During his time as governor, Volpe signed legislation that promoted equality in education and also expanded public housing for the poor. In 1968 he made an unsuccessful bid for president, and in January 1969 the winner, Richard Nixon, appointed him to head the Department of Transportation. Later that year, Volpe chose Pastora San Juan Cafferty (WHF 69–70) to be his White House Fellow.

Cafferty, an instructor at George Washington University, had been a Wall Street Fellow and a Smithsonian Research Fellow before she was selected to be a White House Fellow and Secretary Volpe's special assistant. Her time at the Department of Transportation taught her a lasting lesson about how a leader fosters change. "Volpe used to get together with his immediate deputies for lunch on Saturdays at the Coast Guard mess. The upside of that was the Coast Guard mess had the best food in town, far better than anything at the White House," Cafferty recalled. "And one day Volpe said that I ought to join the group for lunch on Saturdays, and I told him that I couldn't go: They didn't allow women in the Coast Guard mess. He said that was inappropriate, and he made them change the rule. I was the first woman to ever have access to the Coast Guard mess."

Volpe was appalled when he realized that all those working on the upper two floors at the DOT building were white and those working on the lower floors were predominantly black. "He called his assistant secretaries together and he told them that that was unacceptable and that he wanted those floors integrated within the year. And you know what? They were integrated within the year," Cafferty said. "Secretary Volpe taught me a great deal about leadership in the sense that the number one person has to set the agenda for change and has to make it very clear that the markers are measurable, that there's a time line, and that he is going to keep track of it. And once a week in Volpe's office we went over recruitment and promotion statistics to look at diversity. I learned that if a leader said something had to be done and then measured it and held people accountable for it, *it happened*, no matter how difficult it was to do. The DOT was completely segregated when he moved in; in fact, it's hard to believe how extremely segregated the entire city was at that time."

Even though people of color were not given access to many high-profile jobs in Washington in the 1960s, the White House Fellows bucked that trend and included African Americans from day one. Ron Lee (WHF 65–66) was the nation's first African-American White House Fellow, and he made the most of his unique perspective during his year at the U.S.

Postal Service. Of course, it didn't hurt that his principal, Larry O'Brien, practically gave him carte blanche to shake things up. O'Brien was serving as President Johnson's special assistant for congressional relations and personnel when he was named postmaster general of the U.S. Postal Service shortly after the first class of Fellows arrived in Washington in 1965. O'Brien was heavily involved in helping President Johnson get his Great Society legislation passed, and although he was now responsible for the postal service, he would still maintain a White House office and be responsible for finessing legislation through Congress. He told Lee that he would need his help keeping the postal service moving.

Lee enthusiastically accepted that challenge, and while still working in the White House waiting for O'Brien to be confirmed by the Senate, he began studying the practices of not only the postal service's administrative offices in Washington but also those of every post office in the country. In 1966, the U.S. Post Office was the biggest civilian agency in the government, with 600,000 employees, delivering over 70 billion pieces of mail annually to 60 million locations, using a fleet of 70,000 vehicles. What he found appalled him: Out of 44,000 postmasters nationwide, only two were African Americans. "It was disgraceful, and Larry and I agreed that it was something worse than that—it was segregation, because about 30 percent of the postal service employees were minorities at that time," Lee explained. "So O'Brien gave me the go-ahead to find people to promote."

Lee set about finding minority employees who were qualified to be postmasters. Within months he had found three African-American candidates: John Strachan for New York City, Henry Magee for Chicago, and Lester Shaw for Los Angeles—and an Asian candidate, Lim Poon Lee, for San Francisco. "Those cities represented the four largest postal responsibilities in the country. We wanted to put them in those big cities to boost morale," Lee said. "They all came from inside, and they'd all been there a long time and had been passed over for promotions." By the time the year was out, Lee had helped identify ten people for O'Brien to recommend to President Johnson for postmaster appointments. He also helped increase the number of African Americans in the senior management ranks at the headquarters from 5 percent to 12 percent. During the thirty-one months he served as an aide to Postmaster General O'Brien and then as one of the six assistant postmasters general, Lee went on to help hire an additional 50,000 African-American employees for a total of 110,000. He also helped raise their average pay level by 40 percent.

Once that issue was settled, Lee discovered yet another unfair practice: The postal service was not depositing any of its $25 million daily postal revenue into any of the twenty-one African-American-owned banks in the country. "I told Larry that we put all that money into the Treasury and it goes into Federal Reserve Banks and things of that nature, but there are all these black banks in the United States," Lee said. "Why don't we put some of our deposits into those that are just getting started? We're making other people very, very wealthy—why not spread it around?" O'Brien gave the green light for that idea too, and suddenly the playing field became a little more level for American minorities.

Since 1965, the White House Fellows have done exactly what President Johnson and John Gardner had hoped they would do through their Fellowships. They have brought the fresh ideas of a younger generation to the nation's capital, and they have worked with their principals to change the status quo and root out discrimination wherever they found it. Their collective efforts over the years undoubtedly have played a part in making life better for people both inside and outside of Washington, and one hopes that fewer Americans have experienced discrimination because of their dedication to fairness and inclusion.

Great leaders recognize that talent and leadership abilities are distributed randomly. Therefore, they do not form judgments about a person that are based on ethnicity, gender, religion, age, or any other factor. They root out prejudice in themselves and others and ensure that there is an equal opportunity at all levels for everyone to rise to a position of leadership in his or her organization on the basis of merit and character.

CHAPTER 8

LEADERS ACT WITH INTEGRITY

In their personal and professional lives, great leaders demonstrate honor and integrity at all times. When I was a college student at the U.S. Air Force Academy, it was drilled into us that we should always do what is right regardless of the personal or professional consequences.

As chairman of the Cadet Wing Honor Committee at the Air Force Academy, I was responsible for instilling a sense of honor among the cadets in our wing. The honor code we vowed to uphold stated, "We will not lie, cheat, or steal nor tolerate among us anyone who does." During my year as Honor Committee chairman, I conducted over 250 investigations and convened 106 honor boards. I personally served as chairman—which is like being an administrative judge—on seventy-two of those boards. Eight cadets were chosen at random from the cadet wing to serve on juries that studied evidence and heard witness testimony in each case.

In my quasi-judicial role as chairman of the honor board, I participated in the questioning of witnesses and even sat in on the deliberations to make sure that the cadet jurors did not go off on a tangent. On the seventy-two boards over which I presided, sixty cadets charged with an honor violation were dismissed from the academy for violating the honor code.

A senior cadet who was a friend of mine had completed his academic classes and was awaiting graduation ceremonies when some friends of his from high school came to visit him. As his parents drove across the country from Maine to the graduation ceremonies, my friend partied with his high school buddies late into the night and then decided to take them on a midnight tour of the dorms. The problem was that civilians were not allowed in the dormitories. When the cadet brought his friends to the dormitory, an underclassman in charge of dormitory security stopped them and challenged their right to enter. The graduating cadet pulled out his identification card and lied, saying that the visitors were cadets. The underclassman allowed them access because of the graduating cadet's assurance that they were authorized visitors but reported the incident because of the obviously nonmilitary appearance of the friends.

The graduating cadet had committed an honor code violation by lying to the underclassman. An honor board was convened quickly, and the graduating cadet was kicked out on the verge of graduating. The cadet got his academic degree but never fulfilled his dream of becoming a combat fighter pilot.

Whether you agree with the punishment or not, we lived by the honor code at the academy, and everyone knew how important it was to follow it. In too many organizations, integrity is just a catchphrase and leaders can't be taken at their word. It is impossible to lead if you have no credibility with the people in your organization. Leaders must reinforce the company's ethical standards, and it's not enough just to put them in an employee handbook. The penalties for violating the rules must be enforced, and punishment must be more than a verbal slap on the wrist.

In his naval career—and regrettably, even in his White House Fellowship—retired Admiral Charles "Chuck" Larson (WHF 68–69) had to fight to maintain his integrity despite intense pressure to do otherwise. A former Eagle Scout and U.S. Naval Academy graduate, Larson had developed a strong sense of right and wrong that he was not willing to abandon in any circumstances. One of his first challenges came early in his naval career. Larson had just been assigned as a training officer. His squad was preparing for a major inspection, and a superior officer discovered that the squad had not completed some of the required training. "He called me in and asked me to fake the training records and make it look like we'd had all these lectures. I refused to do it," Larson said. "I told him that I would put a good training program together and would guarantee we would execute it, but I wasn't going to fake stuff we didn't do. I told him that if he wanted someone to do that, then he'd better assign someone else as training officer. He backed down. Yes, we took hits on the inspection, but then we put in a good training program. I learned that if you compromise on the little things when you're a junior, it's murder to stand up for the big things when you're a senior."

It wasn't long after the training incident that Larson was selected for a White House Fellowship, and halfway through his Fellowship he was assigned to be a military assistant to President Nixon. His honesty was tested when a two-star admiral asked him to poke around the White House for information. "He said there were some things they needed to know. He wanted me to snoop around in the in-baskets and find some stuff, to be their spy and bring information back to them," Larson explained. "I told him I'd always be loyal to the Navy and I'd always represent the Navy well, but I support the Commander-in-Chief and my loyalty is there, and if he wanted that sort of person in the Fellowship, then he'd better tell the White House they selected the wrong guy and send me back to sea. He backed down, and I was never asked to do anything like that again."

Larson went on to have a stellar career. He served as U.S. Naval Academy superintendent twice and also served as Commander-in-Chief of the U.S. Pacific Command, the highest-ranking officer in charge of all American forces in the Asia-Pacific zone. In 2002, Kathleen Kennedy Townsend, the oldest child of the late Senator Robert Kennedy, chose Larson to be her running mate for lieutenant governor in her unsuccessful run for governor of Maryland. Currently, Larson is a founder, director, and board chairman of ViaGlobal Group, an executive leadership company based in Annapolis, Maryland, that provides training, leadership development, and technical support to the military and to corporations.

Another former Fellow who, like Chuck Larson, served as commander in chief of the U.S. Pacific Command is Dennis Blair (WHF 75–76). Blair is a sixth-generation naval officer and former Rhodes Scholar who served over thirty years in the Navy before retiring in 2002 at the rank of admiral. During Blair's White House Fellowship, he was one of a group of special assistants to Housing and Urban Development Secretary Carla Hills. In that capacity he witnessed how Secretary Hills fought to maintain an honest, aboveboard environment despite ample opportunities for duplicity. "The Department of Housing and Urban Development has been rocked by one scandal after another over the years. It moves a lot of money around and sends it down to the local level, where things can get pretty raw," Blair explained. "Whole parts of the operation can end up on the take and get too cozy with developers. There's just a lot of potential for corruption, but one of the leadership lessons I took away from that assignment was from the tone that Carla Hills set. She was fiercely, unflinchingly determined to do the right thing and never batted an eye about it. Whenever misconduct came to light, she dealt with it quickly and effectively, firing people if necessary and then moving on."

Blair recalled that he and the other special assistants took turns fielding telephone calls from people trying to pressure the secretary and her department to do things for political reasons, perhaps to award a Section 8 housing contract to someone solely on the basis of his or her political influence. "Our instructions were to say, 'Well, Mr. Smith, if you just put that request in writing and send it in, we'll be glad to take a look at it,'" Blair explained with a laugh. "And of course, nothing ever came of it and we never heard from that person again."

During Blair's year in Washington, President Ford was up for reelection. The president and his cabinet, including Blair's principal, Carla Hills, were under intense pressure to run a winning campaign. Although everyone's job was at stake, Blair saw no one abuse his or her power or resort to cheap tactics to influence the election. "It wasn't that the department was completely naive. If there was a good program sitting there waiting to be moved into a key state, then there was pressure to move it and to get the money out the door. But bad programs were never invented for political reasons," Blair said. "Carla Hills never came in and said, 'We're in trouble in Ohio. I want to push some Section 8 money toward Ohio, and I want a big publicity drive so we can turn out a lot of votes there.' There was none of that. They played by the rules and fought fair and always tried to do the right thing. That stuck with me; in fact, it was one of the greatest lessons that came out of my Fellowship. Several times in my own career I was given a choice between doing the right thing and doing something that might have shaded my principles a little bit but also would have gotten me ahead or made things easier for me. I've always tried to choose to do the right thing."

As Blair progressed through the Navy's ranks, he discovered even more important truths about leadership that helped him keep his bearings. He learned that the higher a leader climbs in an organization, the more the rules fall away and the greater the challenge to maintain a strong sense of right and wrong is. "When you're a junior officer in the Navy or a junior plant manager in a company, there is either a written or unwritten 'book' for you to follow. If you go by the book and work harder than other people, you can be a good leader," Blair said. "But as you get higher and higher, the books sort of fall away, and when you get to the very top of the big organizations, there just aren't any books at all. Then it all boils down to your internal gyroscope and your character and what you've learned up until then. The leaders I admire are the ones like Carla Hills who strive to keep it simple, consistent, and honest and who don't try to look for the easy way out. You don't need to be a genius to figure out what the right course of action is, and you don't have to come up with elaborate, brilliant strategies. You just have to pick out the simple, hard things to do and decide you're going to do them. The reason it's so hard to do those things is because the trappings of leadership will give you lots of ways to avoid them, and you'll have lots of other people who will be glad to take that burden from your shoulders and make it all seem very easy and comfortable and pleasant for you as a leader. But if you want to last, you can't fall for that. You have to take it upon yourself."

Blair recalled one occasion when doing the right thing cost him dearly. Although he did not want to provide details—a true leader does, after all, practice discretion—he did reveal that because of his leadership role he had a shot at becoming vice chairman or even chairman of the Joint Chiefs of Staff. To be considered for one of those jobs, he would have had to modify his philosophy and change his leadership style to please a new administration. He chose to stick with the methods and values he had developed throughout his career even though he knew he would not be considered for either position because of that. "It wasn't that difficult a decision," he said. "Certainly I would have relished the chance to make more of a difference in that higher position, but I was still not willing to change my philosophy or my style. I had too much confidence in my approach to change it even though I knew that meant I wasn't going to move up further in the organization."

At the time of this writing, President-elect Barack Obama has appointed Blair to serve as his Director of National Intelligence.

Another former White House Fellow who was not afraid to do the right thing was Jane Cahill Pfeiffer (WHF 66–67). It was 1978, and although more than a decade had passed since Pfeiffer, the nation's first female White House Fellow, had completed her Fellowship, many of her mentors and friends from those days remained close allies and followed her career, cheering her on as she shattered one glass ceiling after another. One fervent supporter was former LBJ press secretary Bill Moyers, who said he was always delighted to work with Pfeiffer because "she was so honest, candid and enthusiastic. Her word was her bond." Another who looked on with great pride was program cocreator John Gardner, who was delighted with the way Pfeiffer had fulfilled her end of the Fellowship bargain. Her accomplishments since completing the program were impressive. She had returned to her former company, IBM, after her Fellowship to work as executive assistant to CEO Thomas Watson, Jr., a demanding but highly regarded executive whose foresight and able leadership continued IBM's journey toward becoming an industry powerhouse.

Pfeiffer's respect for her boss was immense. "Tom was a man who believed so deeply in the customer, and he expected us to move heaven and earth to help the customer. No task was too daunting," she remarked. "IBM had very simple guiding principles and the greatest of attitudes about what a company should be. A company should treat all of its people and its customers with the utmost respect and support. Integrity should be the hallmark of everything the company does. Finally, Tom expected that we should be a vital good neighbor in every community in which we operated. There was a strong core of corporate responsibility at IBM that was started by Tom's father and great respect for people and fairness and integrity. Tom followed the same principles, and they were the fabric of what IBM was."

Watson's dedication to putting people first had strongly influenced Pfeiffer, who ably displayed her problem-solving capabilities to him in the late 1950s during a stint as site manager of a missile tracking station in Bermuda. Once, when her staff's paychecks were late arriving, Pfeiffer took out a loan from a local bank so she could pay the employees. She then fired off a blunt letter to her supervisors at IBM headquarters advising them to "get with it" because the loan would soon be due. Watson was impressed by Pfeiffer's initiative and boldness[19] and called her one of the ablest executives he has ever known.[20]

---

[19] "Pfeiffer, Jane Cahill – Overview," [encyclopedia], (accessed online 1 December 2008), available from http://encyclopedia.jrank.org/articles/pages/6331/Pfeiffer-Jane-Cahill.html.
[20] "Jane Pfeiffer: NBC lassos its own wonder woman," *Chicago Tribune,* 12 November 1978, p. K1.

Pfeiffer's work and attitude at IBM were exemplary, and it wasn't long before she was promoted to vice president of communications and government relations, a job in which she fully absorbed and promoted the company's culture of authenticity and honor. She went on to become an independent management consultant for many companies, including RCA, and was offered a chance to serve as President Jimmy Carter's secretary of commerce, an opportunity she respectfully declined so that she could spend more time with her new husband and her ten stepchildren and also focus on her health—she was recovering from thyroid cancer at the time. Thus, in 1978, when Pfeiffer was appointed chairman of the NBC television network and became the highest-paid woman executive in America,[21] one of the first people with whom she shared the happy news was John Gardner. "I've always been very fortunate in my life to be surrounded by good people who encouraged me," Pfeiffer said. "John Gardner was one those, and he was just thrilled when I got that job at NBC."

But three weeks later, Pfeiffer called Gardner to report that something was dreadfully wrong at her new post: She apparently was sitting squarely in the middle of a major scandal. "I hadn't been on the job a month when I got a phone call with three United States attorneys on the line, and they told me that we had some serious problems with a part of the business not managing funds correctly and that we were under investigation," Pfeiffer recalled. "I remember talking to John Gardner about it, and I said, 'John, you won't believe what's happening with this wonderful assignment that you were so thrilled with!'"

While Pfeiffer cannot offer many details of what transpired next— she is constrained by settlement agreements she signed nearly thirty years ago—I was able to use what little information she provided, along with news archives, to piece the story together. Pfeiffer said the problem first came to light when someone with knowledge of the wrongdoing contacted U.S. attorneys from California, Washington, D.C., and New York to blow the whistle on what a *New York Times* reporter later would call "a seamy scandal involving hundreds of thousands of dollars in padded expense accounts and embezzled NBC funds"[22] in one of the network's divisions.

---

[21] "RCA chief Pfeiffer is best-paid woman exec," *Chicago Tribune,* 12 March 1979, p. 14.

[22] "Television Enters the 80s," *New York Times,* August 19, 1979.

Although the Securities and Exchange Commission was prepared to launch a full-scale probe, Stanley Sporkin, the director of the enforcement division, gave Pfeiffer an opportunity to remedy the matter herself first. Pfeiffer quickly discovered that the unit managers—the ones who took technical and support crews outside the studios to cover sporting events or film television shows on location—were bringing back expense receipts that did not reflect reality. The *New York Times* reported that "unit managers, who carried greenbacks by the briefcase to pay bills for travel, lodging, food and miscellaneous production costs, were not content with garden variety expense-account gamesmanship. They padded payrolls, cashed in unused airline tickets and accepted kickbacks from caterers, hotel managers and equipment salesmen."[23]

"I had receipts coming in from Moscow for all these cables and lighting, so I had them translated at Columbia University and found that they were really for jewelry, vodka, and caviar," Pfeiffer said. "One of the strangest was a receipt for $20,000 for furniture in a studio that already had furniture in it. It was outrageous the ease with which receipts were made." Pfeiffer began personally interviewing the unit managers, many of whom said they had been acting on orders from a higher-level supervisor who had threatened them if they did not comply. "They told me that he would say, 'You bring this stuff back to me from China or you won't have a job,'" Pfeiffer said. "Apparently this kind of thing had been going on for years." Indeed, a *Chicago Tribune* story cited NBC officials who revealed that unit managers were coming back from overseas trips carrying "jade, fancy shoes, Oriental carpets, gold coins, and cash" upon orders from their supervisors, and that kickbacks were used to finance the scheme, which had been ongoing for at least ten years prior to Pfeiffer's arrival.[24] A *New York Times* article stated that one unit manager reported sessions at a massage parlor as "film-laboratory fees." Another unit manager claimed he had lost a briefcase full of important network documents. He received permission from his supervisors to pay a "ransom" of ten thousand dollars for its safe return, only to find the briefcase stuffed with newspapers.[25]

---

[23] Ibid.

[24] "50 at NBC in probe," *Chicago Tribune,* 11 February 1979, p. B24.

[25] "Scope of investigation at NBC widens," *New York Times,* 9 May 1979.

This was not the kind of work Pfeiffer thought she would be doing at NBC. She sought advice from John Gardner and others and came to the conclusion that she had three choices. She could go along with the way things were and stop only the most obvious violations, doing just enough to make the SEC back off; she could quit NBC and find a less chaotic place to work; or she could do her job. "I came from a world where if you had these problems, you got to the bottom of it and fixed them," Pfeiffer explained. "It was an interesting moment to have the chance to see if I'm the kind of person who can work my way through or if I'm the kind of person who will just say 'to heck with it' and quit. I chose to do my job, because it was the right thing to do."

Without taking the time to seek permission from the board or the leadership of RCA, NBC's parent company at that time, Pfeiffer swiftly brought in outsiders—an independent auditing company with 228 accountants[26] and an accomplished corporate crisis manager and lawyer, Victor Palmieri—to unravel the tangled web of issues at the network. "I didn't ask permission to do this because I assumed I was *supposed* to do it," Pfeiffer said. According to *Time* magazine, to preserve potential evidence, investigators had a carpenter close off the office of Vice President Stephen Weston, the unit managers' supervisor. When the investigative team demanded typeface samples from every unit manager's typewriter, one manager's equipment mysteriously vanished after an inexplicable late-night fire in his office. Eighteen of the company's fifty-five unit managers, including their supervisor, Weston, ultimately were fired.[27]

Pfeiffer's take-no-prisoners approach to exposing corruption at NBC caused her to butt heads with more than a few people and made her the brunt of many cruel jokes. At a staff meeting, NBC vice chairman Richard Salant reportedly said it looked as if Pfeiffer "sent in the whole damned Marines to rescue a cat."[28] Disgruntled workers began calling Pfeiffer Saint Jane and Attila the Nun, referring to the time she spent in a convent as a young woman, but she continued to do her work in spite of the disapproval. Whenever the going got rough, she recalled the examples set by her White House Fellows principal, HUD Secretary Bob Weaver, and IBM's CEO,

---

[26] Ibid.

[27] "Struggling to Leave the Cellar," *Time,* May 14, 1979.

[28] "Hell No, I Won't Go," *TIME,* 21 July 1980.

Tom Watson, Jr. Pfeiffer pressed on, fueled by the knowledge that she was doing the right thing. "I had total undermining from the top," said Pfeiffer. "But I also had help along the way, and I received many signed and unsigned notes from people saying they were glad I was there because NBC was a good place with many good people, and they hoped I could fix it once and for all. And we did fix it."

Even though she'd eliminated one of the biggest threats to its reputation that NBC had ever faced, Pfeiffer's chairmanship was to be short-lived. Only two years after assuming her role as the network's chairman, she learned one morning while reading the newspaper that she was about to be ousted. She was fired later that day by the longtime friend she personally had recruited to the network, NBC president Fred Silverman, who yielded to intense pressure from RCA to fire her. According to a source cited by the *New Your Times*, "(Pfeiffer) felt that the people at the top in RCA didn't want the scandal aired and didn't want it to be more than nominally solved, on the ground that it could be embarrassing to key people." The unnamed person also told the *New York Ti*mes reporter that Pfeiffer's prior experience at IBM, where affairs were run "tidily and neatly," did not adequately prepare her for the situation at NBC, where she made "some very powerful enemies (including the head of RCA), very early."[29] Bill Moyers concurred, saying, "Jane wasn't sufficiently coldblooded or unscrupulous enough to make it as a network executive. Had she stayed in television, she would have been one of the industry's few remaining champions of civility and accountability." *Time* magazine called her dismissal an "executive decapitation"[30] and suggested that her chairmanship "produced a predictable mix of envy, admiration, fear and resentment, laced with a dollop of old-fashioned male chauvinism."[31] Reporter N.R. Kleinfield of the *New York Times* wrote that the "stormy affair must have caused beet-red faces at both NBC and the parent RCA Corporation because of the messy way it was handled."[32]

The termination was a blow to Pfeiffer initially, but she now believes the experience was a blessing in disguise. "I walked away from NBC with

---

[29] "Mrs. Pfeiffer Officially Quits NBC Position," *New York Times,* 11 July 1980.

[30] "Hell No, I Won't Go!," *Time,* July 21, 1980.

[31] "NBC's Mrs. Clean," *Time,* May 14, 1979.

[32] "Fred Silverman's NBC: It's Still Out of Focus," *New York Times,* 13 July 1980.

the attitude that this was a great opportunity. I was dealt a different deck of cards than I expected, but I stayed there and fixed it as best I could. I helped change the way a company operated for the better, and then I moved on," she said. "You think you know and have faith in yourself—that you'll act a certain way when troubled times come—and sometimes you get the opportunity to find out. I have not one ounce of regret about any of it."

Like Pfeiffer, two more former White House Fellows—David Iglesias (WHF 94–95) and John McKay (WHF 89–90)—paid a high price for doing what they believed was right. Iglesias and McKay were among the nine U.S. attorneys fired from their jobs by the Justice Department in 2006—seven in one day—for what many consider political reasons. The official cause given for the firings was "performance-related issues," but seven of the nine attorneys, McKay and Iglesias included, had received superlative evaluations for their work. Although U.S. attorneys are appointed by the president and confirmed by the Senate, the position is intended to be unbiased and nonpartisan to protect the integrity of the Justice Department. However, many people, including McKay and Iglesias, believe that high-level White House and Justice Department officials ordered the attorneys' terminations for political reasons.

After graduating from law school, David Iglesias served as a Navy judge advocate general who defended sailors and marines facing court-martial at the Navy base at Guantanamo Bay, Cuba. In that capacity, he became the model for Tom Cruise's character in the movie *A Few Good Men*. He was an assistant state attorney general and prosecutor in New Mexico and an assistant city attorney dealing with civil rights police misconduct cases in Albuquerque before being selected to be a White House Fellow. During his Fellowship year, he worked on aviation and consumer issues with Department of Transportation Secretary Federico Peña, who taught him a valuable life lesson: Keep your word. "When I was at the Department of Transportation I worked with a person who was a long time friend of Federico Peña. Years ago, this friend needed to move to a different apartment. Lots of people said they would help him move," Iglesias recalled. "But when the day came, the only one who actually showed up to help was Federico Peña. That left a real impression on me—the importance of keeping your word. Peña kept his word then, and he kept his word when I was a Fellow, and he keeps his word now, and I try to practice that too in all areas of my life, whether it's to my wife, children, and colleagues or to the oath I took to support and defend the Constitution."

After Iglesias's Fellowship ended, he went to work as an attorney in New Mexico's state government. A Republican, he was defeated narrowly by the Democrat Patricia Madrid when he ran for state attorney general in 1998. He became an associate in an Albuquerque law firm and continued his work as a Commander in the U.S. Navy Reserve Judge Advocate General Corps. In 2001, President Bush appointed him to serve as U.S. Attorney for the District of New Mexico. Iglesias's star continued to rise, and he was considered by many to be on a fast track to high public office. The state's Republican leaders were thrilled with the appointment since there hadn't been a Republican U.S. attorney in the district for ten years, and they were counting on Iglesias to get to the bottom of what they believed was pervasive voter fraud by New Mexico Democrats. However, after investigating the accusations, Iglesias determined that there was insufficient evidence to support the allegations of wrongdoing and declined to file charges. Although he knew it would not endear him to the Republican leadership, he continued to prosecute cases without regard for politics, as he had sworn he would do. Throughout his term, he earned one positive performance evaluation after another from the Department of Justice.

In October 2006, Iglesias received a phone call from someone he considered a friend, a Republican member of the U.S. House of Representatives who asked him for the status of sealed indictments in a high-profile corruption case involving key New Mexico Democrats. The caller was running for reelection against Patricia Madrid, the woman who had beaten Iglesias in his bid to become attorney general back in 1998, and according to Iglesias wanted him to issue the indictments against the Democrats before the November election. "This person wanted to use the federal indictment as a club over the head of opponent Patricia Madrid, who had not filed any state corruption cases in her eight years in office," Iglesias explained. Since prosecutors are barred from talking about indictments, he declined to discuss the matter with the legislator.

It wasn't long before Iglesias received another phone call, this one at his home, from another Republican friend, the U.S. senator who had recommended him to President Bush for the U.S. attorney appointment. "He wanted to know if I was going to file the corruption charges before

November in the same case the previous caller had been asking about," Iglesias explained. "The case wasn't ready for filing yet, but I couldn't tell him that. Instead I told him I didn't think so, and he said, 'I am very sorry to hear that.' And then the line went dead. This guy held my political future in his hands, so to speak, and I didn't tell him what he wanted to hear, which was that I'd move heaven and earth to get this indictment filed now."

A few weeks later, Iglesias was boarding a flight from Baltimore to Albuquerque when he received a phone call from a Justice Department official demanding his resignation—no explanation given. Iglesias's rising star came crashing to earth in an instant. He felt like the world's loneliest man during his long flight home, but he soon would learn that he wasn't alone. Six of his colleagues had received the same phone call with the same bad news that day, and one of them was the only other former White House Fellow in the administration's U.S. attorney class: John McKay.

McKay had been a litigator in a prominent Seattle law firm for several years before being selected as a White House Fellow and serving as a special assistant to FBI Director William Sessions. When McKay's Fellowship ended, he returned to Seattle and became a managing partner of another firm until he returned to Washington, D.C., in 1997 to serve as president of the Legal Services Corporation, a congressionally chartered nonprofit that gives people with low incomes equal access to the civil justice system. As a U.S. attorney appointed by President George W. Bush in 2001, McKay had coordinated federal law enforcement activity for the Western District of Washington from his office in Seattle for five years, doubling criminal prosecutions and leading U.S. and Canadian law enforcement efforts to stem the flow of illegal drugs and human trafficking across the international border. An experienced litigator and prosecutor, he personally handled the office's most important cases, including the sentencing and appeals of Ahmed Ressam, the notorious Millennium Bomber who sought to destroy Los Angeles International Airport in 2000.

In 2006, while some in the Justice Department were preparing to dismiss an unprecedented nine U.S. attorneys, McKay received the Navy's highest civilian award for his innovative law enforcement information-sharing system, which remains in wide use around the country. He undoubtedly had done an outstanding job, as reflected by his recently concluded Justice Department performance evaluation, which lauded him as a strong and innovative U.S. attorney. McKay's refusal to intervene in the hotly contested 2004 Washington governor's race apparently triggered his downfall. In one of the closest elections in American history, the votes had to be counted three times before the Democratic candidate finally was named the winner by a margin of only 129 votes. McKay's fellow Republicans were unhappy that he did not intervene even after a Superior Court judge ruled that there was no evidence Democrats had sabotaged the electoral process. "I was making decisions—and I knew it at the time—that were not going to make me popular with certain politically active Republicans," McKay disclosed.

On December 7, 2006, McKay arrived at work and found a message to call a Department of Justice official—the same one who delivered the bad news to David Iglesias that day. McKay was told that "the administration wanted a change" and that he should "move on" by the end of January. As soon as McKay hung up the phone, images of his White House Fellows principal immediately filled his mind. McKay had been working at the FBI when President Bill Clinton fired Sessions, and the incident was burned permanently in his memory.

"Sessions was fired rather dramatically by President Clinton after mishandling an issue involving a security fence at his house and allegedly misusing government airplanes and other perks for his wife's and his own personal use. After he was fired by the president, Sessions continued to go about his business as if nothing had happened. The president had to call him back within an hour and fire him a second time," McKay explained. "How ironic it is that one of the lessons I learned from working with Sessions was how to get fired with dignity. I hung up the phone from that conversation in which I got fired and didn't want there to be any doubt that I got the message, so I immediately announced my 'resignation' so as to make clear my intention to comply with the president's order. I didn't want them to have to say, 'When are you leaving?' or 'Get out now.' I felt they were capable of that. I thought at the time it was my duty to leave and not do anything to embarrass the White House or the Department of Justice. I set out to swallow my pride and go. And I did."

By February 2007, six of the attorneys fired on December 7, 2006, began talking among themselves about what had happened to them, first by e-mail and then on conference calls. "We started connecting with each other, and we started to see that there was a serious problem," McKay said. "It was a very interesting thing when the six of us came together and realized that one of their main goals was to isolate us and make us think that we'd all been fired because we'd done something wrong. We began to talk about what our responsibilities might be and to speak out about it. None of us had really spoken out."

Iglesias gave a great deal of thought to whether he should comment publicly. "I don't want to portray myself as a saint because I considered not saying anything about the firing and just going with the flow, but it just didn't sit right with me. I kept thinking about how wrong it was and that I had to tell the public what happened," he explained. "It was like an endless loop of tape that began and ended at the same point, which was this: If they're going to do it to me, they're going to do it to somebody else. If I let them get away with it, they're going to lean on some future U.S. attorney and maybe even on a more important type of case. It was really a matter of right and wrong. Partisan politics had nothing to do with it. It was wrong, and I needed to speak out about it. I was just incredibly fortunate that I had other U.S attorneys with similar stories." Iglesias wrote a book about the experience titled *In Justice: Inside the Scandal that Rocked the Bush Administration.*

Congressional hearings into the prosecutors' dismissals took place in early 2007, and although Attorney General Alberto Gonzales dismissed the incident as "an overblown personnel matter,"[33] many high-ranking Justice Department officials ended up resigning in the wake of the investigation, including Gonzales. In September 2008, Attorney General Michael Mukasey launched a criminal inquiry into the matter. He named acting U.S. Attorney Nora Dannehy as prosecutor to investigate whether Gonzales and others should face felony charges as a result of their roles in the firings.

When former White House Fellows Iglesias and McKay appeared together on *Meet the Press*, McKay told the late Tim Russert that U.S. attorneys must "not allow politics into the work that we do in criminal prosecutions." Through it all, neither one of them lost sight of the requirement of every public official to be prepared to pay the price for doing the right thing.

---

[33] Alberto R. Gonzales, "They Lost My Confidence: Attorneys' Dismissals Were Related to Performance, Not to Politics," *USA Today*, March 7, 2007, p. A10. www.usatoday.com/printedition/news/20070307/oppose07.art.htm. Retrieved on August 11, 2008.

When Admiral Chuck Larson was a young officer, he could have bent his principles a little and rationalized to himself that following a direct order from a superior officer was the key to advancing his career and helping his organization advance, but he didn't take any shortcuts where his integrity was involved. Admiral Blair could have followed the leadership philosophy of a new administration in Washington even though he disagreed with it in order to be considered for Chairman or Vice Chairman of the Joint Chiefs of Staff, but he chose to be an authentic leader and accept the consequences. When Jane Cahill Pfeiffer became one of the most powerful businesswomen in the country as the head of NBC, with all the business perks and income potential associated with that position, the easy path would have been to downplay the allegations of wrongdoing, circle the wagons, and defend the organization. In the case of the U.S. attorneys, Iglesias was on the fast track to the governor's office and McKay was one of three finalists to become a federal judge for life. The easy path to fulfill their ambitions would have been to bend a little by using their power to benefit the individuals who could secure their futures. All five—Larson, Blair, Pfeiffer, Iglesias, and McKay—were in an enviable position of power, yet they made the decision to do the right thing and let the chips fall where they might. Larson, Blair, Pfeiffer, Iglesias, and McKay understood that if you're in a position of power and cannot walk away from it, you have no power.

When you say only what others want to hear, you're not helping the organization you're in. It's like being the lookout on the *Titanic*. You're not doing yourself or the company any good by shouting, "All clear ahead," as the iceberg looms ominously on the horizon. By acting with honor and integrity, you build trust with your followers. The actions of great leaders are consistent with their words. Saying the right thing doesn't mean much. Doing the right thing means everything when you want people to follow you passionately.

CHAPTER 9

LEADERS CREATE A SENSE OF URGENCY

When Craig Coy (WHF 83–84) left the White House to return to the Coast Guard at the conclusion of his Fellowship year, he thought that was the end of his time as a Washington insider, and he was okay with that. A helicopter aircraft commander, Coy was thrilled to get back to his choppers and resume flying rescue, drug interdiction, and environmental protection missions for the Coast Guard. However, he had done such an outstanding job as a Fellow working with President Ronald Reagan's domestic policy advisor that it wasn't long before he was brought back into the administration again, this time to work with Vice President George H. W. Bush's counterterrorism task force. Just as he had risen through the ranks in the Coast Guard, Coy steadily climbed the government ladder and soon was named deputy director for combating terrorism at the National Security Council.

In that job he helped implement new strategies to keep the nation safe and also helped devise and carry out responses to threatening acts such as the hijacking of the Italian passenger ship *Achille Lauro*, which was commandeered off Egypt by Palestinian terrorists in 1985. The hijackers murdered the American passenger Leon Klinghoffer, a disabled Jewish man, and threw his body overboard along with his wheelchair. To help bring the hijackers to justice, the United States sent navy jets to intercept a plane attempting to carry the hijackers to freedom, forcing it to land in Sicily. Navy Seals and Delta Force teams were dispatched too, and all the hijackers were captured, charged, and convicted for their crimes. Coy also had a hand in planning the 1986 air raid over Libya, which was staged in response to Libyan leader Muammar Ghaddafi's support of groups blamed for carrying out terrorist attacks in Rome, Vienna, and Berlin. The Berlin bombing, which destroyed a nightclub, had killed two American servicemen. The U.S. government carried out the air strikes to send a strong message to Ghaddafi and other potential or actual backers of international terrorist groups that America would not tolerate radical violence against innocent people.

By then it was obvious that Coy was great at putting out fires and tackling tough problems. Thus, in 1987, when Attorney General Ed Meese needed an assistant to help him carry out his duties as chairman of President Reagan's newly formed National Drug Policy Board, he tapped his former White House Fellow Craig Coy. Levelheaded and extremely bright—he had earned an MBA from Harvard Business School—Coy was charged with creating an implementation plan to support the National Drug Control Strategy. Since the early 1970s, cocaine use had increased dramatically among Americans, and stemming the tide of drugs entering and moving throughout the United States and being used by the populace was of the utmost importance to President Reagan.

"The strategy included getting all the agencies involved in interdiction, investigation, intelligence, prosecution, and incarceration as well as education, treatment, and rehabilitation to identify the resources they had at their disposal and to identify the initiatives they already had under way," Coy explained. "In addition, we wanted to know how these agencies were going to measure whether their initiatives were effective, and that is something the government typically has the toughest time with. Given the inherent slow pace of government activity and the strong reluctance to be held accountable for results, we needed to create a sense of urgency to cooperate. So with Chairman Meese's strong support and his close relationship with President Reagan, we decided to use what I called 'action-forcing events' to generate the impetus for urgency."

Coy knew that people facing a long-term complicated job tend to procrastinate because the task seems insurmountable and the deadline for completion appears to be miles away. To keep all the agencies on track and all the personnel focused on their roles in implementing a coordinated and successful strategy to deal with illicit drug use, Coy and Meese scheduled eighteen individual cabinet meetings with the president over a two-year period. "We would ask each of these individual agencies that were responsible for a specific drug strategy, either on the supply side or the demand side, to come to the cabinet room in the White House and brief the cabinet and the president. There is nothing like the importance and the urgency of briefing the president of the United States to bring people together to get the job done and to fight complacency and bureaucratic inertia. It's amazing what people can accomplish when they have to, so creating action-forcing events is among the top management leadership lessons I have learned over the years."

After leaving the Drug Policy Board, Coy applied his finely honed leadership techniques in the private sector, overseeing highly successful companies in the aerospace industry and business outsourcing. In 2002, in the wake of the 9/11 terrorist attacks, he was selected for a job that would put his leadership skills to the test as never before. It was at Boston's Logan International Airport that terrorists armed with razor-sharp box cutters circumvented airport security and boarded two planes that they ultimately crashed into the World Trade Center Twin Towers in New York City, killing thousands of innocent men, women, and children. Americans were outraged over the Massachusetts Port Authority's (Massport) perceived shoddy oversight of security at Logan. Massport's CEO—a political appointee—hastily resigned, and the governor appointed a task force to take the first step in reforming the ailing agency. Former White House Fellow Marshall Carter (WHF 75–76) led the task force known as the Carter Commission, and when it came time to find a new CEO, he encouraged Coy to take the job.

"At the time I got that call, I did not know much about Massport at all," Coy recalled. "However, after learning more about it, I realized that there was a good match between the job requirements and my background. I also wanted to get back into public service again." Coy took the job and began leading the beleaguered and overwhelmed agency; Massport oversees the Port of Boston, the Tobin Bridge, and Bedford's Hanscom Field and Logan International Airport, which was going through a $4 billion refurbishment. Creating an initial sense of urgency for his workers would not be necessary for Coy in this job; Congress had seen to that by setting January 2003 as the deadline to complete the project. It would be up to Coy to channel that urgency toward a productive and speedy conclusion.

"There are no front lines in this struggle against terrorism. It's being fought half a world away on foreign soil and also in our airports, ports, and tunnels and on our bridges, roads, and highways," Coy said. "When I became CEO of the Massachusetts Port Authority, I took charge of an organization that saw this country's enemy up close and personal, and there is no way to describe the grief that Logan felt—and still feels—at being forever linked to that terrible event. Yet by joining Massport I was given the opportunity to see America's new patriotism hard at work, and it was a remarkable sight."

Although Congress had instituted nearly impossible deadlines, Coy embraced the challenge as part of his turnaround strategy for Massport. A new, never-before-designed $146 million baggage-screening system was needed, and Coy led up to 800 workers who labored through multiple shifts seven days a week to try to beat the clock—and the odds—to finish the job on time. The massive project encompassed 85,000 square feet of new baggage space, 55,000 square feet of renovated space, three miles of conveyor belts, 400 electrical motors, eight electrical substations, and forty-four large screening devices. It was the nation's first fully automated baggage-screening system, a state-of-the-art triumph for Coy and his new Massport team.

"The workers came to Boston from nearly forty states, and few came just for the money. One man who came from Ohio and lived in a trailer hooked to his truck told me that he was there to show his patriotism," Coy recalled. "Patriotism is not too strong a word to describe the motivation of those citizen patriots who did two years' worth of construction in about six months; it was a re-energized American spirit that spurred us on."

In much the same way he had managed the productivity of the National Drug Policy Board, Coy kept the Massport team focused on its short-term goals and maintained a sense of urgency that drove the team ever onward toward its long-term mission of creating a secure facility for the millions of airline passengers who travel in and out of Logan Airport every year. It was a huge undertaking that went beyond baggage screening. Coy was determined to lead his team toward making Massport and Logan a world-class model of efficiency and safety, and he did just that. "We initially came up with four tactical business objectives: operations, facilities, performance, and good citizenship, which dealt with how we affected the neighborhoods surrounding our facilities," Coy explained.

"That gave people a structure they could use to decide whether they were making sound decisions. Then we gave the general managers responsibility for profits and losses, which had a significant positive impact on behavior and team building."

All of Massport's security procedures were reviewed under Coy's watch. In addition to the new baggage-screening system, every fence, door, window, gate, and tunnel was evaluated for its impact on security. More full-time law enforcement officers were added to beef up patrols and ensure proper security checks of vehicles, passengers, and construction workers. Massport checked the fingerprint registries and criminal backgrounds of every single airport employee, construction worker, and contractor associated with the remodeling. Coy's team installed hundreds of surveillance cameras and bomb-resistant garbage bins throughout the terminals and parking garages and put up barriers to keep vehicles away from sensitive structures. Whenever security threat levels were elevated, Massport instituted a zero tolerance policy that entailed the immediate impoundment of all improperly parked cars and trucks on the property.

With input from the Massachusetts attorney general's office and the American Civil Liberties Union, Massport implemented a behavior pattern recognition program in which state police observe and question passengers and airport employees who exhibit specific behaviors that are regarded as suspicious. An elite police unit was created and received training in bomb detection, special operations, antiterrorism, and biological and chemical weapons. Some of those officers became the first airport security personnel in the country to be armed with Heckler & Koch MP5 submachine guns as they patrolled the passenger terminals, curbs, and parking garages. Massport also designed and constructed modern security checkpoints to help the Transportation Security Administration with passenger screening. That system included upgraded equipment and a better layout to keep the traffic flowing. It also included exit lane security doors and video monitoring to prevent the wholesale evacuation of terminals or concourses if a security breach was suspected.

"The list of Logan's security initiatives was long, yet security is more than countermeasures to identified threats. It is mostly about effective leadership," Coy said. "The commitment to use scarce resources to meet potential threats when there are so many other competing demands for those resources; the ability to enlist public support for improved security despite the trade-offs in lost time and possible inconvenience; the determination to remain vigilant despite the inevitable lulls and false alarms—this all required strong, consistent leadership. Because of what happened at Logan we knew that we would be in the national spotlight and that Logan would be the yardstick by which anxious travelers around the country would measure how well the nation, and the nation's airports, had responded to the new day that dawned on September 12, 2001. That put a special obligation on us to make sure Logan got it right. The way we looked at it, rebuilding public confidence in America's air travel system would begin with us at Logan. 'Lead, follow, or get out of the way' was our motto."

A leader's basic task is to keep people energized and focused on accomplishing the organization's mission. As a White House Fellow, Craig Coy saw how a date to brief the president of the United States and his cabinet energized entire departments to get their acts together and get the job done. Years later at Massport, he created a can-do atmosphere in which workers were driven to a nearly superhuman level of achievement—all because he maintained a sense of urgency that neither overwhelmed them nor allowed for a moment's lethargy. Striking that perfect balance is the mark of a great leader, and the first step toward achieving that balance is initiating a dialogue.

That's what effective leaders do: They create a sense of urgency by *communicating with their team* to set a goal and a workable time line for achieving it. They hold team members accountable by *checking their progress* at regular intervals. They encourage their team by *being responsive to their questions and concerns* and by *providing positive feedback*. They are flexible and *always willing to change course* if something is impeding success.

Great leaders create a sense of urgency by conveying a bold vision that captures people's imagination about what can be accomplished in the future. They go one step further by getting all the members of their team to see and feel the need for change.

CHAPTER 10

LEADERS HAVE PASSION

It was 1994, and I had the world on a string. I was a graduate of the Air Force Academy, a highly decorated military officer, a former White House Fellow, and a recent Columbia Law School graduate. I was off to Miami for a plum job—a one-year clerkship with a federal judge—and was about to move my young family from New York to sunny southern Florida to launch what promised to be a marvelous legal career. Everyone was excited about my prospects for success.

Everyone, that is, except me.

Our bags were packed, but as moving day drew nearer, I became more and more convinced that I was not meant to practice law. I knew I had the intellect and skills to be a good lawyer, but I was missing the most critical element: passion. I realized that what made me come alive was using my leadership talents and creative abilities in an entrepreneurial venture. I came to the hard conclusion that I did not want to practice law because it was not my calling: It was not something I was so passionate about that it would sustain me through all the rough spots along the way. Could I muster the courage to forfeit the sure thing—a legal career—to pursue the pipe dream of being the nation's next great businessman? What if I failed? And what about that $70,000 law school loan I was obligated to repay?

After some serious soul-searching and with only two weeks left before I was due in Florida to start my clerkship, I decided to follow my true passion and become an entrepreneur. I was apprehensive, but I was also determined, and after enduring a few bumpy spots along the road, just three years later I founded Sterling Financial Group, which was named the number one fastest-growing Hispanic-owned business in the country and rose to number eight on the Inc. 500 list of the fastest-growing American companies. With nearly sixty offices in seven countries, we became a success, and so did I, because I let my passion guide me.

Passion is the spark that fires every winning endeavor, and many of the White House Fellows I interviewed named it as the driving force behind their successes too. For example, in Chapter 6 we learned how Michelle Peluso and Jeff Glueck (WHF 98–99) turned a bright idea from their Fellowship year into Site59, the wildly successful travel booking Web site that they sold to Travelocity for $43 million. Site59 sounds like an overnight success story, but in actuality Peluso, Glueck, and their partners conquered major challenges in getting their fledgling business off the ground, challenges that might have overwhelmed a less passionate team. The biggest hardship they faced happened on September 11, 2001, when the terrorist attacks in New York leveled the World Trade Center's Twin Towers, just a stone's throw from the Site59 offices.

"That was profoundly challenging because we were cranking along in acquisition conversations and had money in the bank, and the world literally caved in—we were only two blocks off the towers," Peluso recalled. "It was a horrible day. We couldn't find an employee. We were seeing horrendous things. We had a customer stranded, we lost our office, and all of our technology was set up there. Then revenue completely plummeted. We were selling spontaneous last-minute weekend packages, and of course that suddenly stopped, so investors were freaking out and we had to call off the acquisition conversations. I've never been in an environment where revenues went from a big number to almost zero overnight. It was certainly the most profound professional challenge I've ever faced."

The team faced tough personal and emotional challenges too. Not only did Peluso and Glueck have to rebuild their business, they had to rebuild their team and each individual player's faith. To begin the healing process and put things in perspective, the Site59 team reached out to a firehouse in their neighborhood and offered to cook meals every Monday night for the firefighters, a squad of first responders who had lost several of their colleagues when the towers collapsed. Cooking for the firefighters helped ease the team members into talking about what they had experienced and made them feel as if they were part of the healing process; that in turn helped them heal their fractured business. "My business instinct had to be the best that it ever was because we had to build the whole business over again in a much shorter time frame," Peluso said. "But I think my leadership instincts had to be at their finest as well. It was a very challenging period. I remember a lot of sleepless nights where I would be up in the middle of the night scribbling notes, trying to figure out how to pay a big payroll two weeks from now, and if you don't have passion for what you're doing, I don't know what else motivates you."

Site59 not only survived, it ultimately surpassed its pre-9/11 budget. Travelocity bought Site59 and put Peluso, Glueck, and their partners into leadership positions with the goal of saving the foundering company. They accomplished that mission, turning Travelocity from a company that lost $55 million in 2003 to a profitable business with over $1 billion in revenue less than five years later. Peluso says the key to their success was passion—for being a team and for winning.

"I believe being 'the boss' means it's my job to put other people first and to make sure my organization is full of people who are smarter than I am and passionate about winning," said Peluso. "It's incumbent upon us as leaders to dare our team to think big, to be honest and direct with them, to be their champion for career growth, and to obsess about getting obstacles out of their way. We survived and prospered for one reason only: We had a team of people that was committed to each other and that would not accept defeat. And if you look at the Travelocity turnaround, the key ingredient is the same: a passionate team committed to winning. I believe there is no greater correlation for success than how passionate the team is about being a team and winning."

Clearly, the most effective leaders are like Peluso and Glueck: They know how to channel their passion in a way that helps them overcome obstacles. Another great example is Rodney Bullard (WHF 05–06). As a high school student in Decatur, Georgia, Bullard was an academic all-state football player and an all-state mock trial attorney, a standout both on the field and off. When given the chance to attend the U.S. Air Force Academy after high school, he jumped at it. He knew he not only would receive a world-class education at the academy, he also would have the opportunity to realize his dream of playing Division I-A football. A fierce competitor, Bullard threw himself into his sport and his studies, but a devastating knee injury in his junior year sidelined him—and his dreams of ongoing gridiron success—for good.

"It was at this point that I learned from experience that when one door closes, another one really does open," Bullard said. "I couldn't play football anymore, but I could pursue my other passion: the mock trial. I decided to try out for the academy's team, but the advisor told me the team was full. I immediately asked if I could form my own team. He said 'sure,' but I could see the doubt in his eyes. Well, that was all it took. A week later I came back with more than enough people to field a second team. This makeshift team went on to finish second in the nation, and I was recognized as the best collegiate attorney in the West and an all-American collegiate attorney on the national level. As trite as this accomplishment sounds now, these events earned me a scholarship to Duke Law School, which set the stage for many other achievements, including the White House Fellowship in which I worked with NASA administrator Dr. Michael Griffin. It was passion that inspired me to form 'Bull's mock trial team.' Passion inspired my classmates to join it, and passion fueled our success. Regardless of the circumstances, I have always had an irresistible belief in the happy ending." As legislative liaison for the secretary of the Air Force at the Pentagon, where he serves as a link between Congress and senior Air Force leaders, Bullard has found a new channel for his passion for being part of a winning team.

Among all the people I've ever met, George Heilmeier (WHF 70–71) is perhaps the one who has used passion to his—and the world's—advantage better than anyone else. Heilmeier defines passion as simply loving what one is doing, and he says it is an essential ingredient in any recipe for great leadership. As with Bullard, Heilmeier's passion as a youngster was sports. He wanted to pursue a degree in physical education when it came time for him to go to college, but his father encouraged him to go in a different direction. "One night we were sitting around the dinner table—I'll never forget this—and my father said that in every place he'd ever worked, engineers wore clean clothes and made a lot of money. Now, when you grew up in a German household, what your father said pretty much was the way it was. So consequently I decided I wanted to study engineering, and it became a replacement for sports in my life for a while and ultimately became like a hobby for me."

What a hobby it turned out to be. After graduating from Princeton with a Ph.D. in solid-state electronics, Heilmeier went to work for RCA

Laboratories, where he developed the liquid-crystal display technology that would lead to today's flat-screen televisions and computer monitors, among other things. However, a few years later Heilmeier had to rethink his career path. "I had become disillusioned by the slow progress in commercialization of our discoveries at RCA, and I needed a change," Heilmeier explained. "I had lost my passion and excitement for liquid-crystal display work, and it is my view that when your passion and excitement for work in a specific technical field leaves you, you should leave the field with it. I left RCA Laboratories to serve what I thought would be a one-year term as a White House Fellow."

At the end of Heilmeier's Fellowship in the Defense Department, he was asked to stay on as an assistant director for the Defense Advanced Research Projects Agency (DARPA), and it wasn't long before the word *assistant* was removed from his title and he was running the place. "That was the best job I ever had because I was working with people who were really, really passionate. They were like entrepreneurs," Heilmeier said. "They had the interest and the drive and the intelligence to really make things happen." Under his directorship, Heilmeier's team created the first stealth aircraft, an accomplishment that required great tenacity, teamwork, and faith. "Those were some of the most rewarding years of my professional career, and I learned some powerful lessons that I carry with me to this day," Heilmeier said. "I learned that you must practice 'no excuses' management. That means that you must remove all of the bureaucratic impediments to success. 'Breaking glass' and going around the bureaucracy can be done if you believe in your cause and refuse to quit. And I learned that your best memories will be those that center on hard work and sacrifice with a great team that's totally passionate about the mission of the organization. Money rewards are irrelevant in situations like this. It's about passion, and it's why I'll never fully retire."

Like George Heilmeier, I feel blessed to have found and followed my true purpose and passion in life. We're not alone, George and I. Everywhere I look, I see others who have managed to do the same, and they're reaping the rewards. You can spot a passionate leader from a mile away: She's the one with the spring in her step, a smile on her face, and an enthusiastic, productive team by her side. Perhaps her passion is serving her country as a military, law enforcement, journalism, or political leader. Or maybe she's a teacher aspiring to be a principal whose dream is to lead young people toward the knowledge necessary for them to have a successful future. The first step toward greatness came when she listened to her inner voice and heeded its call.

A great example of this is my friend Theresa Park. Park's family wanted her to pursue a legal career, and she succumbed to their wishes. After double-majoring in political science and creative writing at the University of California, Santa Cruz, she went on to Harvard Law School. Upon graduation, she made her family proud by taking a job as a corporate lawyer in a prominent firm in California. Park was earning great money in an impressive career, but after fifteen months she was unfulfilled and disappointed. The money and prestige just weren't enough—Park had no passion for being a lawyer. When her husband, who was also a lawyer, accepted a job in New York City, she gave herself permission to consider trying something new.

Park had always loved books, and she believed that good ones have the power to make the world a better place. She knew she wanted to have something to do with creating books, but she did not necessarily want to be the one to write them. After thinking about it and studying the way books are created, Park realized that what she really wanted to do was help aspiring writers bring their stories to life. She became fascinated with the role literary agents play in the publishing industry, and so she decided to abandon her lucrative legal career and become a literary agent. After all, New York City is the literary capital of the country; surely she would have no trouble finding a job there.

Park studied the industry and reached out to working agents for guidance. Few responded, but some of their assistants did offer advice, telling her that she'd have to start at the bottom of the pecking order and work her way up. It was a rocky road, but at last Park found a small agency willing to give her a job as an assistant: a glorified secretary. "I think they saw how passionate I was about wanting to be in the business," Park recalled. "After all, I was making a major financial sacrifice to get my foot in the door." Her salary was only $18,000—less than half what her former secretary had made at the law firm—but although the pay was low and the work hardly glamorous, Park loved her new job.

After nearly a year spent shuffling through mountains of manuscripts from hopeful authors and finding nothing that really stood out, Park stumbled upon a story that captured her interest and her heart. It was a love story written by an unknown twenty-eight-year-old pharmaceutical salesman. The manuscript had been rejected by dozens of other agents, but Park had a gut feeling that it would be a hit. She called the author and offered to help him polish the manuscript and then submit it to publishing houses. When he learned that she was only an assistant, he was hesitant. His dream was to snag a big-time literary agent, and Park was the opposite of that. But Park's enthusiasm was infectious, and he agreed to pin all his hopes on her untested ability to make the sale.

The duo worked together through extensive rewrites, and at last Park began pitching the manuscript to publishing houses around the city, boldly billing it as the next *Bridges of Madison County*. Park could hardly contain her excitement when she received a call from Time Warner Books offering $500,000, an impressive bid for an unknown author's manuscript, but she took a deep breath and made a leap of faith and refused the offer. She believed the manuscript was worth much more and was willing to stake her reputation—and her client's future—on it. Thirty minutes later the phone rang again. It was Time Warner Books, and this time the representative offered the sum of $1 million. Park heartily accepted the offer on behalf of her client, Nicholas Sparks, and the rest is history. The manuscript that Park had pulled from the slush pile and titled *The Notebook* became an international bestseller, the first of many books that Sparks and Park would create together. Sparks and Park are two people who followed their passion's call, and let it lead them directly to greatness.

The common thread running through all these stories is that when you gamble on your passion, the payoff can be greater than you ever imagined. It's been said that if you do what you love, personal success will follow. But I think it's also true that if you do what you love, the team will follow. Thus, the first step in being a great leader is to identify your calling. What makes you come alive as a human being? What makes you get out of bed and start the day with a smile? Whether it's business, the military, government service, or helping aspiring writers tell their stories to the world, pursue it wholeheartedly. Be a maverick. Passion will give you the strength to overcome any obstacle in your team's path.

I could have been a good lawyer, but "good" wasn't good enough for me. Is "good" sufficient for you, or do you aspire to greatness as a leader? If you'd prefer greatness, remember this: If you want people to follow you, you must follow your passion, because if you don't care about what you're doing, you can be sure that no one else will care either.

CHAPTER 11

LEADERS ARE PERSISTENT

Although the purpose of the trip to Israel with his principal was diplomatic—to study American foreign assistance efforts there—Wesley Clark (WHF 75–76) was far more interested in military matters. After all, he was an army officer first and foremost. Before being selected as a White House Fellow, Clark had graduated from West Point, earned a Rhodes Scholarship and graduated from Oxford, and commanded a company in Vietnam. Just one month after assuming command of his unit early in 1970, Clark was shot four times by a Vietcong soldier armed with an AK-47 assault rifle, but he continued to direct his troops as he lay bleeding on the battlefield, leading them through a counterattack that crushed the Vietcong offensive.

As a White House Fellow, Clark was assigned to work with James Lynn, the Director of the Office of Management and Budget, who had taken his young Fellow along on a trip to Israel in 1976. So it was that Clark found himself in Prime Minister Yitzhak Rabin's dining room, preparing to enjoy an evening of fine food and captivating conversation with some of the most powerful men in the Middle East.

"It was late at night, as Israeli dinners usually are," Clark recalled. "There were seven of us at the dinner. I was with Jim Lynn and Don Ogilvie, who was Associate Director of the OMB, and on the other side were Prime Minister Rabin, Defense Minister Shimon Peres, Foreign Minister Yigal Allon, and Minister of Finance Yehoshua Rabinowitz. I was the only one on the American side who had had military service, and naturally that made me able to converse in a slightly different way with Rabin and the others who had been in the military. We were talking about Israel and its history and what Rabin had done in the military. I was listening to his war stories, and I just felt compelled to ask him a question, so I said, 'As a veteran soldier, what would you say is the most important military lesson that you could pass on to a young officer like me?' And he replied that it was persistence."

Prime Minister Rabin told Clark that during the War of Independence in 1948, he was a brigade commander of three battalions assigned to hold East Jerusalem. The Jordanian Arab Legion charged in a fierce assault, and Rabin's troops bravely repelled the attack. The Arab Legion stormed the Israeli position once more, and again Rabin's troops held them off. "But then the battalion commanders came to Colonel Rabin and said, 'We don't have any more ammunition! We're out of machine gun ammunition—we've got four or five rifle rounds per man. We're down to one or two grenades per squad, and if they come at us again, we'll be destroyed. We must pull back now to save the forces.' And Rabin said, 'No, we're not going to do that. Our mission was to hold and we will hold, and we'll fight right here. This is *our* Jerusalem.' I guess it was pretty heated with the battalion commanders, but Rabin held his ground and the brigade stayed there, and it turned out that on the other side, the Arab Legion troops had gone to *their* brigade commander and they too were out of ammunition! They were down to two or three grenades per squad, and they didn't have enough firepower to succeed. Well, the Jordanian brigade commander said, 'Okay, let's fall back,' and they retreated. Rabin had carried out his mission and held East Jerusalem. That was the major success he had in the War of Independence, and it all came from persistence—he refused to give up."

After the dinner was over, Clark reflected on Rabin's words of wisdom. He was right, Clark thought, and he compared Rabin's experience in 1948 to his own in Vietnam just six years before. "As a captain in Vietnam, I had seen that when we would come under attack, the senior person on the ground would often call for artillery," Clark explained. "Well, sometimes he'd get the artillery and sometimes he wouldn't. If he didn't get it right away, the question would be whether he would keep asking. I then put that experience together with what Rabin told me, and I realized that you have to be persistent not only in your aims but also in your assessments. If you say you need something, you have to persist until it's either provided to you or you're ordered to quit asking."

After his Fellowship was over, Clark continued to move up through the Army's ranks, eventually becoming a four-star general and NATO's Supreme Allied Commander for Europe. His greatest challenge during that tenure would be the war in Kosovo, which was waged in 1999 in response to Yugoslavian President Slobodan Milosevic's grisly ethnic cleansing crusade in Kosovo. Clark commanded combined U.S. and NATO forces during Operation Allied Force, which was NATO's first major combat experience.

"When I was in the Kosovo campaign, there were a lot of people who suggested that it would be over in a day or two, that all you had to do was bomb them. But unfortunately that didn't happen," Clark said. "It became a matter of persistence. We decided to use coercive diplomacy. We seized control of the escalation ladder, and we established escalation dominance. No matter what Milosevic tried to do, he was always going to be outescalated by the NATO forces. We brought in more aircraft and attacked more targets. We eventually threatened to institute a ground campaign. Ultimately, despite the problems of the campaign, despite the difficulties of coalition warfare with all these frictions and differences between America and allied contentions of war and how to fight this one, we were able to hold together. Nothing we did—no single target, no single strike—was more important than maintaining a persistent NATO strategy. Through seventy-eight days of persistent strategy implementation, we broke his will. It was strictly a lesson in the power of persistence. *You don't give up.*"

NATO forces saved an estimated one and a half million Albanians from Milosevic's bloody rampage, and General Wesley Clark retired from the U.S. Army after thirty-four years of exemplary service. He ran for president in 2003, winning the Oklahoma primary before setting aside his campaign to help other Democrats win public office. He is also a writer, businessman, and commentator on CNN, MSNBC, and Fox News.

Achieving a positive outcome in a high-stakes situation such as the Kosovo campaign required great persistence, and the same has been true of the war on terror. In late 2006, the Bush administration put together a team to formulate a new strategy to counter the increased violence and terrorist buildup in Iraq, and that team included former White House Fellow Ahmed Saeed (WHF 04–05). During Saeed's Fellowship, he was assigned to the Treasury Department, where he worked on Social Security reform and Treasury issues related to the Middle East. When his assignment drew to a close, Treasury Secretary John Snow offered him a permanent position as deputy assistant secretary for Africa and the Middle East, and he accepted.

In December 2006, a bipartisan study group headed by former Secretary of State James Baker and former U.S. Representative Lee Hamilton released its final report with its recommendations for proceeding—or not—with the war in Iraq. Among other things, the group recommended that the United States begin withdrawing its troops from Iraq. But President Bush did not agree with the Baker–Hamilton report, and he directed Deputy National Security Advisor J. D. Crouch to lead a group in formulating an alternative response.

"The president asked each of the national security agencies to appoint two people at the undersecretary level to this group, and I was one of those appointed," Saeed said. "He basically said that he wanted our calendars cleared for a month, and we were to do nothing else but work on that issue. There were about fifteen of us. The cabinet secretaries were all involved, including Secretary of State Condoleezza Rice, Secretary of Defense Robert Gates, Chairman of the Joint Chiefs of Staff Peter Pace, Director of National Intelligence John Negroponte, Treasury Secretary Hank Paulson, and then the rest of us. We basically looked at different proposals about how to proceed. All these options were debated in front of the president, and then the president made the decision that a troop surge was the right thing to do. On January 7, 2007, he gave a speech announcing the surge."

News of the planned surge was met with widespread and thunderous disapproval, but President Bush defied the naysayers and carried it out anyway, sending an additional 20,000 troops to Iraq. It appears that his dogged persistence paid off: In mid-2008, the numbers of multiple-fatality bombings and resulting deaths in Iraq plummeted from presurge levels.[34] Not only are U.S. and coalition troops safer, Iraqi civilians are safer too. "I think this was one of those examples where a leader—in this case, President Bush—needed to know when to listen and when to stop listening," Saeed

---

[34] Michael E. O'Hanlon and Jason H. Campbell, *Iraq Index: Tracking Variables of Reconstruction and Security in Post-Saddam Iraq,* Brookings Institute, July 17, 2008. Available from www.brookings.edu/saban/~/media/Files/Centers/Saban/Iraq%20Index/index20080717.pdf.

said. "The president took in a lot of input and he knew it was going to be a very controversial decision, but he made that decision about where he wanted to go and then he stuck to it. In this instance it seems to have worked." Saeed took that lesson along with him to his newest venture: In 2008, former Treasury Secretary Snow, in his capacity as chairman of Cerberus Capital Management LLP, tapped his former White House Fellow as the company's new managing director and president of Cerberus Middle East. Cerberus is one of the world's foremost private investment companies.

As White House Fellows, Wesley Clark and Ahmed Saeed both learned that a successful leader never gives up even when faced with seemingly insurmountable obstacles. When you say to yourself that you will never, never, never give up—that's persistence. Lack of persistence is the major cause of failure. Effective leaders have the staying power and persistence to follow through on their goals regardless of circumstances or what other people say, think, or do.

Persistence will mark you as a leader and separate you from others. You must learn to cultivate a habit of persisting, since all things are possible if you persist. Calvin Coolidge said, "Nothing in the world can take the place of persistence. Talent will not; nothing in the world is more common than unsuccessful men with great talent. Genius will not; unrewarded genius is almost a proverb. Education will not; the world is full of educated derelicts. Persistence and determination alone are omnipotent."

CHAPTER 12

LEADERS ARE GREAT COMMUNICATORS

In his job as chief strategy officer and executive vice president for Univision Communications, America's premiere Spanish-language media company, Cesar Conde (WHF 02–03) has worked with great communicators every day and has had contact with some of the biggest stars in the Spanish-speaking entertainment world. Thus, the day he watched his White House Fellows principal, Secretary of State Colin Powell, deliver a speech in person, he knew he'd just seen something extraordinary. While riding together in a limousine after the speech, Conde complimented Powell on his speaking abilities, and Powell revealed something that Conde never would have guessed: Communicating well with others had not come naturally for Powell. Perfecting his communication skills had taken years of study and hard work. "He was very humble," Conde said. "General Powell explained that very few people are born with that ability, and he said he really had to work at it. He realized early in his military career that great ideas and intentions weren't enough; he would have to become an effective communicator in order to maximize his impact."

I asked General Powell to explain how he developed his exemplary communication skills. He told me that it all started when he was sent to the infantry school at Fort Benning, Georgia, in the mid-1960s to become an instructor. "I had to go to a three-week course on how to give a class—how to talk to a bunch of lieutenants who were all heading off to Vietnam and who really didn't care what I had to tell them about filling out a readiness report," Powell recalled. "So I learned how to communicate as a young major for the purpose of keeping 200 second lieutenants awake. That's where I got my basic training, and I just sort of learned on the job. As I went through the rest of my career, I was constantly being pressed to communicate. I learned what works and what doesn't work. I learned how to use stories and gestures, how to put a simple message together, and how to take complex issues and break them down in ways that average people can understand. You can't be afraid to stand up and speak in front of people, because that's how you learn. You'll stumble and you'll mumble, but you'll gain confidence and you'll do fine in due course. In my early years I really bombed on a few presentations, but I learned."

Conde said that Powell gave him the same advice, encouraging him to practice and prepare. "He said not to fool myself into thinking that the best speakers don't prepare. They all prepare, but he said that the most effective are the ones that can communicate their message with a conversational tone," said Conde. "He felt that the strongest public speakers were those who used their notes in a smooth, nondistracting way. Some of the best communicators have the ability to look down at their notes and digest the whole page with only a glance, whereas most people would have to look at a page three to five times. Everyone has his or her own style, but the best speakers work hard to fully develop their personal style and make it seamless."

During his Fellowship, Conde also had the chance to watch how Powell prepared for and carried out one-on-one meetings. He was impressed with how much time his principal devoted to meeting with people at all levels both within the State Department and outside it. Powell did not just meet with the CEO of an organization or the head of a foreign government or entity. He talked to people with a variety of different responsibilities and viewpoints. He used his finely honed communication skills to dig deep into organizations, and although the meetings or telephone conversations he had were often brief, they broadened the scope of the information he received and helped him make well-informed decisions. "He was approachable, but he was very demanding. He was extremely effective at those initial meetings with someone who was about to work with him," Conde explained. "He was very good at giving you direction as to how to succeed with him. In my particular case, he gave me great advice on how to be successful with him in the White House Fellowship year."

Another important aspect of communication that Powell has mastered is establishing and maintaining healthy media relations. By personally opening the lines of communication with journalists, Powell assured that giving access to the media empowered him, and he took the time—even when there was no need and he was in a position of strength—to meet with journalists just to hear what they were observing and get their input on world events. Of course, he would give them his perspective and what he was observing too. Indeed, Powell confirmed that as he progressed in his career, he became increasingly more aware of the importance of effective communication with journalists. "You have to learn how to communicate with the press in a way in which they can use and carry your story," Powell said.

Another strategy that Conde witnessed during his Fellowship involved the daily staff meeting that brought Powell together each morning with his deputy secretary, his four undersecretaries, his sixteen assistant secretaries, and his chief of staff. Conde attended most of those meetings during his year in the State Department, and he counts them among the most constructive experiences of his Fellowship. Having come from the private sector, Conde equated the State Department with a multinational Fortune 500 company, and he was struck by how effective the daily staff meeting was at keeping Powell and his team abreast of the day-to-day workings of their massive global organization. Powell ran a tight ship when it came to the daily meeting. The gathering started promptly at 8:30 a.m., and those who arrived after the secretary—who was always on time—understood that they were not supposed to enter the room. There was no set agenda. Powell simply went around the room in a clockwise direction and asked each person if he or she had something to contribute.

"This was not a meeting for just stating what you were busy with or to show off what you were doing," said Conde. "It was extremely efficient. He wanted to know if there was something that was going to move the needle for the department on a macro level that day. He wanted to know what would be meaningful for you today in your region of the world or in your function. He encouraged people to pass if there was nothing important to say, and they often did, so meetings ran anywhere from fifteen minutes to forty-five minutes. It just depended on what was on the plate. This meeting gave the secretary a quick snapshot of where people felt his attention should be focused that day. And the flip side of it was that he also let people know where he was going to be spending his time that day, and so it had a double effect of ensuring that the organization was focused on priorities. He was quite aware of the ripple effect of his words. He wanted his direct reports to go out and speak with their people and say, 'I heard X message or X words directly from the secretary this morning.' So he was very successful in using those meetings to communicate, and people really had a sense that they were part of the process and understood the direction he was trying to take the department."

Through the daily staff meetings, Conde saw firsthand how a world-class communicator such as Colin Powell was able to reach down into his extremely complex organization and quickly and efficiently get a firm grip on the information he needed. With the input he received each morning from his people on the front lines, Powell created a cache of information that he could use later to make better, more informed decisions. Conde often sensed that when Secretary Powell asked someone a question during a meeting, he wasn't asking the question just to get an answer for his own benefit. "My belief was that he was trying to ensure that the other people in the room were hearing certain information in addition to himself," Conde explained. "General Powell had a very good eye for what the rest of his team needed to know, and he was essentially just getting all the information out there so everyone else could have access to it. He was great at getting everyone on the same page."

Powell was also great at making sure the people on his team understood that they mattered to his department's mission and to him personally. Louis O'Neill (WHF 04–05) was Secretary Powell's special assistant for Russian affairs during his Fellowship. He traveled with Powell to Japan, Korea, and China and also sat in on many of his daily staff meetings. "I'll never forget the first time I went to one of his staff meetings. He warmly welcomed me and introduced me to everyone. It immediately made me feel like part of the team and not simply a spectator," O'Neill recalled. "It's those little things I saw him do that carried over when I became a leader myself. Those lessons will stay with me forever. General Powell once told me, 'Take care of the people, and the people will take care of you.' So after my Fellowship when I was ambassador and head of mission to Moldova, I had a staff of sixty, and I saw to it that everyone's birthday was remembered. Or if someone was having a particular problem, I made sure they got the training or the help they needed. Another thing he told me was that it doesn't matter how smart you are—everyone in Washington is smart. What matters is how you make people feel. And that's really key when you're a leader. You don't have to prove anything to anyone. You've just got to communicate with them, inspire them, take care of them, and give them the chance to be part of something larger than themselves."

Former White House Fellows Conde and O'Neill consider themselves incredibly fortunate to have worked so closely with Colin Powell, one of the nation's great communicators and a leader who knew the value of talking with and learning from everyone in his organization regardless of a person's position. In contrast, Mel Copen (WHF 70–71) saw quite a different leadership style in his White House Fellow principal. Copen, who was associate dean of the University of Houston's School of Business when he was selected for a Fellowship, worked with Secretary of Agriculture Cliff Hardin, a man he described as "an academic . . . one who would sit back in his chair and puff on his pipe as he thought through ideas. He was a very private individual."

Copen had not wanted to go to the Department of Agriculture at first, but after meeting Hardin and learning more about the assignment, he enthusiastically accepted it. "I had no background in agriculture. As far as I knew, the Agriculture Department was only some place that paid farmers not to grow things," said Copen. "But I went in and met with Cliff Hardin, and I was fascinated. I learned that the Agriculture Department had the largest financial institution in the world—at that time the commodities exchange was part of Agriculture—and it had the largest welfare program and the largest home lending department. It was so much more than I thought. I used to joke we even had our own army, navy, and air force. The 'army' was armed with recoilless rifles to knock the snow off the side of the mountains. The 'navy' had 200 ships to do river basin surveys, and we had an 'air force' that used heavy bombers and dropped paratroopers to fight forest fires. It was an exciting place. But the thing that sealed the deal for me was Cliff Hardin and the reason he picked me. Hardin had been chancellor of the University of Nebraska system. He went into an Agriculture Department that had thirty-six separate agencies and 116,000 employees in 16,000 offices in roughly 3,000 counties in the United States, and he was wrestling with the task of how to get control of it. He saw my academic background and the business part of it, along with some other things I had done, and he was comfortable with all that. When we met, the chemistry was incredible. Basically he said, 'I've got to get control over this department, and I don't know how to do it. I need somebody like you here.' To have a cabinet officer tell you he needs you—well, I was sold."

Because Secretary Hardin believed that direct access to the secretary was a privilege to be earned, he granted it to only three people: his secretary, his executive assistant, and Copen. People within the department were forced to fight for time to communicate with the secretary, and as a result, he lost touch with many of those who could have made his job easier. Copen compiled a weekly report designed to keep the secretary as informed as possible in the circumstances. He asked each agency to send relevant news items, which he condensed to two pages and gave to Hardin. "He was a wonderful person to work with. He was receptive to new ideas, but he was also quite closed when it came to granting access," Copen explained. "It was nice for me that I could just walk into his office whenever I wanted, but I could see he was hurting himself by not being more open, by not communicating with others."

At the end of Copen's Fellowship, Hardin asked him to stay for three more years to help consolidate the department's 16,000 offices into a network of forty-eight "one-stop-shop" computer centers. Copen agreed to take on the massive project, but before the three years were up, Hardin left the department and was replaced by Earl Butz, a man who was as different from Cliff Hardin as night is from day. Copen was already somewhat familiar with his new boss. The two had served on a board together years before, and Copen did not have a high regard for him. He thought Butz was the most arrogant, opinionated person he had ever met, and he was certain that Butz's tenure at the Department of Agriculture would be a disaster. However, he was in for a shock.

"I haven't had to reevaluate my assessment of people very often, but I sure did with Earl Butz. He was so much more open with people. He had his finger on the pulse of the agency, and even though he wasn't a great analytical mind, he was more effective," Copen recalled. "The one thing that Butz provided that Hardin didn't was the charismatic side of leadership. Hardin was too remote; no one understood him. He may have had better ideas than Butz, but he didn't inspire. He didn't have close interactions with the people under him, whereas Earl Butz was always out slapping everybody on the back and talking. He'd sit in the employee cafeteria and talk with a lower-level employee about her children. The employees loved him. If you're trying to do things of the magnitude that we were trying to do back then, that I guess any cabinet officer is trying to do today, you've got to build political capital. You've got to give people a sense of being involved, of having a bond, because the forces against what you're doing are just too great. Hardin was brilliant and a wonderful mentor for me, but he just couldn't establish that bond because of his aloofness."

The bond between Marsha "Marty" Evans (WHF 79–80) and her principal, U.S. Treasury Secretary William "Bill" Miller, was strong from the moment Evans arrived for her Fellowship. At that time, Evans was a U.S. Navy lieutenant commander who never had held a job outside the Navy. Secretary Miller had a soft spot for people in the military, having served in the Coast Guard. He gave Evans the title of Executive Secretary of the Treasury and, along with it, the opportunity to do meaningful, demanding work that built her self-confidence and inspired her to pursue even greater challenges as the year progressed. Miller invited Evans to attend important meetings and called on her to write speeches and prepare materials for congressional testimony. He also tapped her to write the weekly Treasury Department summaries for President Carter, who often would send handwritten feedback to her.

"Here I'm thinking, I'm a lieutenant commander in the Navy—I'd been in the Navy about eleven years at that point—and here's the Secretary of the U.S. Treasury, a principal economic officer of the government, and he believes that I can do this significant work for him," Evans said. "I had never had a real job other than the Navy, so it was an amazing time of confidence building for me, and it reinforced in my mind that I could do anything I set my mind to do. Secretary Miller was a wonderful, inclusive boss. He always communicated in a positive way—praise in public, criticize in private—and he always communicated that there's a way to get over, under, or around every problem."

Having worked in such a positive environment with an effective communicator like Secretary Miller during her year in Washington had a strong and lasting effect on Evans. At the end of her Fellowship she returned to the Navy and continued to move up in the ranks. In 1986, former Fellow and Naval Academy Superintendent Chuck Larson (WHF 68–69) tapped

Evans to be one of six battalion officers at the Naval Academy—the first female battalion officer in Navy history—placing her in charge of the training and well-being of hundreds of midshipmen. The academy was meant to be a place of discipline and decorum, but occasionally a lower classman would slip up by wearing nonregulation clothing, which caused the academy's commandant to crack down on the youngster's battalion officer.

"We'd go every Monday morning for a meeting with the commandant, and he'd wring his hands and embarrass my fellow battalion officers about their midshipman turning up in Budweiser T-shirts and that sort of thing," Evans explained. "So when I saw one of my third classmen in a Budweiser T-shirt, I summoned the entire chain of command between me and that youngster. I remember the lecture so well. I said, 'You know, my own basic leadership belief is that people generally want to do the right thing, and if they're not doing the right thing it's because they haven't been trained properly. They haven't somehow had the benefit of the teaching and the leadership of their seniors. So, I can only come to the conclusion that this youngster is wearing this T-shirt because he has suffered from faulty communication by his midshipman chain of command.' Each person in the third classman's chain of command was held accountable and punished. That's the last T-shirt problem I had in my battalion. And, it was simple and maybe silly, but word went out far and wide that Commander Evans was not fooling around about holding accountable the people that were up and down the chain."

Evans's commonsense approach to encouraging better communication in her organization helped her create a more cohesive team and also garnered the Navy's attention. She was promoted steadily throughout her thirty-year career and retired as a two-star rear admiral, one of only a few women to attain that rank. Since leaving the military, Evans has used her outstanding communication skills in her roles as director of the Girl Scouts of the USA and president and CEO of the American Red Cross.

Great leaders communicate through their spoken and written words and their nonverbal actions. For instance, when you "set the example," that communicates to your people that you would not ask them to perform anything you would not be willing to do. When someone fails you and you hold the highest people in the chain of command responsible instead of the little guy, you communicate that you are serious about this issue because you choose to hold those truly responsible accountable.

The leadership trait of communication is critical to almost every task. Leadership is about influencing others, and this cannot be achieved without the ability to communicate. Effective communication is such an obvious component of successful leadership that it is often overlooked. But not by Colin Powell, who strongly encourages aspiring leaders to master the English language in reading, writing, and speaking. "The English language is the way you gain and communicate knowledge," he said, "and if you're going to be successful, you must master its use."

Through decades of effective leadership, Colin Powell became a world-class communicator by becoming a master of language and practicing tried-and-true techniques for making his point in an informative and, if circumstances permitted, entertaining way. He learned how to use words to form *connections* with people, because he instinctively knew that the greatest leaders are those who understand that what matters most is how they make people feel.

Once you master the ability to influence individuals intuitively by first connecting with them, and then choosing words that are impactful to carry your message, you need then to figure out how to communicate to a larger audience. Always keep in mind that your actions truly speak louder than your words. Marty Evans demonstrated that holding the right people accountable delivers an unspoken message to the entire organization of what will not be tolerated and raises everyone to a higher standard. Leaders who strive for greatness work hard to master the art of communication in all its forms.

CHAPTER 13

LEADERS ASK THE TOUGH QUESTIONS THAT NEED TO BE ASKED

The eighteenth-century French writer and philosopher Voltaire, who had a great influence on Franklin, Jefferson, Paine, and other leaders of the American Revolution, once said, "Judge a man by his questions rather than by his answers."

Effective leaders have the guts to ask the tough questions that have to be asked. At the foundation of Western thought is the Greek philosopher and teacher Socrates, who believed he had a duty to present incisive and profound questions to his young students. Nothing was taken as absolute fact, and Socrates would challenge his students' answers, sparring with them intellectually and requiring them to back up their responses with logical thought. The Socratic method still is used in American law schools.

Voltaire and Socrates understood that leaders must elicit the best information from others and listen carefully to make sure the answers are based on credible facts, real knowledge, and logical thought. Incisive questions also frame the focus of all those thinking through an issue.

Unfortunately, in the presence of powerful people, some people tend to fade into the background out of fear that they will say something foolish, and they avoid asking provocative questions that might make waves.

When the opportunity arises to learn something new, leaders do not linger in the shadows. They take a deep breath, step forward, and ask the tough questions. That's what Mark Vlasic (WHF 06–07) did when he met President George W. Bush.

Vlasic was a Fellow in the Department of Defense, and he described what it was like for his class to visit the forty-third President of the United States. "We were a bit excited and a bit nervous, all at the same time. We had all met famous people before, and we'd all just met President Bush the week before at the White House Christmas party, but to my knowledge this was the first time any of us had sat down for a chat in the Roosevelt Room with the leader of the free world. After a few minutes, President George W. Bush opened the door and walked in just like any other person. He invited us to sit down, and he sat at the middle of the table. He was relaxed, and although he was wearing a suit like the rest of us, he was still informal. He immediately put the room at ease. My first impression was that President Bush in some ways is very different in person than he is on television. The man that sometimes seems awkward on television is both passionate and articulate in person. I knew some of my friends would never believe me. Still, the president is just a man, as human and fallible as every one of us. But as I look back at it today, he really is, in person, a guy you'd want to go have a cold beer with."

Indeed, Vlasic, a Californian who had spent a year backpacking around the world and over three years studying and working in "Old Europe," had taken some ribbing from a few friends and former colleagues for accepting the White House Fellowship appointment from President Bush, although he doubted that any of those disparagers would have turned down the chance to talk face to face with the president. "I decided to ask him about something I was passionate about and something my friends might be proud of me for asking—how to fight genocide," Vlasic explained. Vlasic had spent nearly three years working for the United Nations as a prosecuting attorney at the International Criminal Tribunal for the Former Yugoslavia, where he was a member of the Slobodan Milosevic and Srebrenica genocide trial and investigation teams. Milosevic and others were implicated in the most terrible mass execution in Europe since the Holocaust, in which Bosnian Serb forces rounded up more than 7,500 Muslim men and boys and slaughtered them in cold blood, thousands with their eyes blindfolded and their hands tied behind their backs. "The mass slaughter of humanity is not just a thing of the past, like the genocide that I had seen through the witnesses I worked with and the crime scenes I had visited in Bosnia, but it is also part of the present in Darfur," Vlasic said. "And thus, I asked my question:

> Mr. President, on the topic of evil, you have done more than any other world leader to highlight the evil that is going on in Darfur, and as someone who spent nearly three years of his life helping prosecute genocide, I thank you and applaud you. But why haven't you done more to push the issue at the United Nations Security Council and, if need be, dare China's veto— especially before they host the Olympics—and let them say they are okay with genocide?

"The President's answer was great, and frankly, having talked to a number of politicians about the issue, it was more than I expected," Vlasic said. "While his answer is off the record, I can say that it was not a stock response. It was heartfelt and well informed. And it was even saddened. Here was arguably the most powerful man in the world, and while he appeared passionate about the issue, there was much, it seemed, he couldn't do without *real* international consensus and United Nations support. Amazingly, the president referred to Darfur three more times during our two-hour meeting, which went about an hour past our allotted time. This was not a mere public relations issue for the president—this was a heartfelt issue for him."

At the conclusion of their meeting, President Bush brushed off his staff's attempt to move him along to his next appointment and invited the Fellows into the Oval Office for a tour and a photo session. He discussed the history of the room and several of its relics and then posed for a picture with each Fellow. "When it was my turn, I shook his hand for the camera and I thanked the president for his time," Vlasic said. "But before I could walk off, the president grabbed me by the elbow and said, 'Thank you very much for your interest and passion on the Darfur issue. We have to find a way to do more. You should spend some time with my friend Andrew.' Well, Andrew is Andrew Natsios, the president's special envoy to Sudan. So, on the president's advice I called

Andrew Natsios, met with him, and later had the opportunity to work with him."

A few days after the meeting with the president, the United States announced that it had demanded that Sudan allow a team of United Nations personnel into Darfur and formally accept an international force by the year's end or face immediate unspecified consequences imposed by the United States, such as travel bans on Sudanese officials, freezing of their assets, and a no-flight zone over Darfur.[35] Although Vlasic said it was just a coincidence, his Fellows classmates teased him about it anyway.

During Vlasic's first meeting with Special Envoy Natsios, he told Natsios about how he had served on the Slobodan Milosevic prosecution team and later, while in private practice, had donated his time to help train the Iraqi judges who tried Saddam Hussein. Natsios explained that he was trying to persuade Sudanese President Omar al-Bashir to sign on to a United Nations–African Union peacekeeping agreement to help stop the bloodshed in Darfur, and he invited Vlasic to join him on his next trip to see Bashir in Sudan. "He told me that Bashir was worried about two things: getting bombed and being prosecuted in The Hague," Vlasic said. "Since I had worked on the Milosevic case and helped with the Saddam case and was now working for Defense Secretary Gates, he thought just having me in the room—*if I could get into Sudan*—might send a strong signal and possibly help motivate Bashir to sign the peacekeeping agreement."

Sudan is the largest country in Africa, with a population of 39 million, and the Darfur region in the western part of that country has a population of about 6 million people, mostly living in small villages. Sudan's people consist of nomadic Arabs and ethnic African farmers, with most power in the hands of those of Arab descent. The killings began when the ethnic Africans in Darfur demanded a greater role in the government. The Sudanese government then armed and paid northern Arab tribes known as Janjaweed as their proxies to take up arms against the ethnic

---

[35] "U.S. Tells Sudan to Accept U.N. Force by Year's End," *New York Times*, December 21, 2006.

Africans, resulting in widespread atrocities and rapes.[36] Sudan has powerful friends, especially China, which buys its oil and supplies it with arms. Since 2003, it is estimated that up to 300,000 innocent men, women, and children have been murdered on the basis of their ethnicity and nearly 2.2 million have seen their villages and livelihoods destroyed. In 2004, Secretary of State Colin Powell labeled the Darfur conflict as genocide and said it was the most terrible humanitarian crisis of the new century.

However, as Natsios feared, the Sudanese Embassy pushed back on Vlasic's visa application, and he was the only member of the delegation who wasn't able to go to Sudan. It seemed Bashir's Sudan had no room for someone with Vlasic's background.

However, Vlasic still traveled extensively with the Secretary of Defense and even with Andrew Natsios (though not to Sudan), including an official visit to Saudi Arabia during which he joined Secretary Gates, Secretary of State Condoleezza Rice, and a number of others at a dinner with King Abdullah at his summer palace in Jeddah. The meal was served buffet-style from a serving area that seemed to go on forever. The dinner table was covered with even more platters of food, leaving barely enough room for the diners to set down their already overflowing plates. "We were in a massive ballroom, with a beautiful tiled pool in the middle," Vlasic recalled. "One side of the ballroom was a huge aquarium, from the floor to the ceiling, filled with beautiful corals and hundreds of fish from the Red Sea, but it also had two big sharks about eight feet long swimming around in the tank. And as the Saudis fed us dinner, they fed the sharks their dinner at the same time. It was surreal. I was in a palace in Saudi Arabia, dining with a king, princes, cabinet secretaries, generals, and sharks—all at the same time!"

At the end of Vlasic's Fellowship year, it was time for his class's final visit with the president. Each Fellow was given the chance to ask the president a question or make a comment, and when it came time for Vlasic to speak, he thanked President Bush for suggesting that he spend time with Andrew Natsios. He told the president about how he been able to meet with Natsios and even travel with him to Europe and Africa. President

---

[36] Andrew S. Natsios, president's special envoy to Sudan, Testimony before the Senate Foreign Relations Committee, Washington, D.C., April 11, 2007.

Bush asked if Vlasic had made it to Sudan. "I said I had not and told him the story of the Sudanese Embassy pushing back on my visa and that it may have been related to my past and current work. The president joked that it was a good story and that I should be proud of the fact that I was rejected by Sudan!"[37]

A few minutes later, the president announced that he needed to finish up so that he could meet with the Saudi ambassador. As he and the Fellows made their way from the Roosevelt Room, through the Oval Office, and out to the Rose Garden for a final photograph, Vlasic suggested that the president should feel free to ask the Saudi ambassador to pass on his thanks for the fantastic dinner King Abdullah had hosted for the American contingent the previous week. "The president looked at me with surprise and asked, 'Were *you* at that dinner?' I told him that I was," Vlasic said. "The president smiled and said he had heard about that dinner. I asked if he'd heard about the sharks, and, laughing, he said he had, adding, 'Wow, you've had a great year!'

"The president was right: I had an outstanding year. I came away with a clear understanding of how personal relationships and international diplomacy are vital to America's commitment to international peace and security in the world, and I also learned that you do neither the president nor yourself any favors by not asking the tough questions. As Edmund Burke once said, 'All that is necessary for the triumph of evil is that good men do nothing.' As leaders we have an obligation to speak up, *especially* in closed-door discussions. It's easy to doubt yourself, but when it comes down to it,

---

[37] In July 2008 Prosecutor Luis Moreno-Ocampo at the International Criminal Court (ICC) in The Hague filed ten charges of war crimes against Sudan's President Omar al-Bashir: three counts of genocide, five counts of crimes against humanity, and two counts of murder. The case was referred to the ICC by the United Nations Security Council in March 2005. The ICC was founded in 2002 to extradite individuals to an international court whom a country's own weak justice system could not prosecute. The ICC claims that al-Bashir "masterminded and implemented a plan to destroy in substantial part" three tribal groups in Darfur because of their ethnicity. Moreno-Ocampo is expected to ask a panel of ICC judges to issue an arrest warrant for al-Bashir. Although 106 nations have signed the international convention establishing the ICC, its authority is hampered because powerful countries such as the United States, China, India, and Russia have refused to endorse it. See Peter Walker, "Darfur Genocide Charges for Sudanese President Omar al-Bashir," *The Guardian*, July 14, 2008.

you're talking to the president for a reason. If he didn't want your thoughts, you wouldn't be there, so you might as well take a deep breath, make every sentence count, and walk away without any regrets."

During his Fellowship year, Mark Vlasic learned firsthand the value of stepping up and asking the tough questions when it matters most. Luckily for him, he learned this lesson early in his career and will have the rest of his life to put it into practice. In contrast, history is rife with examples in which people in leadership positions did not speak up, and the results were disastrous. Case in point: the Bay of Pigs invasion.

It was 1961, and President Kennedy, the CIA, military leaders, and a brave group of Cuban exiles decided to take bold steps to overthrow Fidel Castro's Cuba and quash the spread of communism in the Western Hemisphere. The Kennedy administration—particularly President Kennedy, Secretary of Defense Robert McNamara, Secretary of State Dean Rusk, Secretary of the Treasury Douglas Dillon, Attorney General Robert Kennedy, and foreign affairs advisor McGeorge Bundy—hatched a plan for 1,400 Cuban exiles to invade the island at the Bay of Pigs. They expected that the invasion would spark an uprising among Cubans that would overrun what they considered a weak military and topple the Castro regime. They also believed that the CIA-trained rebel exiles would be able to escape to the mountains to hook up with guerrilla operations already established there in case something went wrong. Kennedy advisor and White House historian Arthur Schlesinger, Jr., was part of the group planning the maneuver and had grave misgivings about it. He detailed his concerns in a memorandum to President Kennedy, but Attorney General Robert Kennedy privately warned him against challenging the president's plan. Schlesinger kept his thoughts to himself from then on and watched in silence as the group agreed to carry out the invasion even when President Kennedy asked if everyone was in agreement with the operation.

The exiles landed at the Bay of Pigs and within three days were overrun by 200,000 rough and ready Cuban troops whose commanders had been tipped off by newspaper articles predicting an invasion the week before. Furthermore, critical air strikes against the Cuban Air Force were canceled, and a series of other mistakes were made that led to 1,200 Cuban exiles being captured and most of the others killed, unable to make their planned escape to the mountains because strategists had overlooked the fact that the mountains were over eighty miles away, on the far side of impassable swamps. Two years later, the United States paid a ransom of food and medicine worth $53 million to secure the hostages' release. Schlesinger berated himself for not speaking out, saying, "In the months after the Bay of Pigs I bitterly reproached myself for having kept so silent during those crucial discussions in the cabinet room. I can only explain my failure to do more than raise a few timid questions by reporting that one's impulse to blow the whistle on this nonsense was simply undone by the circumstances of the discussion."[38]

One who is not afraid to speak up and ask a tough question is Colin Powell (WHF 73–74). It was August 3, 1990, and President George H. W. Bush called an emergency meeting of the National Security Council to discuss the American plan to defend Saudi Arabia against Saddam Hussein's Iraqi forces. The Iraqis already had invaded Kuwait, and many feared that Hussein intended to keep rolling until he had gained control of much of the region, including Saudi Arabia. The United States and its allies were not going to allow that to happen; it was their intention to defend Saudi Arabia. As chairman of the Joint Chiefs of Staff, it was Powell's job to inform the NSC and the president of all military options toward that end. Powell put forward the military's plan to defend the Saudi border from an Iraqi invasion. Everyone agreed that the United States was committed and that it was time to prepare the troops for deployment to Saudi Arabia.

However, Powell was not ready to roll quite yet. During the Vietnam War, he had been appalled by the lack of pressure put on political leaders to give clear objectives to their military strategists. Before he could participate in sending American troops into harm's way in the Persian Gulf, there was something he needed to know. Therefore, Powell asked this question of those assembled that day: Is it worth going to war to liberate Kuwait? Powell immediately detected a chill in the room. Apparently he had overstepped his bounds. No one answered his question before the meeting adjourned. Afterward, Defense Secretary Dick Cheney chastised Powell, reminding him that he was the chairman of the Joint Chiefs, not the secretary of state or the national security advisor or the secretary of defense, and told him to attend to military matters, not policy. However, Powell

---

[38] Irving L. Janis, "Groupthink," *Psychology Today*, November 1971, p. 74.

was not sorry that he had spoken out; he believed that his question had to be asked. "Many people have made a lot of this, asking, 'Who were you to be asking these questions?' I'll tell you who I was," Powell said. "I was the senior military advisor and the principal military advisor to the president, the secretary of state, the secretary of defense, and the vice president. It was very much my responsibility even though it rankled people. But rankling people comes with the job, and if you're not prepared to rankle people, you shouldn't have the job."

The next day General Powell and the national security team gathered at Camp David with the president while General Norman Schwarzkopf gave everyone an in-depth briefing on the military options, including what it would take to eject the Iraqi forces and liberate Kuwait. When President George H. W. Bush returned to Washington from Camp David on Sunday armed with a credible plan, he stepped off the helicopter, walked to a podium on the south lawn of the White House, faced the reporters and the television cameras, and confidently told the world that this aggression against Kuwait would not stand. "'This will not stand,' his famous expression on that Sunday morning, did not mean he was going to use military force. It meant that this will not stand, and what did he do? He took it to the United Nations," Powell explained. "He got a variety of resolutions telling Iraq to get out, and, frankly, it was our policy until January to try to resolve the issue peacefully and get the Iraqis to leave. The best evidence I'll give of this point is that Secretary of State Jim Baker went to see Iraq's deputy prime minister, Tariq Aziz, at the very last minute and he was rebuffed. That's when war became inevitable. We were ready for it. We had deployed 500,000 troops, and we succeeded in carrying out the mission."

Slightly more than ten years later, General Powell found himself on the opposite side of the policy-making table when, as secretary of state, he served as an advisor to President George W. Bush on the impending 2003 invasion of Iraq. In early September 2002, two days before a scheduled briefing of the National Security Council in Washington, Powell called U.S. Army General Tommy Franks, who was to lead the invasion. Powell had grave concerns that the forces would be insufficient to carry out the mission.

"I was secretary of state, neither secretary of defense nor chairman of the Joint Chiefs of Staff anymore, that's true. But I was a retired four-star

general who had been chairman of the Joint Chiefs of Staff, and I probably had more experience than anybody in the room with respect to conducting large-scale military operations, especially against Iraq," Powell
explained. "So when there was discussion about the military force needed to
decisively deal with the problem in Iraq, I was concerned that maybe there
was not enough force, not enough troops going in for the mission that had
been assigned. I called Tommy Franks to ask him if he thought he had
enough and to tell him I thought it was something that we should discuss
in front of everybody. He took my call and treated it somewhat cavalierly.
Then he quite correctly called his boss, Defense Secretary Rumsfeld,
because I was out of channels, and Secretary Rumsfeld thought it was
appropriate to have me raise the issue at the meeting. So I did. It was
discussed."

Powell made sure President Bush understood that he had concerns
about the troop levels, but when the president made it clear that he
intended to take the advice of General Franks, Defense Secretary Rumsfeld, and Chairman of the Joint Chiefs General Richard Myers, Powell had
to step aside. "People have asked why I didn't press my case even more
strongly, and the answer is because I had pressed my case and it was not
my responsibility," Powell said. "I was not the chairman of the Joint Chiefs
of Staff. So you press your case, but then, after a while, the president can't
keep hearing you press your case when he is getting different kinds of
advice from the people who have to execute the mission."

Against Powell's better judgment, the invasion was carried out in early
2003 by 150,000 troops. Powell believes history will show that he was correct: The numbers of troops deployed in 2003 were insufficient to complete the mission once the fall of Baghdad was carried out. Indeed, in 2007
President Bush ordered another 20,000 troops into Iraq and extended the
tours of thousands more already on the ground there.

By raising his concerns over certain aspects of both wars in Iraq, Colin
Powell did what any effective leader would do: He gave his best advice and
asked the tough questions even if it meant he stood alone. As it happened,
he resigned from his post as secretary of state in 2005. "I didn't feel constrained to just offer stovepipe advice, totally in my own lane; I gave the
advice that was expected of me," Powell said. "But presidents deserve even
more than that. They deserve your *best* thinking and your *best* judgment,
whether it's in your lane or not and whether you're taking a risk by doing

it or not. I think I did take a risk, and it may have affected my future role within the administration, but that's not my concern. My concern was giving my best advice."

No matter what your station in life is, there will come a day when you'll have to decide whether to speak out or forever hold your peace. When that day comes for you, remember that great results begin with great questions. On a frigid morning in January 1961, John F. Kennedy asked each American citizen in the country a question when he spoke these words: "Ask not what your country can do for you—ask what you can do for your country." This powerful question inspired a whole generation of Americans to consider serving something much greater than themselves.

CHAPTER 14

LEADERS TAKE RISKS

It was 1964, and Robert Patricelli (WHF 65–66) read with great interest the front-page story in the *New York Times* about the White House Fellowships, a program being launched by President Lyndon Johnson to give young Americans a chance to work for a year in Washington, D.C. It was perfect timing. Patricelli was in his third year at Harvard Law School, and although he planned to practice international law after graduation, he thought a detour via the nation's capital might be not only be interesting but good for his career. A former Fulbright Scholar, he applied for the Fellowship, was accepted, and spent a year under the tutelage of Secretary of State Dean Rusk.

Rusk gave the twenty-six-year-old Fellow practically unlimited access to the workings of the State Department. "He told his scheduler and personal assistant to share his schedule with me every week so I could check the meetings I wanted to sit in on," Patricelli recalled. "Ninety-five percent of the time he agreed to let me attend. Often in those meetings it would be the secretary and some visiting foreign minister, a translator, and me. I was also invited to travel with him to lots of international conferences all over the world. I was barely dry behind the ears, and as you can imagine, the Fellowship was very much a life-changing experience for me." Rusk also gave Patricelli the job of organizing his briefing materials in preparation for the first major congressional hearings on the Vietnam War and took his young Fellow along to sit in on the hearings. No matter what the occasion or the pressures, Patricelli was impressed by Secretary Rusk's grace under pressure. "I always tried to follow his example of maintaining composure and not getting rattled," Patricelli explained. "His job was extremely high-pressure. People were always coming at him, and he was always a model of calmness and steadiness."

At the end of his Fellowship year, Patricelli went to work for nearly three years as counsel to a U.S. Senate subcommittee on employment, manpower, and poverty whose members included Senators Ted and Bobby Kennedy, Jacob Javits, and Fritz Mondale, among others. After that, Patricelli served as deputy undersecretary at the Department of Health, Education, and Welfare and then as administrator of the U.S. Urban Mass Transportation Administration.

Bob Patricelli never made it to that international law firm he had his eye on while at Harvard Law School. Instead, when his time in Washington, D.C., was done, he decided to forgo his promising legal career and try his hand at business; he went to work in the government relations section of Connecticut General Insurance Corporation, which later became CIGNA. "My government experience from the White House Fellowship got me in the door," Patricelli recalled. "I said I'd do government relations for Connecticut General to start, but I wanted the opportunity to move into the mainline of business at some point, and that's exactly what happened." After one and a half years, Patricelli moved into a position managing corporate staff and then, after a merger, was given his first full business responsibility when he was assigned to lead one of the company's four divisions. His division oversaw Connecticut General's fledgling health maintenance organization (HMO). Over the next four years, as Patricelli built the division into a national health care organization, he realized that the next logical step was to merge the company's health plan segment with its group health insurance segment. "The world was moving toward health plan–type organizations with networks of care, and I had a number of ideas I wanted to implement," Patricelli explained. "But it became clear there was going to be an organizational tussle between me and the longtime head of the group insurance operation—a twenty-five-year veteran of the company—and he ultimately won out. That was fine with me. I knew I had some good ideas, and I was ready to go out and test them."

However, there was a fly in the ointment. Patricelli needed money to finance his dream company but had no idea how to go about raising venture capital. A family member introduced him to the people at Warburg Pincus, a private equity firm based in New York that helps entrepreneurs finance new businesses, among other things. "I didn't have a management team, but I had the prospect of recruiting some former colleagues. I also didn't have what you'd call a Harvard Business School–style business plan. It was just a three- or four-page narrative, but I took it down to Warburg Pincus to see what they thought," Patricelli said. "I told them that I had some specific targets—two or three entities that I wanted to acquire—so I had the outline of some platform companies that could be bought into to start this new organization. Warburg Pincus had made several previous major investments into the changing nature of health care, and they signed me up. From this experience I learned that it's all about the people. It's not about the specific business plan and financial models of the moment, because those will change. It's about whether or not you've got good people, and whether or not it's a good market opportunity, because then the good people will work their way through the inevitable problems and produce a positive result."

One of those "inevitable problems" surfaced a bit more quickly than Patricelli would have liked. As he was negotiating with the acquisition prospect, a mental health management company, they gave him an ultimatum: commit to buying a 40 percent share of the company within the next two weeks or the deal would be off. That company was to be an essential part of Patricelli's new organization, and he wasn't about to give it up because of bad timing. He called upon the greatest lesson he'd learned from his White House Fellows principal, Secretary of State Dean Rusk, and kept a level head while he gave calm consideration to his next step. "I wasn't even done with my paperwork for Warburg Pincus yet, but I did something that I don't think would happen in this day and age. I took out a personal loan, a demand note from Warburg Pincus for $4 million, so that I could go ahead and make this investment in the new entity before we were even done with the Warburg Pincus paperwork," Patricelli said with a laugh. "The loan was all done on handshakes and trust. It was a very big risk for me. Fortunately, about a month later we got the legal documents straightened out and just converted that loan into the initial equity investment. But that's how I got started back in 1987."

Warburg Pincus invested approximately $25 million in Patricelli's venture, Value Health, Inc., which was listed on the New York Stock Exchange. For ten years Patricelli served as Value Health's chairman, president, and CEO until 1997, when the company was purchased by

Columbia/HCA for $1.3 billion. A week later, Patricelli started a new company with his own funds and named it Women's Health USA, Inc., a firm that provides management and administrative services to doctors and also manages two *in vitro* fertilization clinics in Connecticut. In 2000 he founded Evolution Benefits, a company that provides debit card payment solutions and related services to health plans and other entities. He attributes it all to the day he decided to stick his neck out and risk everything for the chance to make his entrepreneurial dream come true.

"As I think back on it, taking on a $4 million personal loan to make an investment in a company before I even had a staff or anything else was pretty heady," Patricelli said. "But you have to have the courage to take risks. You've got to be willing to be a ball carrier and take the lumps if you want to lead a winning team."

Bob Patricelli took a risk that would have wiped him out financially if things had not gone his way, but great leaders assume all sorts of risks, not just the monetary kind. Sometimes a leader has to make life-and-death judgments, and it is then that his or her leadership skills are put to the ultimate test. Such was the case for former White House Fellow Ron Quincy.

At the time he was selected for the White House Fellowship, Quincy (WHF 85–86) was serving as executive director of Michigan's Department of Civil Rights, where he was, at that time, the youngest person in the state's history to serve as a cabinet-level department head. Day in and day out, he and his staff conducted research into the most effective ways to reduce the numbers of civil rights complaints in the state and also created and implemented innovative community and industry-based programs designed to protect people's civil rights.

While Ron Quincy was working within Michigan's government to eliminate acts of discrimination, across the Atlantic Ocean the South African government was working to perpetuate *more* discrimination. Since the late 1940s, the white South African minority had set up and maintained a formal system designed to keep blacks and other people of color subjugated by any means necessary, an apartheid system of institutionalized racism that undermined the basic human dignity of nonwhites. Blacks were segregated and forced to live in slums, their movements restricted and their labor exploited. They were denied the right to participate in the political system and saw their leaders arrested, convicted of treason, and sentenced to life in prison. One of those imprisoned was former African National Congress leader Nelson Mandela, whose wife, Winnie, remained an outspoken opponent of apartheid despite herself being incarcerated and harassed repeatedly. In the mid-1980s, antiapartheid activists were stepping up the pace of boycotts, protests, and uprisings in response to the regime's racist practices, and violence was bloodying the region. Black South Africans and their sympathizers desperately needed help dismantling the apartheid system.

That's why Ron Quincy was thrilled when he was assigned to work during his Fellowship as a foreign affairs advisor in the State Department, where his focus would be on South Africa. After successfully handling some small in-office projects, Quincy was tapped to organize an education mission to South Africa for fifteen presidents of historically black American colleges and universities that were going to team up with colleges and universities in South Africa. Faculty exchanges, research collaborations, and student scholarships would be part of the program, and Quincy was in charge of planning and carrying out the advance trip for the college presidents. "It was so funny because I had never traveled abroad in my life. But suddenly here I am with a diplomatic passport, off to South Africa," Quincy said. "We stopped first in London to meet the U.S. ambassador to the Court of Saint James's, and then we moved on for two weeks over to South Africa. It was a very successful mission. They all said I was all right for a guy who had never been anywhere!"

Quincy was so "all right" that at the end of his Fellowship year he was asked to stay on at the State Department to work with the South and Southern African Working Group. In that role he helped craft the Comprehensive Anti-Apartheid Act of 1986 which imposed economic sanctions on the South African government and required U.S. corporations working in South Africa to divest their holdings. It also mandated that the U.S. government work with and provide financial assistance to black South African human rights organizations and labor unions and barred South African government leaders from traveling to the United States without special permission.

During his tenure at the State Department, Quincy again had to dust off his diplomatic passport for a trip to South Africa, and although travel throughout the region was always risky in that era, this trip would be especially perilous. He would have to watch not only his own back but also that of a very special traveling partner. Secretary of State George Schultz had assigned Quincy to be the diplomatic escort officer for Dr. Martin Luther King's widow, Coretta Scott King, during her mission to South Africa. "The secretary briefed Mrs. King in his office prior to departure on how very difficult the political landscape was there in South Africa. He informed her that a number of high-level missions to South Africa had not succeeded," Quincy explained. "But Mrs. King was determined to meet with a cross-section of South African leaders to discuss the political and economic situation there. It was imperative for high-level U.S. leaders to have dialogue with South African leaders. It was particularly important for someone of Mrs. King's stature to do so because she was universally respected for her own work in human rights."

Despite extensive advance work by the American Embassy staff in South Africa, high-level State Department officials, and National Security Council staff, the delegation was met with incredible challenges on the ground. Mrs. King was scheduled to meet with black South African leaders at Winnie Mandela's home in Soweto, an African township just outside Johannesburg known for its violence. South African President P. W. Botha sent word to the American delegation that his government would not be responsible for Mrs. King's safety and notified them that he had pulled all his security forces from inside the township. Only the township's entrances and exits had security personnel, and Botha had ordered them not to enter Soweto under any circumstances. Consequently, the U.S. ambassador to South Africa ordered the State Department security force officers accompanying Quincy and Mrs. King not to go into Soweto either and ordered all U.S. personnel to leave Soweto immediately. Mrs. King's mission was on the brink of being a complete failure.

"Mrs. King summoned me to her hotel suite. She was in tears, and she told me that she could not leave the country without meeting with Winnie Mandela and the other black antiapartheid leaders, many of whom were under house arrest. She said, 'Look, I've gone through an awful lot, and my husband could not have led the civil rights movement if he was in fear. He led without fear for his life and he led without fear for his reputation.' So she felt that if she was going to be a leader in the mirror of her husband, she had to be courageous and not worry about her safety—to be conscious of it, but not to worry about her safety—and not to be concerned about preserving her reputation. She was willing to take that risk," Quincy said. "So I told her that I would figure out a way to get her into Soweto."

However, when Quincy phoned his superiors in Washington for advice, he was told that he was on his own. It was then that he took matters into his own hands. The hotel manager let him use the company's large black Mercedes-Benz. Quincy mounted U.S. flags on both front bumpers, put Mrs. King and Dr. King's sister, Christine King Farris, in the backseat, and set out to pay a visit to Winnie Mandela.

At the entrance to Soweto, the American delegation was greeted with chaos and violence as the South African security forces were engaged in a clash with black protesters, but the Mercedes wended its way through the township. At one point the protesters realized that Mrs. King was in the car, and it was surrounded by an estimated 20,000 people with others in close pursuit. However, they made it safely to Winnie Mandela's house, and Quincy took Mrs. King inside to meet her.

"The two of them stood in the middle of the room and embraced and cried," Quincy recalled. "Winnie was the face of the antiapartheid movement in South Africa, so for her message to be delivered to the U.S. government by Mrs. King—someone she respected and trusted—was extremely important. This meeting opened the door for Mrs. King to meet with many of the black opposition leaders and hear about the issues they believed could lead our countries toward ending apartheid. She listened to what they had to say, and she told them that she would go back and report their concerns and suggestions. No one else had done that, certainly no one else with the integrity that Mrs. King had. There were plenty of high-level Americans that had gone over there and had summarily been sent home. She carried a message of hope, and she was able to complete the majority of her South African mission because she wasn't afraid to take a risk."

In 1991, Coretta Scott King asked Quincy to serve as executive director of the King Center for Nonviolent Social Change, a living memorial and institutional guardian of Dr. King's legacy that she established in Atlanta.[39] It was through that work that Quincy was given the opportunity to travel with Nelson Mandela after his 1990 release from prison after twenty-seven years of incarceration. Just four years later, Mrs. King danced with Mandela to celebrate his inauguration as president of South Africa.

---

[39] *The King Center's Mission.* Accessed 31 July 2008. Available online at www.thekingcenter .com/tkc/mission.asp.

Ron Quincy took a tremendous personal and professional risk in assuming responsibility for getting Coretta Scott King safely in and out of Soweto that day, but if he had it to do all over again, he wouldn't change a thing. "To have had the opportunity to play a very, very small role in the reshaping of U.S. and South African relations is one of my proudest moments as a White House Fellow and in my entire career," he said. "Was it worth the risk to go into Soweto? Absolutely."

Both Patricelli and Quincy knew exactly what it was they wanted to achieve, and so they plotted a course that led to that goal. As opportunities and obstacles arose, they dealt with them decisively. They let nothing deter them, thus inspiring confidence in the people around them. A confident team guided by a bold leader willing to assume large risks is an undeniable force.

Leaders take personal risks and sometimes lay it all on the line to meet a challenge. Dale Carnegie once said, "Take a chance! All life is a chance. The man who goes the furthest is generally the one who is willing to do and dare. The 'sure thing' boat never gets far from shore." Leaders also create a culture that encourages their people to take risks and learn from the inevitable mistakes that occur when risks are taken. Leaders constantly challenge their team to take risks, and that encourages creativity and leads to organizational breakthroughs.

CHAPTER 15

LEADERS UNDERSTAND THAT NOT EVERY BATTLE IS THE END OF THE WAR

Today's White House Fellows represent the American population in all its amazing diversity, but the first class of Fellows was far from representative. It was made up entirely of men even though several highly qualified women made it to the national finals, including Mary Elizabeth (Hanford) Dole, who was educated at some of the world's most prestigious schools: Duke, Oxford, and Harvard. Dole was disappointed but not bitter over the rejection and went on to have an incredible career in public service, working in five presidential administrations. In fact, she served in President Reagan's and President George H. W. Bush's cabinets and even made a bid for the presidency in 2000. In 2003 she was elected to the U.S. Senate from her home state of North Carolina. The first lady, Lady Bird Johnson, made her disappointment very well known when she saw the roster of Fellows that first year and demanded that all those involved in the selection process give women candidates an equal opportunity. Program director Tom Carr pledged to ensure greater diversity in future classes, and he made good on his promise the next year when Jane Cahill Pfeiffer (WHF 66–67) became the first woman to be selected as a White House Fellow.

Pfeiffer was a thirty-three-year-old IBM executive on the company's fast track when she learned about the White House Fellows program. "They didn't know what to do with me at IBM. They just weren't ready for a female branch manager yet," Pfeiffer recalled. "So I saw this ad about the White House Fellows, and I thought, 'With my ten years working with IBM's government division it would be great to further my understanding of how the government really works.'" Pfeiffer was awarded the Fellowship and received a plum assignment: to work as administrative assistant to the new Secretary of Housing and Urban Development (HUD), Robert "Bob" Weaver. When Weaver was told that Pfeiffer had been assigned to work with him for the year, he allegedly exclaimed, "My God, it's a girl!"

"Now, you have to put that into the time sequence, and when you do, you realize how legitimate and absolutely hilarious that reaction is," Pfeiffer explained with a laugh. "But he got used to the idea, and it wasn't long before he moved me into an office near his, and I had a real job and was part of everything."

Weaver had been HUD secretary for only a few months, and everyone in President Johnson's administration had very high hopes for him. He had earned a Ph.D. from Harvard and had been the administrator of the federal Housing and Home Finance Agency for several years. He was an expert on two of the most important issues of the day—black labor and urban matters—and had written highly regarded books on those topics. "He was like a superstar. He lived right down the street from my mother in Washington," Pfeiffer recalled. "Back then I had a convertible white Corvette Sting Ray with a red interior—I love sports cars—and I used to pick up Secretary Weaver on Saturday mornings and drive him to the HUD office in that Corvette. He loved it. He became one of the dearest people in my life, a lifelong mentor who taught me so many valuable leadership lessons."

The lessons Pfeiffer learned that year would serve her well when, in 1978, she was named chairperson of the NBC television network and became one of the nation's most powerful women. The lessons of her year at HUD were especially significant because of one noteworthy fact: Secretary Robert Weaver was black, the first African American ever to be appointed to a presidential cabinet post. When he accepted President Johnson's historic appointment, Weaver carried the hopes and dreams of millions of African Americans on his shoulders, and he did not disappoint them or the influential leaders who had helped propel him into the national spotlight. In fact, one who had played a vital behind-the-scenes role in Weaver's rise to the top was the Reverend Dr. Martin Luther King, Jr.

It was January 15, 1965, and Dr. King, who had just won the Nobel Peace Prize, waited patiently for President Lyndon Johnson to accept his telephone call. The civil rights movement had made great strides over the last few months, but there was still much to do, and King intended to issue a challenge to the president that day that, if Johnson chose to accept it, would signify a momentous step on the road to equality for minorities in the United States. The president recently had signed into law the Civil Rights Act of 1964, which put an official end to segregation in employment, public places, and schools, making it illegal for the federal government or state governments to discriminate against people because of their race, color, religion, sex, or national origin. However, despite the new legislation, discrimination was still rampant throughout the country; the old social order was proving difficult to dislodge.

The fight for the Civil Rights Act had been a long and bitter one during which President Johnson and like-minded congressional leaders had squared off against an indignant band of Southern lawmakers led by the president's old friend and former mentor, Georgia Senator Richard Russell, who had declared, "We will resist to the bitter end any measure or any movement which would have a tendency to bring about social equality and intermingling and amalgamation of the races in our [Southern] states." After a filibuster lasting fifty-four days and much political wrangling, the historic measure passed the Senate in spite of the southern bloc's opposition and was sent to President Johnson for his signature on July 2, 1964.

It had been six months since the president had signed that bill, and the dust had begun to settle, relatively speaking. King believed the time had come for President Johnson to make perhaps his boldest move yet and set a precedent for establishing racial equality at the highest reaches of the federal government. It was time for him to appoint an African American to his cabinet.

"We have a strong feeling that it would mean so much to the health of our whole democracy, to the Negroes of the nation, to have a Negro in the Cabinet," King said during the call that President Johnson secretly recorded.[40] "It would be a great step forward for the nation and the Negro and our international image, and would do so much to give many people a lift who *need* a lift now. I'm sure it could give a real sense of dignity and self-respect to millions of Negroes. . . ."

President Johnson responded, "I'm going to concentrate all of the executive power I can to get that done," telling King that it was his intention to create a new cabinet-level department that dealt with housing and urban issues and revealing that he already had the perfect person in mind to run it: Housing and Home Finance Agency Administrator Bob Weaver. "I'm going to shove as strong as I can to get the biggest department—housing, urban affairs, city, transportation—everything that comes in that department that involves the urban areas of America, in one department," Johnson told King. "And then if I can get that done, without having to commit one way or the other, my hope would be that I could put the man in there, and probably it would be Weaver because I think we have a more or less moral obligation to a fellow who's done a good job and he hasn't disappointed anybody."

"This is very encouraging," King replied. "This would be another great step toward the Great Society."

"It's like you being assistant pastor of your church for ten years with the understanding of your deacons that you would take over . . .," the president continued. "And finally the good day comes and they say, 'Well, you get back and sit at the second table.' I just don't feel like saying that to Weaver. Weaver's not *my* man—I didn't bring him in. He's a Kennedy man. But I just think it would be a pretty revolutionary feeling about him."

One year and three days after that telephone call, Robert C. Weaver became the first African American to serve in a cabinet post when President Johnson appointed him secretary of the newly created Department of Housing and Urban Development. Eight months later, Jane Cahill Pfeiffer broke through yet another barrier when she became the country's first female White House Fellow. However, despite the major advances in race and gender relations in Washington that year, it wasn't all smooth sailing; unfortunately, discrimination was still alive and well in the nation's capital.

---

[40] Telephone Conversation between President Johnson and Martin Luther King, Jr., January 15, 1965, 12:06 pm, Citation #6736, Recordings of Telephone Conversations, Lyndon B. Johnson Presidential Library.

"Weaver was the coordinator of the Model Cities program recently enacted into law to collectively channel federal, state, and local resources for urban renewal of slums in sixty-three inner cities. He asked me to figure out a place where all the task force members could have an offsite meeting, a place President Lyndon Johnson could come to," Pfeiffer explained. "I told him I knew just the place, a country club in Bethesda, Maryland, that IBM often used for conferences. I knew a high-level person at the club, so I called him up and he said we couldn't come. And I said, 'What do you mean we can't come? Gosh, we've got the cabinet secretaries and even the president of the United States,' and he said, 'Weaver can't come here.' They didn't allow blacks at that club! Now, can you imagine having to go back to Weaver and tell him that?"

Pfeiffer informed the club representative that she would see to it that IBM boycotted their facility until they rescinded their discriminatory practices, and she got a colleague at IBM to promise that the company would back her up. She decided not to tell Weaver that he was unwelcome at the club; she would book another facility for the Model Cities meeting quietly and move on. But when Weaver asked her point blank why she had changed venues, she broke down and told him the sad truth: The club's doors were closed to him because of the color of his skin.

"He did not brood over it, and that was the end of that. He was such a dear man—he never said anything more about it," Pfeiffer said. "That's what Weaver could always do. He could rise above the slights."[41] It was a good lesson for a young woman trying to function in a male-dominated workplace. Pfeiffer learned that becoming angry or resentful just makes you bitter; it's a virus that can enter your pores without warning and spread silently, infecting your entire being. If you allow that to happen, you contaminate everyone around you with a negative attitude, especially your subordinates, who quickly will lose respect for you and make it difficult for you to lead. Although pressing ahead, rising above the slights, and not becoming bitter is a good advice for those facing discrimination, leaders should draw inspiration from Martin Luther King, Jr., who gave his life trying to bring the

---

[41] In a profile Robert Weaver said: "The lash of prejudice is not the overt lash; it's the subtle lash of feeling yourself up against an iron block of prejudice that is the most cutting." A. H. Haskin, "Washington Gets the Weaver Treatment," *New York Times Magazine*, May 14, 1961, p. SM16.

nation together and who dreamed of a country in which people were judged by the content of their character. Great leaders treat everyone with respect and ensure that what matters most is competence and character.

Like Pfeiffer, many years later Ronald Quincy (WHF 85–86) was a Fellow at HUD. One of his assignments was to represent the HUD secretary at an interagency effort led by the Department of State to promote fundamental change in South Africa. This task force was formed at the direction of President Reagan in 1985 to organize opposition to apartheid, South Africa's system of legally enshrined racism.

Quincy's role was to help organize high-level diplomatic and private missions to South Africa at a critical time in that country's history. Halfway through the Fellowship year, his success led to a transfer from HUD to the State Department as a foreign policy advisor to the Africa Bureau. On one key assignment, Secretary of State George Schultz chose Quincy as the diplomatic escort officer for a mission led by Mrs. Coretta Scott King, the widow of Martin Luther King, Jr., to South Africa to meet with a cross section of that country's leaders. After her return to the United States, she personally urged President Reagan to approve sanctions against South Africa. Through that experience and over two dozen subsequent trips to South Africa, he developed friendships with leaders such as Bishop Desmond Tutu, Winnie Mandela, Oliver Tambo, and Walter Sisulu that led to an opportunity to work and travel with Nelson Mandela after his Fellowship year.

Nelson Mandela is today one of the world's most respected, beloved, and admired leaders. "I was inspired by his lack of bitterness after spending twenty-seven years in prison despite appalling atrocities committed against his fellow citizens and even his own family by the apartheid regime," said Quincy. In 1991, Mrs. King hired Quincy as the executive director and chief operating officer of the Atlanta-based King Center for Nonviolent Social Change, an organization charged with carrying on Dr. King's legacy. One of the projects the King Center undertook after Mandela was released from prison in 1990 was to work closely with a group of American students and their South African counterparts to help train over 50,000 South Africans in the election process, which was a precursor to a much broader international effort for nonpartisan voter education. Quincy remembered, "We hosted Nelson Mandela at the King Center in Atlanta as part of this effort for a couple of days, and then I had the privilege of escorting him around the United States and then flying back with him to Johannesburg."

At one point during the eighteen-hour South African Airways flight, Mandela and Quincy were standing up talking with each other in the aisle when one of the male flight attendants rudely told Mandela to sit down so that they could serve dinner. "I was shocked. The attendant shouted at Mandela in a loud, rude, and disrespectful manner. I was hardly able to restrain my own anger because I'm a part of this humiliation," recalled Quincy. However, he decided to hold his tongue and see how Mandela wanted to handle it. "Mandela then turns and points to me and says, 'Actually, sir, I'm with him,' shifting the blame to me as if I was the culprit, the important American. He said it jokingly in a mischievous way, grinning with a blink of the eye to me, and completely disarmed the situation and quietly returned to his seat."

Quincy reflected that in an era in which divas have to be escorted off the plane for throwing temper tantrums when one of their bags is mishandled, here was a man of enormous international stature who chose to sit down quietly without making a scene. Reflecting on the incident, Mandela later told Quincy that when he was active in the African National Congress (ANC) as a young man, "I learned that leaders who last are those who understand that every battle is not the end of the war. That little incident was not the war. It was not important, absolutely of no consequence."

Quincy learned that not only was Mandela not bitter, he did not have an ego that required that he be treated as royalty. Mandela cautioned Quincy to "never take your condition so seriously that it impedes you from accomplishing your personal mission, which, in my case, is a free democratic election in South Africa."

Less than a year later, in April 1994, the ANC won a landslide victory and Nelson Mandela was elected the first black president of South Africa.

Effective leaders display the kind of grace and humility under pressure that characterized Mandela and Weaver. Great leaders keep their eye on the bold vision of their organization and focus on executing the objectives of their mission, not allowing themselves to be distracted by other people's prejudices. This applies to any broad personal attack on you by someone with his or her own agenda. Too often leaders allow themselves to be sidetracked by these minor irritants and then focus too much of their attention on counterattacking those individuals and wasting precious energy and time on irrelevant issues. Leaders who demonstrate grace under fire with a laserlike focus on their true mission are the ones who will achieve greatness one day.

CHAPTER 16

LEADERS ENERGIZE THEIR PEOPLE

Each year in a small conference room right across the street from the White House there are seventy-five to a hundred off-the-record lunches with very prominent individuals from all walks of life. One of the questions I asked White House Fellows alumni when I was gathering anecdotes for this book was, "Who was the most memorable person who spoke to your White House Fellowship class and why?" There were as many different answers as there were Fellows, with one notable exception: Every Fellow I interviewed from one recent class chose General David Petraeus, at that time the commanding general of the Multi-National Force in Iraq, as the most impressive speaker they heard all year. Petraeus's question to the Fellows was simple but unforgettable: "Are you the kind of leader that fills your subordinates with energy, or do you suck the energy out of them?"

Without a doubt, General Petraeus is an authority on leadership principles and ways to put them into practice to accomplish a mission. His abilities and intellect have garnered worldwide praise and recognition. A graduate of West Point with a Ph.D. from Princeton in international relations, Petraeus was the top student in the U.S. Army's Command and General Staff College's class of 1983. In 2007, *Time* magazine named this soldier-scholar one of the most influential leaders and revolutionaries of the year, and he was one of four runners-up for the *Time* Person of the Year. In 2008 he was named "America's most respected soldier" by the German weekly magazine *Der Spiegel*. He was chosen 2007 Man of the Year by

Britain's *Daily Telegraph*. When General Petraeus talks about leadership, people listen. U.S. Major John Patrick Gallagher (WHF 07–08) certainly did.

Petraeus was a colonel in the 82nd Airborne Division at the same time Gallagher was assigned to the division as a second lieutenant. Gallagher, a graduate of West Point and the University of Chicago with degrees in philosophy, sociology, and public policy, remembered the day Petraeus called the troops into the chapel and asked if anyone could tell him the number one leadership priority of the brigade. "We all said integrity, professional and tactical competence, things like that. Gosh, we went through every quality we could think of," Gallagher recalled with a chuckle. "We even mentioned marksmanship and good vehicle mainte-nance, but he kept saying that was not the answer he was looking for. Finally someone said, 'Physical fitness?' And he said, 'Yes, that's right. That's the number one leadership priority.' Well, we thought he was kidding, and we couldn't for the life of us figure out how that could be the number one priority in the brigade. But we learned later that he was right: Self-discipline and being able to perform under pressure and exist outside our comfort zone would be the key that unlocked our success."

Petraeus began leading his troops through seventy-five minutes of intense exercise every morning on the parade field, working them to exhaustion and then pushing them farther. With every pull-up, push-up, and sprint, the brigade began to change. The troops became more alert during the day. They had more physical and mental energy. Their individual and team pride increased markedly.

"All those other things we wanted to do well got better, whether it was marksmanship or vehicle maintenance or soldiers going on leave and not getting arrested for DUI," Gallagher said. "All these other indicators went up when Petraeus created this climate of self-discipline. He boiled down his leadership approach to this: Am I giving my subordinates energy or am I taking it away? Put another way, am I leading in a way that causes my subordinates to be more enthusiastic and creative about doing their jobs— to believe more deeply in what they are doing and why they are doing it—or am I leading in such a way that it is stifling growth and enthusiasm? If the latter is true, the job may still get done by the sheer force of your legitimacy or presence, but it doesn't get done as well and it doesn't last after you're gone. Petraeus knows how to lead in such a way that it gives his subordinates energy. That's an incredibly powerful leadership tool."

Since leaving his Fellowship, Gallagher has been using that tool daily in his role as Director for the War of Ideas and Strategic Communications at the National Security Council's Office of Iraq and Afghanistan Affairs.

Another former Fellow who is determined to energize her team every day is Court TV news anchor and legal analyst Jami Floyd (WHF 93–94). Floyd, who earned a juris doctor degree from the University of California–Berkeley and a master of law degree from Stanford Law School, spent the bulk of her Fellowship year working in the office of Vice President Al Gore alongside his chief domestic policy advisor, Greg Simon. From both men she learned the power of positive energy.

"Greg was the kind of person who inspired energy. Even if you were exhausted, he lifted you up with his good spirits and his positive attitude. I know he had to be tired, but he never *seemed* tired," Floyd explained. "Greg and Al Gore had very different personalities, but they were both energizing leaders. Greg was lighthearted and jovial, a very talkative and friendly person. He'd encourage you to take your lunch break and go for a walk around the block or to the museum or the Corcoran Gallery of Art to get out and stretch your mind a bit and then come back reenergized. How many bosses do that? Then there was the vice president's energy, which was much more focused and directed, and you felt its intensity even without words. When I think back to all the great people the vice president had working for him, I realize they were all people, like Greg, who gave energy more than they drew it away. So obviously the vice president appreciated those who motivated through enthusiasm rather than fear and dissension, and he selected people who thrive under stress, who cope well with it without taking it out on others."

It would take seven years and a horrific event for Floyd to understand the full power of that lesson. As Floyd strolled through the streets of New York to her job as the law and justice correspondent for ABC News one sunny morning in September 2001, terrorists crashed two hijacked planes filled with innocent passengers into the World Trade Center's Twin Towers. Floyd's first instinct was to rush home to her two-year-old daughter, but knowing the toddler was safe with her husband, she placed her duty as a journalist before her own interests and dashed to the newsroom to receive her assignment. "I was immediately dispatched to the World Trade Center with a single producer and a crew—one cameraman and one soundman," Floyd recalled. "We were about to cover the biggest story of our lives and one of the most significant events in the history of our country. This was a transformational moment, and we knew it. And with that knowledge, we felt the awesome responsibility to get it right."

Floyd and her crew drove the news van toward the scene of destruction, but the road became impassable a few blocks from the Twin Towers, and so they abandoned the vehicle and started walking. Burning ash filled the air. As Floyd's crew walked through the streets of Manhattan toward the World Trade Center, the first tower fell. Floyd and her team couldn't see what had happened, but they heard the noise and felt the earth rumble and shake. They froze, confused and frightened. The rumbling was followed by an eerie calm that slowly was filled with the sound of distant cries. Suddenly a gray plume appeared that looked like smoke but smelled like wet concrete. The crew then saw waves of people covered in ash and soot running toward them, crying, gasping, and screaming. Some of the people waved frantically, trying to warn Floyd's crew of the danger ahead and imploring them to turn around.

"Our team didn't speak to one another. Instead, what had seemed like slow motion suddenly came to life and we started walking again, toward the Twin Towers, my cameraman shooting what he could along the way," said Floyd. "We pressed down the West Side Highway, and then the horror began again: The rumbling. The sonic boom. The cries. The plume. This time we didn't stop. We just kept walking toward the World Trade Center. And here is where I think leadership comes in. I don't know what makes a person rush toward danger while everyone else is rushing away from it. Reporters, after all, are not first responders, working to save lives. We aren't in search of loved ones. And we aren't soldiers defending life and liberty. But we are serving our country just the same."

Floyd and her crew were the first to gain access to "the Pile" and the first to bring Americans the initial horrible images of the devastation. She and her team worked tirelessly at ground zero every day for nearly three weeks. They reported on Marines who showed up to dig for survivors with their bare hands and volunteer firefighters who came from across the country to assist their brothers and sisters from the New York City Fire Department. Floyd and her crew located the day care workers who saved scores of children before the towers fell and filmed those children being reunited with their families. Floyd's team was at ground zero when the last two survivors were pulled from the rubble days after rescue workers had all but given up hope of finding anyone else alive.

As the pressure mounted and fatigue set in, Floyd recalled the positive energy with which Vice President Gore and Greg Simon motivated their teams during her White House Fellowship year. In the same way, she was determined to inspire and energize her young crew members to do their best work despite the incredible stress and round-the-clock toil associated with covering the 9/11 terrorist attacks. "The news business is a young person's game. At thirty-six years of age, I was not only an accomplished news correspondent but was also one of the oldest people in our unit. I had a staff of much younger people working with and for me," Floyd recalled. "When those young people confided to me their fears or, as happened on more than one occasion, they began to cry, it was my job as a leader to be compassionate. But it was also for me to gently remind them of our duty to the network, the public, the victims, and the truth. Using that positive leadership approach renewed their energy and gave us the strength to fulfill the awesome responsibility of reporting the events of 9/11 accurately and dispassionately."

Like Jami Floyd, Robert "Bob" Joss (WHF 68–69) learned great leadership lessons during his White House Fellowship. Currently serving as professor and dean of the Stanford Graduate School of Business, Joss was assigned to the Treasury Department for his Fellowship. It was the transition year between the Johnson and Nixon administrations, and when Richard Nixon took office, he appointed David Kennedy, chairman of the Continental Illinois National Bank and Trust, to be Secretary of the Treasury. "Kennedy was a wonderful, kind banker from Chicago," Joss said. "He had no ambition to be a politician, and in some ways he seemed almost uncomfortable in a public role. So he was happy for others in his staff to get the public credit."

Joss became such a valued member of the Treasury team that he was asked to stay on for two more years at the end of his Fellowship. "I was the luckiest of all the White House Fellows," Joss remarked. "It was like having a three-year Fellowship." Joss traveled the country giving speeches on legislation relating to the Treasury and also spent time alongside Treasury administrators lobbying legislators on Capitol Hill. For such a young man, Joss tackled one weighty economic issue after another and earned the respect of his supervisors, but his supervisors earned his respect too.

"I learned so much in that environment, just realizing how great it is to work for positive people who will give you lots to do, as much as you want, and who will give you all the credit when you do it well and who will also back you up when it doesn't go so well," Joss said. "I learned that a leader's job is to energize, motivate, and inspire younger people to achieve everything they can for the good of the cause. That's why in all the leadership roles I've had, I try to give people all the responsibility and give them all the credit, because I know that when they do well, it will make me look good too. But when it doesn't go well, you've got to back them up and take responsibility off their shoulders so they don't get crushed by it and yet learn from it. Of all the things I learned in my Fellowship, that was probably the most valuable."

In 1971, Joss had a chance to observe a different kind of energy at work in Washington when President Nixon appointed former Texas governor and U.S. Navy secretary John Connally, Jr., to be Treasury secretary. Unlike David Kennedy, Connally was an outgoing, charismatic politician of the highest order. He was flashy, engaging, and energetic and was a household name because of the fact that he had been riding in the convertible when President John F. Kennedy was assassinated and had been injured seriously in the shooting.

"I'll never forget something Connally once did that was so impressive. You might think it was contrived, but it wasn't—he did it so naturally," Joss said. "We were on the Hill one day when we ran into a congressman who had a group of little school kids visiting from his district. When Secretary Connally and I came in, the congressman said, 'Boys and girls, this is the Secretary of the Treasury. This is John Connally.' That congressman was so proud to get to introduce his constituents' kids to the famous John Connally. But then Connally did the most amazing thing. He sauntered over in his big Texas way and he put his arm around this congressman, and he turned to the kids and said, 'Now boys and girls, I want you to know that your congressman is the most fantastic member of Congress,' and on he went about how great this gentleman was, and it was just the most amazing thing to watch. That congressman was just beaming because John Connally made him look so good in front of the little kids from his district. I learned that day that a very important aspect of leadership is to build relationships with others through positive actions."

Frederick Benson III (WHF 73–74) was influenced by a similar positive leadership approach he learned during his time in Washington, D.C. After his Fellowship, Benson served as military assistant to Assistant

Secretary of Defense Bill Brehm. Benson called Brehm "the greatest mentor I've ever had," and the two became such close friends that more than thirty years after the Fellowship they still talk to each other weekly. "From Bill I learned this: Speak softly, give people a lot of room, give them general guidance, and make sure they have the resources to do what you've asked them to do," Benson said. "He was running against incredible opposition from the services about getting women into West Point, and he just knew how to deal with every person on their level to get to the right outcome. His motto was: 'Do what's right.' He was once threatened by a member of Congress who said, 'If you don't do what I want you to do, I'll get you fired,' and Bill didn't even answer the letter—he just said, 'Let him try.' He had incredible strength, and his ethics were impeccable. I never once heard him raise his voice. He taught me that you've got to take care of your people."

Years later, when Benson was running his own office as vice president for federal and international affairs at the Weyerhaeuser Company, he practiced the positive approach he had learned from Brehm. "I had that position at Weyerhaeuser for eighteen years, and several of the people I hired early on stayed the entire time I was there. I created a 'no-risk environment' in which I encouraged everybody to step in to do whatever they thought was right to help the company, without fear of making a mistake," Benson said. "I told them to come up with new ideas and new programs, and I would give them bonuses if they came up with something that worked. If something went wrong, I simply asked, 'Okay, what did we learn? What can we do differently next time?' It reaped dividends. A twenty-nine-year-old secretary I hired in my first couple of years in the company is now the president of her own trade association in Washington. I mean, if you let people go and grow and give them the resources and help them when they stumble, they will dearly respect your leadership and want to break through barriers for you. I've seen it happen in both military and civilian life, and I truly believe that creating a bubble of positive energy, a no-risk environment, is the way to go."

Benson's energy helped him and his employees become a productive and happy team. Lincoln Caplan II (WHF 79–80) became part of a similar winning team during his Fellowship, largely as a result of former White House Fellow Colin Powell's humorous brand of leadership. Caplan, a graduate of Harvard University and Harvard Law School and now a celebrated author and journalist, was assigned to the U.S. Department of Energy for his Fellowship and was one of ten aides serving the secretary and deputy secretary. One of his coworkers was Colin Powell, who had been borrowed from the Army to serve as the energy secretary's top aide. "During the summer of 1979, when my class of Fellows was placed, energy was, as it is now again, in the headlines," Caplan explained. "Car lines at gas stations stretched for blocks. President Jimmy Carter declared the energy challenge the moral equivalent of war. A placement at the relatively new Department of Energy felt like a patriotic opportunity, and when I was offered it, I took it."

Caplan's writing skills were put to good use in developing a lengthy document called the "Posture Statement on U.S. Energy Policy," which was designed to lay out the Energy Department's rationale for its budget requests. The young Fellow witnessed round after round of intradepartmental squabbling as each section of the department jockeyed for a higher-profile position in the report. Whenever pressure threatened to overwhelm Caplan and his colleagues, they looked to Powell to alleviate the stress. "Colin Powell was the largest presence on the team," Caplan said. "When he signed out of the department garage each evening, his signature was emphatic and took two lines. Powell used humor as a tool of management and leadership better than anyone I had ever worked with. He used it to dispel tension, redirect discussion, and, most of all, create the spirit of a team."

For some White House Fellows, becoming part of the team might have been impossible if not for their principal's positive energy and open leadership style. Such was the case for Lynn Schenk (WHF 76–77), a San Diego attorney and fervent Democrat who was selected for a White House Fellowship in the waning days of the Gerald Ford administration. The heated presidential race between President Ford and Georgia Governor Jimmy Carter was in full swing, and the White House was pulled in a million different directions trying to campaign for Ford while also running the country.

Schenk, who recently had attended the Democratic National Convention as a delegate for candidate Jerry Brown, was assigned to work with Jack Veneman, counselor to Vice President Nelson Rockefeller. Even though President Ford had dropped Rockefeller and chosen Kansas Senator Bob Dole to be his running mate for the 1976 election, Rockefeller still planned to campaign for Ford's election. Schenk's first meeting with Rockefeller came just one week after the close of the Republican convention. "He called me into his sitting room, and he said in that gravelly Rockefeller voice, 'Look, whatever happens in the fall, I'm not going to be vice president, but I'm still going to campaign for my party between now and November. If you come on the campaign trail, we'll keep you busy and you'll learn a lot. Will you come on the campaign trail with me?' I told him I was a Democrat, and he said he suspected that but still thought I ought to go on the trail. It took me a quarter of a second to say yes, and I spent the next two and a half months on the campaign trail with Nelson Rockefeller for the Republican ticket even though I had just come from the Democratic convention. The vice president was right. I learned a lot. Being in Nelson Rockefeller's office for my Fellowship was the turning point in my life."

Although the polls indicated that Ford's campaign was faltering, Schenk was impressed by the way Rockefeller kept a positive outlook; his enthusiasm never wavered. His boundless energy filled every room he entered, and in Schenk's words, "he just blew energy and enthusiasm into the room. You came away buoyant as if you'd been filled with helium. He had an incredible spirit and belief in what he was doing." Although some might have questioned Rockefeller's wisdom in allowing a passionate Democratic supporter such as Schenk to tag along on the trail, he still included her in everything. "From the beginning he had me sitting in on senior staff meetings. He would have a lovely catered lunch for senior staff, about eight or ten people. They sat around the dining table in his office," Schenk explained. "He made it clear to everybody that he wanted me to be there not by saying, 'Include Lynn,' but rather by bringing me in himself. He would say, 'Lynn, come sit here by me.' When others saw that I was sitting at his left arm, it made them unconsciously more inclusive of me. He was larger than life but as open and welcoming as your uncle."

In January 1977, President Jimmy Carter and Vice President Walter Mondale assumed office, and Schenk made the transition to a new principal and a vastly different leadership style. Although she admired Mondale greatly, he did not include her in higher-level functions. "Mondale was new in the office and at a different stage of life than Nelson Rockefeller," she said. "Rockefeller was older and at the sunset of his political career. He had been governor, a statesman, and a vice president, and he was just more open. He left a trail of enthusiasm wherever he went."

When her White House Fellowship came to a close, Schenk returned to California, determined to emulate Rockefeller and leave her own trail of enthusiasm. At age thirty-three, she became a member of Governor Jerry Brown's cabinet as secretary for the Department of Business, Transportation and Housing. She was elected to the U.S. House of Representatives and served from 1993 to 1995. In 1998 Schenk was tapped by California Governor Gray Davis to be his chief of staff, a position she held until 2003. She currently practices corporate law and sits on a variety of boards.

Just as Jami Floyd, Bob Joss, Frederick Benson, Lincoln Caplan, and Lynn Schenk learned the power of positive energy during their time in Washington, D.C., so did I. White House Fellows cocreator John Gardner once spoke to our class, and each of us had the privilege of asking him a question. This was mine: "What do you think is the number one trait of a great leader?" I imagined he would say integrity, competence, courage, or optimism. Instead, he said the one common trait of every outstanding leader he ever worked with was energy. Without energy, a leader physically cannot accomplish all the things he or she sets out to do. In John Gardner's opinion, energy is the most essential leadership trait. "Physical vitality, stamina, good constitution—the moral is to stay in shape," Gardner said. "It not only gets you through a tough schedule, it comes through to the people you're working with. They get vitality from your vitality—there's no question about it. Very few people follow a tired leader."

A great leader needs stamina and vitality to be physically energized, emotionally connected, and mentally sharp. Physical energy is the key to mental sharpness, which boosts one's confidence and enables one to get the job done. As General Petraeus taught his young leaders, the number one leadership priority is to develop a high degree of personal energy through physical fitness and a healthy lifestyle, which provide fuel for emotional and mental skills. Leaders like Jami Floyd, who reported for ABC News in the wake of the terrorist attacks on September 11, are often under intense stress and need to have deep emotional reserves if they are to be capable of displaying empathy, patience, and optimism to their subordinates. As she set out to motivate her team in the gut-wrenching moments, days, and weeks after the Twin Towers crisis, Floyd often recalled the way Vice President Al Gore's focused determination energized his staff and tried to emulate that approach.

Always remember that great leaders are the stewards of their organizations' energy, giving all the people around them the boost they need to accomplish extraordinary things. Fred Benson called this the creation of a no-risk environment in which people are free to make mistakes, learn from them, and grow professionally. Take a long look at yourself to see if you are a leader like Nelson Rockefeller, who, as Schenk recalled, supercharged those around him with energy so great that they came away as buoyant as if they'd been filled with helium. Instead of being the type of leader who sucks the energy away from others, resolve to be the kind of leader who strives to bring passion and positive energy to the workplace every day.

CHAPTER 17

LEADERS ARE GREAT LISTENERS

When Cesar Aristeiguieta (WHF 02–03) was only fifteen years old, he emigrated alone from his homeland of Venezuela to the United States in search of better opportunities. He certainly made the most of what he found here. After graduating from high school, Aristeiguieta worked as an emergency medical technician and volunteered for the National Ski Patrol and the American Red Cross. He was accepted to the police academy and was the top graduate in his class. He worked as a police officer while attending California State University full-time. After graduation, Aristeiguieta was accepted to the University of Southern California's School of Medicine. He graduated and began a residency in emergency medicine.

As he was finishing his residency, Aristeiguieta began to have doubts. The prospect of jumping directly into a career as a doctor did not appeal to him. He wanted to do something different—something in the realm of public service—but did not know what it might be. Aristeiguieta shared his confusion with a close friend. Coincidentally, she recently had heard about the White House Fellows program. "She gave me the Web site address, and I checked it out," Aristeiguieta recalled. "As I started reading through the description of the Fellowship and what they were looking for, I realized that I had been preparing for this program all my life." Aristeiguieta applied and was accepted for the Fellowship. He was assigned to work with Department of Health and Human Services Secretary Tommy Thompson.

Secretary Thompson was an attorney who had been governor of Wisconsin and a state assemblyman for twenty-five years before that. He did not have a background in medicine, and so he counted on Aristeiguieta to put health-related issues into context for him. Aristeiguieta had nearly total access to Secretary Thompson's schedule and often attended meetings with him. It wasn't long before the young White House Fellow noticed an important leadership trait in his principal that he hoped to nurture in himself: Secretary Thompson was an outstanding listener. Aristeiguieta confessed that at that point in his life, he was rather impatient when it came to conversational give-and-take. By watching the secretary in action, Aristeiguieta saw for himself how listening made Thompson a more effective leader.

"Childhood obesity was a hot topic at the time I was a Fellow, and one part of that debate centered on what responsibility the food industry may or may not have with that. So the secretary brought in all these food industry executives to begin a dialogue on childhood obesity," Aristeiguieta explained. "From the start of the meeting it was clear that the food industry people were concerned that they were going to be regulated, and it progressed to the point where I was starting to feel uncomfortable with how aggressive some of those folks were. They were addressing some comments toward the secretary about how this wasn't the government's role and the government really should stay out of their business. But the secretary just sat there patiently and listened to them. He didn't say a word. He didn't try to defend himself—not once—for almost an hour. Then, after all those executives from the food industry had spoken, the secretary said, 'I've heard you. I understand your concerns. Now I need you to tell me how you, as an industry, can help address this public health issue.' Then he just sat back and listened again. Pretty soon they were talking about how they could step up and participate without being forced into it—how they could begin putting more healthy food choices on their menus and those kinds of things—and by the end of the meeting the tone had changed dramatically. They weren't attacking the secretary anymore. They were actually pleased, and they felt that they were part of the dialogue, and in fact, they probably went further than the secretary really expected them to go at that point. From that meeting I learned the value of listening. I've tried to incorporate that into my own leadership style in my work as director of emergency medical services and disaster preparedness for Emergent Medical Associates and also in my role as an assistant professor in emergency medicine at the University of California–Davis."

Aristeiguieta saw how Secretary Thompson's listening skills helped him earn the trust of those on the opposite side of the table during a conflict. In contrast, Ron Quincy (WHF 85–86) learned the flip side of that lesson during his Fellowship. As a result of being a White House Fellow, Quincy got to know and work with the South African leader Nelson Mandela. Mandela often reminded Quincy to listen carefully to people to determine whether they were trustworthy, because one of the greatest tools a leader possesses is the ability to identify those on whose judgment he or she can rely. Mandela told Quincy that when he was in prison, he cultivated relationships with certain prison guards by establishing a dialogue with them. He would speak to the guards, but more important, he would listen. "Mandela would listen to the guards and, from doing that, decide which ones he could count on to relay important messages to his family, friends, and comrades on the outside," Quincy said. "Even in prison there were guards he was able to actually trust versus those who sent signals showing they were not trustworthy. He never attempted to engage with the latter. Just imagine what would have happened if he had made a mistake. The listening part of being a leader is so very important."

Quincy recalled a Chinese fable in which a teaching master is ordered to prepare a young prince for his future leadership role as king. The first thing the master does is to send the prince out alone into the forest. The master tells the prince he is to stay there for one year, and then he is to return to the master and describe what he heard. "After a year has passed, the prince comes back and starts talking about how he heard the birds singing and the leaves rustling and the wind whispering," Quincy said. "And the master orders him to go back into the forest again and listen some more—there was more to be heard. The prince went back into the forest and after sitting there for a very long time, one morning he actually *did* hear something different. He returned to the master and said he had heard the 'unheard'— the sound of flowers blooming and the sun warming the ground. And the master nodded and told him that he was finally ready for the throne, because the ability to hear the unheard—to go deeper than the obvious— is necessary to being a great leader."

Another leader who taught Quincy the value of listening was Correta Scott King, the widow of Dr. Martin Luther King, Jr. As a Fellow, Quincy had accompanied Mrs. King on a mission to South Africa and had helped her pass safely through a violent clash in Soweto so that she could visit with Nelson Mandela's wife, Winnie. Years later, Mrs. King interviewed Quincy for a position as executive director and chief operating officer of the Martin Luther King Jr. Center for Nonviolent Social Change. The interview was scheduled to last no more than two hours, but it ended up taking ten hours.

"I missed four flights back to Boston," Quincy said, chuckling. "And when Mrs. King told me she was choosing me for the job over 200 other people, I couldn't believe it and I told her so. But she told me that much of her decision rested on that day in South Africa when I listened to her reasons for wanting to meet with Winnie despite the risk. She appreciated that I listened to her that day and that I used an effective process to determine how I could help her achieve her goal while still keeping her safe. She felt comfortable that I was the right person to help her turn the King Center around to where it needed to be."

While at work at the King Center, Quincy received a call from the director of the FBI, who had an upcoming trip to Atlanta. He wanted to make an appointment to stop by the center and visit Mrs. King while he was in town. Quincy knew that the King family and the FBI, under the leadership of former director J. Edgar Hoover, had not had a comfortable relationship during the civil rights movement, and so he was prepared for Mrs. King to reject the offer. Instead, she told Quincy she would love to meet the FBI director. "She told me to set it up, arrange it," Quincy said. "The FBI director was as shocked as I was. But they had a great meeting, which led to the King Center getting involved with providing nonviolent conflict resolution training for FBI agents. It was remarkable."

Mrs. King's uncommon willingness to set aside differences and listen was a source of surprise for Quincy more than once. He remembers receiving a call from the wife of James Earl Ray, Dr. King's assassin. Mrs. Ray wanted to offer portraits of Dr. King that her husband had painted in prison. "Mrs. Ray admitted that the paintings weren't very good ones," Quincy said. "Well, I knew how sensitive this would be for Mrs. King, so I sat down with her and explained the situation. She told me she would have been interested in seeing Ray's paintings had they been good ones, but since she already had enough marginal paintings of her husband, she would pass on these. Mrs. King just had an extraordinary capacity for listening with an open mind."

During his Fellowship year, Mitchell Reiss (WHF 88–89) also saw how the ability to listen enhances a leader's effectiveness. Reiss worked for National Security Advisor Colin Powell, and he often marveled at his principal's willingness not only to hear dissenting views but to encourage them actively. "It was an open-mindedness to get all ideas, all options, out on the table without judging them in advance so that people wouldn't self-censor. He encouraged people to speak truth to power, because he knew it was very hard to go in and tell a powerful person something that you know he absolutely does not want to hear," Reiss explained. "Powell knew you can't function in any environment—government, private sector, academia, think tank, it doesn't matter—unless you have a culture that encourages people to come to you with problems, preferably while the problems are still small. Powell was terrific at that. He knew he wasn't going to be effective if you couldn't tell him the truth."

Reiss recalled once giving Powell two short memos asking him to reverse course on two different policies. Reiss was certain he was right and confident that Powell would go along with his recommendations. Instead, Powell lectured Reiss for almost half an hour, ripping apart the younger man's reasoning. "At the end of it he asked if we understood each other," said Reiss. "Of course I said, 'Yes, sir.' He threw the memos at me as I was leaving, but when I reached the doorway, he said there was one more thing he wanted to tell me. I turned around, and he said with a smile, 'Keep the memos coming.' He recognized that even though I had just wasted twenty-five minutes of his time, there weren't that many of us who were willing to tell him stuff like that. Even if he disagreed, he still valued it. That makes all the difference in the world."

Like Reiss, Bill Cotter (WHF 65–66) learned a great lesson in listening during his Fellowship. At the Department of Commerce, Cotter was assigned to a task force charged with bridging the gap between the senior civil servants and the political appointees. In that capacity he got to see a wide variety of leadership styles in action among the department's assistant secretaries and undersecretaries. Cotter came away with a crystal-clear picture of the leadership type that was the most effective.

"Those senior civil servants were very smart and dedicated, and they cared a lot about the mission," Cotter said. "But the ones who were most enthusiastic about the department's agenda were the ones who had the best communication with their superiors. Their assistant secretary or under-secretary met with them regularly, talked with them, explained things to them, and incorporated their ideas. They really felt part of the team, and even when they disagreed, at least they knew their opinions had been heard and treated with respect, and they had been given explanations as to why it wasn't possible to do the thing they were advocating. That lesson of listening carefully to people throughout the entire organization and then communicating back to explain why you were taking one action over another helped to bring a larger group of people together to achieve a common aim, no matter what their level in the organization." For that reason, Cotter implemented weekly staff meetings in every organization he led after his Fellowship so that he could not only communicate his priorities but also listen to his people and hear their concerns and ideas.

As a Fellow in the Department of the Interior, Richard Northern (WHF 79–80) had the opportunity to watch how his principal, Interior Secretary Cecil Andrus, used his listening skills to resolve a major dispute facing the department and, indeed, the country. Northern, a lawyer from Kentucky, admired his principal a great deal. "Andrus looked the part of Secretary of the Interior. He was a tall, fit outdoorsman who preferred to be pictured on horseback rather than in a suit. He taught me to take my work—but not myself—seriously. He never got caught up in the arrogance of Washington despite his large responsibilities. He never seemed full of himself," Northern said. "He played first base on the department's softball team. His driver also played on the team. Andrus treated the driver with the same respect he did any of the assistant secretaries, maybe more because the driver was a better ballplayer than the executives."

Andrus, who served a total of four terms as a popular governor of Idaho, gave his young Fellow a plum assignment working on the Central Arizona Project, the biggest and most costly water diversion system ever built in the United States. The centerpiece of the project was a 336-mile canal that would bring water from the Colorado River down through the state and into Phoenix and Tucson. The Department of Interior's job was to decide how to allocate the finite water supply among three competing interests: the cities, the farmers, and the Native Americans.

"It was a major chore of his to get the allocations done before the end of his term, so I got very involved in it. Secretary Andrus was determined to do the right thing as trustee of the Native American lands," Northern explained. "He listened to these three competing interests, all of which had strong claims to the water. Certainly at that time the municipal and the agricultural interests were much more powerful politically than the Native American interests. The easy way would have been to not push for ground-water reform and to make large allocations to the cities and to the farmers and give less to the politically powerless Native American interests. But that's not the direction the secretary took. After listening to all the arguments, he upped the allocations to the Native Americans. In Arizona there was a sense that the recommendations favored the Native Americans more than they should have, but it was important to Secretary Andrus that we do the right thing anyway, as the trustee of the Native American lands."

Every week Andrus would host staff meetings that began at 8 a.m. During the winter, before the assistant secretaries, undersecretaries, and key staff people arrived, Andrus would come in early to start a cozy fire in the fireplace. The group would gather around it, and Andrus would start the meeting by asking each person to speak out and tell him his or her concerns, ideas, triumphs—whatever they wanted to share.

"I knew that he might have a different opinion about what those assistant secretaries were saying, but he always listened with respect and conducted himself at all times like the Secretary of the Interior should," Northern said. "He developed an atmosphere in which everyone could speak out with the assurance that he would listen, and that made him extremely effective. I took his lessons to heart and have used them many times since returning to Louisville, Kentucky, after my Fellowship. They were especially helpful to me when I worked on a complex project to merge two large health care organizations in Louisville: the Jewish Hospital and the largest Catholic hospital system in the state, Caritas Health Care. It was a fascinating and challenging venture to merge those two organizations with significantly different cultures, but we were able to put together what is now known as the Jewish Hospital & St. Mary's Health Care System. There's no doubt many of the lessons I learned during my White House Fellows year helped me rise to that challenge." Because of his community involvement in projects such as the health care organization merger, Northern was named Louisville's Community Leader of the Year in 2007.

Whereas Rick Northern's principal exhibited a consistent, laid-back leadership style during his Fellowship, Alexander Rodriguez (WHF 80–81) dealt with two starkly contrasting principals during his year in Washington. Rodriguez, a psychiatrist who earned his medical degree from Emory University School of Medicine, was assigned to work in the Department of Health and Human Services, where he dealt predominantly with the settlement of thousands of Cuban refugees who had sailed to the United States in what was known as the Mariel boat lift. His principal was Secretary Patricia Harris. The first African-American woman to hold a cabinet position, the diminutive Harris had learned leadership techniques from her onetime mentor Lyndon Johnson, whose forceful, commandeering style was well known.

"While Patricia Harris was physically petite, she stood upright and absolutely took over any room she entered. She dominated any gathering not just because she was the secretary but because of her leadership 'presence,' including her upright posture, purposeful stride, and stentorian voice. When she spoke, she always articulated her ideas clearly and forcefully, often hands on hips," said Rodriguez. "Her body language said, 'I'm a leader, so everybody listen up.' She was the personification of a field commanding general such as George Patton. She would walk in with a clear agenda and a clear strategy of exactly what she wanted to accomplish in each and every meeting."

Like the skilled attorney and law school dean she was, Patricia Harris was always organized, plainly stated her thoughts, and was adroit at getting others both to see her logic and to agree with her action plan. She was effective because she scared people into action and then inspired them with her brilliance. The most important lesson she taught Rodriguez came by way of a tactic she utilized repeatedly whenever a power position had to be established through discussion and negotiation.

"As the individual or group of individuals would initiate greetings and socially typical warm-up exchanges, she would unleash from her four-foot ten-inch frame a torrent of vitriolic verbiage that would invariably leave the perceived adversary reeling in defense," Rodriguez recalled. "Following her greeting, she would then calmly offer a cup of tea or coffee and then proceed to dominate the discussion to achieve her alpha-female objectives for the meeting. The first time I witnessed this, I almost literally ducked behind the curtains in her office. I had never seen anything quite like it before in a supposedly civil setting, and I was afraid the next barrage would be headed in my direction."

Later, Harris took Rodriguez aside and told him that Lyndon Johnson had taught her that technique to help her establish her position of authority quickly whenever she was faced with resolving disputes. Although Rodriguez liked Harris, he was reasonably anxious about her. "As a psychiatrist, I was trained to listen to my body and my thoughts. How I feel about people when I'm with them tells me something about the way they are communicating with me and the way I'm responding," he explained. "I decided that her approach to establishing rapport was not my personal style and would not serve me very well, especially since respect and trust are so important for negotiations in my field."

When President Jimmy Carter lost his bid for reelection and Ronald Reagan took office, Rodriguez received a new principal at Health and Human Services: Secretary Richard "Dick" Schweiker. Rodriguez was relieved to find that he and Schweiker had similar personalities.

Schweiker was an intense observer, listener, and team leader. When it came time to make leadership decisions, he asked his people to give him information so that he could process it with them. He then would lead the team toward making a collective decision. Schweiker employed a disciplined, methodical approach to collecting and sorting through information, and he took an impatient young Rodriguez to new levels of critical thinking.

"He repeatedly impressed on me that I hadn't stretched my mind and, in some instances, my soul adequately in preparing my work," Rodriguez recalled. "He could point those kinds of things out in a very effective, kindly way. He taught me a lot about decision making by critically listening and probing, by crystallizing thoughts, and by extracting the four or five things that are most important for a decision so as to lead to effective priority setting and consensus building within a defined time frame. He helped me organize my executive thinking and my planning skills in ways that really served me well in my subsequent professional and personal life. During my Fellowship, as I struggled with many months of negotiation with the Office of Management and Budget over proposed cuts in Great Society health and social service programs, I was always impressed with the strength that Secretary Schweiker brought to negotiations by conveying dignity, respect, and a sheer command of facts that allowed him to always make a salient business case for any proposed strategic policy decision."

Rodriguez, who currently serves as chief clinical officer and medical director of Harmony Behavioral Health, knew that since he aspired to be a leader of a health care organization someday, he needed to understand more than just facts. He needed to understand the people and the processes he would lead, and he knew that one important tool for achieving that level of understanding would be active listening. Engaging in active listening entails trying to understand more than just a speaker's words. Active listening involves responding to the speaker in a way that demonstrates that he or she has been heard and that his or her feelings have been considered.

Rodriguez, who served in the Naval Reserve, said the military offers great examples of why the technique is so important and why every leader should learn to use it. "One of the lessons we had learned in all the debriefings following the U.S. experiences in Vietnam was that the best field leaders at the platoon and company levels were those who listened actively to their noncommissioned officers before making life-and-death decisions," Rodriguez said. "The leadership objective was not to lead the unit through a truly democratic process. But it was critical to form up a team of followers by tapping into the unit's best collective judgment in order to lead those people toward a common objective that might even kill them but could only be achieved with a clear plan and a commitment to teamwork for their collective survival. So it is that even in more mundane situations, leaders best achieve their objectives through active listening—always with a clear goal in mind. It is imperative for the functioning of any effective group that each participant, including the leader, must sacrifice some part of the individual self to the larger group identity and purpose. Effective leadership, then, requires an extraordinary talent—to be able to steer each member of a group to psychologically give up his or her narcissistic needs to a shared group need. This can be accomplished in any number of ways: verbal eloquence, appealing to people's sense of self-worth or purpose, or appealing to just their sheer greed, their narcissistic negative needs. Leaders can take people down the right path or the wrong path. They can take them to a higher social level or a lower one, including criminal acts. Some of the best leaders are leaders of psychopathic groups. Fortunately for me, I had the benefit of role models who led by inspiration toward higher group goals, including Secretary Schweiker. Like all effective and inspiring leaders, he led by personal decorum, expression of positive social values, and clear respect for others, including those with whom he had disagreements."

Author, political scientist, and educator Dr. Thomas Cronin (WHF 66–67) shares Rodriguez's opinion that the ability to listen is essential to effective leadership. Cronin was assigned to work with former White House Press Secretary Bill Moyers for most of his Fellowship year and also developed a close relationship with John Gardner, who became a mentor to him. Cronin calls listening "squinting with one's ear" and says it's the most important yet underrated leadership tool there is. "The capacity to listen much better than other people is what sets a leader apart from others," Cronin explained. "Leaders are asked to represent, to rally, to mobilize, to be coalition builders, agreement builders, all those things. But if they're not very good at listening to their constituents and to the people that are in conflict with them, they're destined to fail. I see leaders faltering along the wayside all the time who aren't able to listen. This is a lesson that comes from the ancient classics. Sophocles's *Antigone*, for example, is really a story about listening, and many of Shakespeare's plays are really about the capacity to listen and understand and appreciate."

Chances are that you've run across a hapless leader or maybe even two or three who simply issued a directive on the fly without ever bothering to consult team members for their thoughts or suggestions. There was no buy-in, no collective judgment, and no focus. When the team members gathered around the water cooler later, they probably muttered things to each other such as "She doesn't care what we think," "Once she has her mind made up, that's it," or "I'm not going to bust my hump for something I know isn't going to work." If that leader had taken the time to solicit input and then respectfully listen—*really listen*—to her team with a clear goal in mind, she might have inspired them to develop their own plan, one to which they were truly committed and one they believed they actually could carry out. Cesar Aristeiguieta, Ron Quincy, Mitchell Reiss, Bill Cotter, Richard Northern, Alex Rodriguez, and Tom Cronin all learned during their White House Fellowships that the most effective leaders are the ones who take the time to listen not just to their team members' words but to the priceless hidden meaning beneath them.

CHAPTER 18

LEADERS ARE PERSUASIVE

John McGinty (WHF 67–68) was a young architect with degrees from Rice and Princeton when he was accepted for a White House Fellowship, the first and only architect ever selected. Sent to the Department of the Interior to work alongside Secretary Stewart Udall, McGinty was given several significant assignments that greatly expanded his professional and personal perspectives. He had a hand in the restoration of Ford's Theatre, the historic site of President Lincoln's assassination, and helped Udall with his speeches and books, injecting into them fresh ideas about design and planning. McGinty also was sent to scout out and report on development initiatives in the Virgin Islands and the Pacific Trust Territories.

Closer to home, McGinty was assigned a task that taught him one of the most critical leadership lessons he ever learned. In the early summer of 1968 after Dr. Martin Luther King's assassination, the Reverend Ralph Abernathy, a close King associate, carried out what was called the Poor People's Campaign, which was to be a massive Washington, D.C., "sit-in" in support of an Economic Bill of Rights that would guarantee that poor people had access to jobs, housing, and food. "They came by the thousands, on foot, in symbolic mule trains, by bus, and by air, from all over America, but particularly they came from the South. Their destination was the National Mall of the United States, where they intended to camp until progress was forthcoming on civil rights," McGinty recalled. "The Mall is a national park and, as such, under the care and custody of the Department of the Interior. Rather than resist the invasion, as many urged him to do, Secretary Udall made the courageous decision to welcome the campaign as an appropriate use of this national treasure. And he assigned me—I suppose because I was an architect and knew about urban planning and plywood-floored tents—to inspect the camp daily and report to him on problems."

Unfortunately, there were plenty of problems to report. It rained incessantly, turning the makeshift streets between the rows of tents into impassable quagmires. Port-A-Cans could not be reached for servicing. Azaleas were trampled into the mud. The reflection pool in front of the Lincoln Memorial became a community bathtub. McGinty's daily reports to Udall became bleaker and more heartbreaking, softened only by Udall's steadfast conviction that the cause was worth the sacrifice. For several weeks, the protesters lobbied the government for passage of the Economic Bill of Rights. They staged demonstrations and engaged in acts of civil disobedience aimed at drawing attention to their plight. However, infighting soon emerged among the group's leadership. The *New York Times* reported that a rift developed between protestors living in the filth and squalor on the Washington Mall and Abernathy and other high-ranking campaign officials, who were all staying at a comfortable midtown hotel.

The group's support on Capitol Hill and in the White House began to wane. A *New York Times* reporter wrote, "The anxious observers . . . include a number of high officials in the Johnson Administration, whose interest is in giving the Poor People's Campaign what one of them called today 'the maximum possible victory under very unpromising circumstances.'" Halfway through the campaign, on June 5, 1968, Senator Robert Kennedy, a beloved champion of civil rights, was assassinated. The protestors' morale plummeted. Violence erupted not only in the tent city but also throughout Washington, D.C. The American people, the Johnson administration, and the country's lawmakers turned their backs on the Poor People's Campaign. The defeated campers returned home.

"By sunset of the final day the tent city was abandoned. The National Mall of the United States consisted of nothing more than a sea of grassless mud and mountains of soaked canvas, plywood, and human household debris," McGinty said. "Looking at the dismal scene, I thought about how and why the Poor People's Campaign failed. The group might have achieved its goal had its leadership taken the time to become better organized. Perhaps if they had worked to build a strong, broad-based constituency first, they might have been able to overcome the setbacks and realize at least some of their objectives."

The Poor People's Campaign was an eye-opener for McGinty, who also gained valuable insight from studying his principal, Stewart Udall. Udall had a keen intellect and a creative approach to problem solving. He was passionate about the environment and was an idealist in the best sense of the word. However, he lacked one vital characteristic that would have made him even more effective: the charisma to persuade. In stark contrast to his magnetic and outgoing brother, Arizona Congressman Mo Udall, Stewart was very much an introvert. He was quiet and thoughtful and often had difficulty getting people to buy into his progressive, somewhat revolutionary ideas, whereas his brother Mo's wit and charm were legendary. When Mo Udall lost to Jimmy Carter in his bid to become the 1976 Democratic presidential nominee, columnist James Kilpatrick declared that he had failed because he was "too funny to be president." In 1988, Mo Udall, still a popular congressman from Arizona, pocketed Kilpatrick's phrase and titled his autobiography just that: *Too Funny to Be President.* Many believe that Mo Udall, who was elected to fourteen terms in the U.S. House, might have achieved the presidency if he had not been diagnosed with incurable Parkinson's disease at a relatively young age. It was the obvious dissimilarity between the Udall brothers, coupled with the failure of the Poor People's Campaign, that taught McGinty his most important leadership lesson: If you want to be a great leader, develop your ability to persuade others.

When his Fellowship came to an end, McGinty returned to Houston, where he resumed working for an architectural firm. His cutting edge, award-winning designs and his teachings, writings, and congressional testimony on architectural design propelled him into the national spotlight. In 1976 he was elected first vice president of the American Institute of Architects (AIA), the nation's primary professional association for licensed architects. McGinty's rise to president of the institute came at a time when several social movements were having an effect on the AIA, one of which was the consumer rights movement led by Ralph Nader. Nader's grassroots efforts had renewed a focus on antitrust laws designed to protect consumers from monopolies, price gouging, predatory pricing, and other threats to the establishment and maintenance of a healthy competitive market.

"For years and years architects had a code of ethics that had a prohibition against competition on the basis of fees; they had fee schedules that were set," McGinty explained. "The Justice Department ordered the AIA to stop all that. At the same time, there were architects in the AIA who were looking for new roles in society such as doing construction themselves, which had also been prohibited. And then, of course, the environmental movement was coming on, and the civil rights movement too. There was a great effort to widen the profession, to be more diverse, and to bring in more women and minorities, because architecture had always been a white gentlemen's profession until then."

McGinty was in favor of all the new trends facing the AIA and believed the time for change had come. Through his new leadership position he planned to modernize the concepts of architectural practice to address societal trends such as consumerism and conservation, and he planned to waste not one minute in doing so. He proposed a series of resolutions to the convention while he was president-elect of the AIA. "So, being young and thinking I knew everything, I was certain everybody would agree with me and we would revolutionize the profession and reform it overnight," McGinty said. "But I was wrong: Everything got voted down. I was defeated in my effort to rewrite the canon of ethics and redefine membership qualifications and professionalism."

The young president-elect could not believe he had lost in his bid to revolutionize the organization. He wondered where he had gone wrong when it suddenly became clear to him that he had made the same mistake as the organizers of the Poor People's Campaign. He had not taken the time to build a solid foundation for his ideas; he had not utilized the power of persuasion.

"As soon as I realized my mistake, I decided I would devote my year as president to making sure the reforms did happen. I went back to work and spent the following year building a greater intellectual basis for reform and building a broader constituency." McGinty set out to develop a grassroots movement for change within the AIA. He organized a task force that included people with a broad range of opinions and experience, from the institute's youngest associate members to its veterans, as well as industry-related professionals such as engineers. He traveled around the country visiting local groups of architects, talking with them about ethics reform and listening to their concerns. On the basis of the membership's input, he developed a new set of resolutions. "A year later at the convention when I was president, the reforms passed overwhelmingly," said McGinty. "And it was a better product too, because it was more carefully designed and more thoughtful. So the lesson I learned was that you've got to bring people along and engage them if you want to persuade them. You can't get too far ahead of your troops."

Another leader who learned this lesson as a White House Fellow and used it years later to help bring the Cold War to a peaceful conclusion was Robert "Bud" McFarlane (WHF 71–72). McFarlane was assigned to work with Clark McGregor, counsel to President Nixon, but was transferred to President Nixon's congressional liaison Bill Timmons when McGregor left to become head of Nixon's reelection committee. The first U.S. Marine to be selected as a White House Fellow, McFarlane had served two tours in Vietnam. During his initial tour he commanded the first artillery battery to land in Vietnam. On his second tour he served as a regimental fire support coordinator for the Third Marine Division during the Tet offensive, a particularly fierce and lengthy Vietcong military campaign aimed at bringing down the Saigon government.

McFarlane spent much of his Fellowship year watching how President Nixon and his advisors—unknown to the American public—laid the foundation for establishing more open connections with the People's Republic of China. Sino-American relations had been tenuous for decades, and they were damaged seriously after World War II when the American-backed Republic of China government was driven off the mainland by communists led by Mao Zedong. Mao created the People's Republic of China (PRC) on the mainland, and the Republic of China was relegated to Taiwan under its leader, Chiang Kai-shek. The United States refused to recognize Mao's government and fought its attempts to gain a seat in the United Nations.

During the Korean War, American and PRC troops were on opposite sides of the battle, and that strengthened U.S. resolve to support Chiang's Republic of China government on Taiwan. Years later, when the Chinese Communist Party provided support and troops to its North Vietnamese counterparts during the Vietnam War, the United States became even more committed to crippling the PRC. The United States established a trade embargo against that country and rallied its allies to support it, and that began to chip away at the PRC's foundation. Border disputes in 1969 between the PRC and its longtime backer the Soviet

Union led the mainland Chinese to feel diplomatically strained and isolated. President Nixon, National Security Advisor Henry Kissinger, and other top-ranking U.S. officials were convinced that improved relations with the PRC would tip the balance of power toward the United States in its Cold War rivalry with the Soviet Union. Opening up trade with the PRC would be a windfall for American commerce too. However, the White House was worried: Would President Nixon be able to convince the American people that the time was right for détente between the United States and China? Was the nation ready to see its president embracing "the enemy"?

"Here was China, a country that was killing millions of their own people in the middle of their cultural revolution," McFarlane said. "Here was a country that was providing arms to Vietnam, that was killing Americans, and here was a communist government. I mean, if the president had just announced that he was going to China to open talks with that government and that was that, people would have said, 'What in the dickens are we doing, Nixon?' But he first employed strategies to engage his three key constituencies—Congress, our allies, and the American people—and those are the constituencies a president has to tend to if he's going to get his ideas adopted, shared, supported, funded, and ultimately made successful. So it was only through privately, clandestinely nurturing the idea and, importantly, publicly outlining all the strategic advantages it would give us against the Soviet Union that he achieved such a dramatic, historic leap forward."

In July 1971, President Nixon secretly sent Kissinger to China to meet with Chinese Prime Minister Chou En-lai to make all the arrangements for Nixon's upcoming visit. Kissinger was supposed to be in Pakistan that day, but he pretended to be sick and gave the press the slip. Less than a week later, President Nixon announced that he had been invited to the PRC and would be meeting with Chairman Mao. A majority of Americans supported the trip, and in February 1972, McFarlane watched along with the rest of the world as President Nixon and Chairman Mao greeted each other with a warm—and historic—handshake. Nixon's approval rating soared.

Although McFarlane's Fellowship year ended in August 1972, his time in Washington did not. Henry Kissinger asked McFarlane to stay on and be his military assistant. In that role he engaged in sensitive intelligence interactions with Chinese officials and accompanied Dr. Kissinger on trips to China. McFarlane was involved in every facet of U.S. policy in the Middle East and the Soviet Union, including arms control issues. When Vice President Gerald Ford assumed the presidency after Richard Nixon's resignation, he appointed McFarlane to be his special assistant for national security affairs. McFarlane served in that capacity until 1976, when he returned to the Marine Corps. After accepting a series of additional congressional and presidential appointments, McFarlane became President Ronald Reagan's national security advisor, a position in which he helped design and carry out a course of action that led to the end of the Cold War and the reduction of nuclear weapons.

Throughout the Cold War, the Americans and Soviets had engaged in a dangerous game of one-upmanship when it came to accumulating nuclear weapons. The doctrine of mutually assured destruction (MAD) had deterred the launch of any catastrophic weapons from either side, but President Reagan did not think the offensive strategy of hoarding more arms was sustainable. He wanted to explore a different policy, a switch to a defensive mode. "Reagan didn't believe in deterrence through massive offensive power, but his Defense Department didn't agree with him for the first couple years of his presidency," McFarlane recalled. "Indeed, they never enthusiastically went along with the idea of shifting from offense to defense, but Reagan said that he didn't think it was moral to base our stability in the world on the ability to destroy everybody, because the chaos theory tells you that at some point an accident is going to happen as you keep building more and more and more. From my point of view and Reagan's, we were militarily in an unsustainable position. So what were we going to do? Well, if we couldn't build up our own side and deploy them, and we couldn't get the Russians to unilaterally reduce, our only choice was really to go to defense."

McFarlane's opinion was based in part on something he discovered during his Fellowship year: The Russians had enormous respect for and fear of American technology. McFarlane had long been a student of military strategy, and he often thought about the role economics plays in defense. He came to the conclusion that if the United States was to develop a way to deter a ballistic missile launch, the Soviets would be both financially and scientifically unable to match it.

McFarlane queried the country's leading scientists engaged in national security research and development, including Edward Teller, the creator of the hydrogen bomb, and learned that it was possible to calculate with confidence a warhead's flight path; that was the first step toward being able to intercept a missile. "As for guidance and propulsion, there had been a lot of gains in that too. The scientists didn't all agree uniformly, but there was a consensus that yes, if you threw a lot of money at this, we would advance our ability some day," McFarlane said. "None of them said that we could build this during Reagan's term. But we could advance our ability to some day defend against a missile attack, and it would bankrupt the Soviet Union. I told the president that if he were to invest money in this, the Soviets would see the writing on the wall and they would come his way on arms control because they wouldn't want to go bankrupt. They'd reduce their systems, and we'd win."

The trouble was that the MAD doctrine had worked for more than three decades. Getting the public, Congress, and the allies to abandon that successful strategy in favor of unknown and seemingly far-fetched technology would be a challenge. However, Reagan was committed to putting an end to the arms race, and he and his advisors launched a systematic approach to drum up support for the Strategic Defense Initiative (SDI), dubbed by some "Star Wars," a space-based defense system that relied on laser beans and infrared, radar, and optical detection systems not only to protect the United States physically from nuclear attack but also to break the Soviets' confidence in their ability to compete. Reagan decided to take his pro-SDI campaign straight to the American public first and attempt to persuade them that it was the right thing to do.

"If he had gone to the leadership of the Congress and said he wanted to overturn thirty-five years of successful strategy for something that might not even work, it would have been strangled in the crib, and I think that he was right about that," explained McFarlane. "Starting with the people at the grass roots was a perfect situation from my point of view because it made Ronald Reagan the advocate, and he could sell ice cubes to Eskimos. He was just great at selling things. So the idea was basically for him to tell the public, 'We don't have any way of defending you right now against a missile coming in, and I'm going to build one for you,' and that's a winner. The economy was just beginning to turn around after the recession of 1981, and Reagan's tax cuts had begun to produce a rebound at the end of 1982. His political capital was relatively high at that point."

President Reagan began to build his case for the major policy shift in a series of speeches around the country in spring 1983. Finally, in a televised address, he publicly announced his plan to pursue the Strategic Defense Initiative. Although he received withering criticism from leaders at home and abroad, he garnered the support of the American people. With that battle won, the president and his advisors turned their attention to getting Congress and U.S. allies to warm to the idea. McFarlane recalled the most crucial leadership lesson he learned from Henry Kissinger and President Nixon during his White House Fellows year: A great leader develops the ability to persuade. "In most public policy pursuits your success will be rendered far more likely if you are persuasive. The ability to define a problem and its solution persuasively is decisive," McFarlane said. "If you are to win over congressmen, senators, or other key constituencies, you must come into the meeting having studied their interests and how those interests will be served by your solution to the problem. In getting SDI funded, we had to convince a lot of smart people who really didn't like the idea. It took many meetings where I just talked candidly and honestly about what I thought was going to happen. I said that if they invested this money in this initiative, we would expose the relative backwardness of the Soviet Union."

President Reagan's powers of persuasion had the desired effect. Congress funded the initiative, and development of the technology started in earnest. In summer 1984, the Army had success with its first Homing Overlay Experiment when personnel intercepted a mock ballistic missile warhead outside the earth's atmosphere. Other triumphs followed, and most of the allies changed their opinion of the new American defensive strategy. Less than a year later, Mikhail Gorbachev assumed leadership of the Soviet Union, and President Reagan initiated contact with him. The two agreed to a series of summits to negotiate arms control and the resolution of other conflicts. The lessons about persuasion that McFarlane learned from Dr. Kissinger and President Nixon came into play again as he helped President Reagan prepare for his first meeting with Gorbachev. In the six months leading up to the first summit meeting, the president focused on building support among his key constituencies: the public, Congress, and the nation's allies.

"In the run-up to the first summit, we wanted our president to arrive with maximum strength—strength in the measures that count in the bilateral context. With the Soviet Union, for example, the president needed to arrive in Geneva with a very high approval rating at home so there would be no issue about whether Americans agreed with what he was advocating at the table," McFarlane said. "He needed to have the ability to pay for his proposals as indicated by congressional support, and that had to be demonstrated in a visible way through polls, articles, and public statements. Then he needed to have the allies concurring so the Russians wouldn't think they could drive a wedge between the Europeans and us. So during the six months running up to that November 1985 encounter with the Soviet Union, Reagan totally focused on those constituencies. He gave four major policy speeches on each dimension of our relations with the Russians: bilateral, human rights, regional disagreements, and arms control."

It was a systematic approach to persuasion. President Reagan used every opportunity to spell out his position publicly and explain why he believed it was sound as well as why he believed the Soviets' position was not. The president and his advisors held weekly bipartisan meetings with congressional leaders and met with the Republican leadership weekly too. The purpose of those gatherings was to drive home the message and get sufficient resources appropriated to demonstrate that the United States was serious about SDI. The president courted his allies, and one month before the first summit meeting in November 1985, the nation's most powerful friends—leaders from the United Kingdom, Japan, France, West Germany, and Italy—stood together at a press conference and professed their support for President Reagan's positions, signaling that the United States and its allies were indeed a united force.

"By coordinating the lead-up to the 1985 summit, we were able to send Reagan to Geneva with strong allied support and two solid years of appropriations for SDI. By that time, there was no question that he could fund his program," said McFarlane. "Going into those summit meetings, as I recall, Reagan also had a 73 percent approval rating at the grass roots too. It took a lot of bureaucratic effort to get all those speeches written, the trips to Europe done, and the background sessions with the press that took about a third of my time by the time I left office, but that's how it works in a major democracy."

President Reagan and Mikhail Gorbachev met five times in all, and their efforts resulted in the signing of the historic Intermediate-Range Nuclear Forces Treaty (INF) in 1987, which eliminated certain nuclear missiles and allowed for cross-inspections between the two countries. Four years later, the Soviet Union collapsed after years of economic hardship brought on by excessive defense spending.

As a leader, your success depends on your ability to get things done. Persuasion is an essential proficiency for all leaders, requiring you to move people toward a position they don't currently hold. Before you even begin to articulate your position, consider your proposal from every side. You must not only make a rational argument but also frame your ideas, approaches, and solutions in ways that appeal to diverse groups of people with basic human emotions. Know how your audience will react by trying to understand things from its position. Like John McGinty, you must go out and meet the people you are trying to persuade and invite their opinions about the merits of your position and let them offer constructive feedback so that your final proposal reflects their concerns.

Bud McFarlane was able to convince the U.S. Congress, our allies, and the American people that President Reagan knew exactly what he was doing by adopting the Star Wars initiative despite widespread opposition. He learned that the ability to persuade takes hard work and discipline, and he demonstrated that to persuade you need to be methodical in following all the steps necessary to leverage the correct response from different constituencies.

CHAPTER 19

LEADERS KNOW WHEN TO COMPROMISE AND WHEN TO STAND FIRM

Compromise. Few words in the English language have such starkly contrasting definitions. According to the Merriam-Webster dictionary, *compromise* means "to find or follow a way between extremes," which sounds like a good thing, but as an alternative definition, the dictionary lists "to make a shameful or disreputable concession," which doesn't sound like a good thing at all. One of the most difficult choices a leader must face is when to compromise and when to stand firm. The wrong choice on a critical issue can destroy a leader's effectiveness.

As a White House Fellow during the Reagan administration, Craig Coy (WHF 83–84) was assigned to work with Jack Svahn, assistant to the president for domestic policy, and Edwin Meese, counselor to the president. The first Coast Guard officer ever to be selected for a Fellowship, Coy attended nearly every meeting his principals attended, including meetings of the president's Budget Review Board, which consisted of Chief of Staff James Baker, Ed Meese, and the director of the Office of Management and Budget, David Stockman. The board was trying to hammer out the fiscal year 1985 budget, and it was through this process that Coy learned one of his most valuable leadership lessons.

"I learned why Jim Baker was able to get things done and why he was so successful in his career," Coy said. "There was a conflict, if you will, about how much to budget for the Coast Guard for drug interdiction. Meese was running the Drug Policy Board at the time, and he was arguing that the Coast Guard needed $100 million. David Stockman said that $50 million was all they were going to get. So they grabbed me, as I was still in the Coast Guard, and said, 'Let's go talk to the president.' Before I know it I'm in the Oval Office with President Reagan, Jim Baker, Ed Meese, and David Stockman, and Ed Meese is talking about how the Coast Guard needs its money, and he turned to me and said, 'Craig, tell them why the Coast Guard needs the money,' and I said that the Coast Guard has been underfunded. They've got old ships and old assets and old equipment, and in order to be effective they need to upgrade, and that takes money. Then Stockman made his case that the Coast Guard already had plenty of money. At that point Baker instantly jumped into the middle of it, before the president had a chance to say anything, and essentially said to Meese, 'Now, Ed, you know that $100 million is going to be tough to get in this kind of a budget, and David Stockman, you know $50 million isn't going to cut it. Why don't we just split the difference and make it $75 million and keep the president from having to make a tough choice here, and then everybody will be happy?' And that's the way it settled out. Jim Baker showed me the art of compromise. He made sure everybody won something, and he also kept the president from having to make a decision that he really didn't need to make."

Through that experience, Craig Coy learned that a good compromise can save the day. In contrast, another former White House Fellow, Francis "Fran" Harvey (WHF 78–79), learned just the opposite: Sometimes refusing to compromise is the right thing to do. Harvey was working as an engineer for Westinghouse Electric Corporation when he was selected to be a White House Fellow. He was assigned to the Department of Defense, where he worked to develop energy policy, and also served as a Defense Department representative on a task force charged with promoting the Strategic Arms Limitation Treaty to the American public. Harvey was assigned to work with Secretary Harold Brown, a brilliant but introverted scientist who had earned three degrees—including a Ph.D. that he received at the age of twenty-one—from Columbia University and had served as a deputy defense secretary in the Lyndon Johnson administration. "The lesson I learned from Dr. Brown was that you really do have to understand the environment in which you operate, and you can never get separated from that environment and that understanding, whether it's a market environment or a national security environment," Harvey said. "In the corporate world there are so many examples of leaders that get disconnected from the realities of the marketplace, and they make stupid decisions and issue stupid orders."

Harvey watched Secretary Brown grow the defense budget in spite of the Carter administration's pledge to cut defense spending drastically in the aftermath of the Vietnam War. "If you ask people when the buildup of the defense budget started in response to facing up to the realities of the Soviet Union, everybody would say it started under President Reagan. But the fact of the matter is that Harold Brown, in what ended up being a pretty liberal democratic administration, actually got real increases in the defense budget, and I think it's because he really did understand what the Soviet Union was doing," Harvey explained. "I can remember all the rhetoric of the strategic nuclear balance, and even though we were ahead, the Soviets were catching up. We needed to ensure that we had the strength, and the numbers didn't matter. It was the *parity* that mattered, and Secretary Brown went after that. I don't know how he did it—it was amazing, and in reflection, it was all based upon his understanding of what was really going on in the environment. You've got to give Brown a lot of credit for what he did there."

Harvey left his Fellowship and returned to Westinghouse, where he applied the lessons he learned in Washington to a sterling career in the private sector. For the next twenty years, he filled a variety of senior leadership roles at Westinghouse, including general manager of the Electrical Systems Division, general manager of the Marine Division, vice president of science and technology, president of the Government and Environmental Services Company, and president of the Defense and Electronics Systems Group. Harvey retired from the company in 1997 as the chief operating officer of the Industries and Technology Group. He served on a variety of corporate boards during the next several years, until the day in November 2004 when he returned to public service in what would become his most demanding leadership role ever: President George W. Bush had appointed him to be Secretary of the Army.

As secretary, Harvey assumed responsibility for the Army's manpower, training, equipment, communications, budget, and more. All told, over a million active-duty Army, National Guard, and Army Reserve soldiers as well as nearly half a million civilian employees and contracted service personnel were in his hands. Harvey also oversaw more than 15 million acres of land and nearly 1 billion square feet of facilities. It was a job of mind-boggling proportions, but Harvey knew exactly what his first task would be: get to know and understand the new environment. He traveled extensively, visiting U.S. soldiers in the Middle East and at over 150 Army installations, camps, and bases in the United States and abroad. Once he had a clear understanding of the situation, Harvey realized that the Army was significantly underresourced. He learned that in the 1990s, in the aftermath of the Cold War, the Army went from 780,000 to 480,000 personnel, and he classified those personnel as inadequately trained and equipped.

"I think it's ingrained in the national psyche that when the war's over, you just decrease the army. It goes back to World War I," said Harvey. "We went into World War II totally unprepared, and then we won that big war and said, 'Hey, it's over! We don't need an army anymore,' and we decreased again. We went to the Korean War unprepared, the Vietnam War unprepared, the Iraq War unprepared. Right away it was very apparent to me and my partner, Army Chief of Staff General Peter Schoomaker, that the budget, personnel, training, and equipment were all inadequate."

When Harvey took over as secretary, the 2005 Army budget was $98.6 billion, and it was his responsibility to prepare and submit a new five-year financial plan. The Office of Management and Budget and the Secretary of Defense recommended a decrease in the Army's budget. "From the beginning, my number one priority, which is well documented, was the well-being of the soldiers and their families. You see, when you're Secretary of the Army, there are some tough things you have to do," Harvey said. "You have to sign condolence letters. You have to go to the hospital and visit the wounded and sit with them and try to console them. And you have to go to the funerals. The fact is that the Army went into Iraq unprepared, and when you see soldiers die on the battlefield, it changes you, and as a leader; you have an obligation to the Army to get them the funding they need."

Harvey's wife, Mary Louise, concurred and said, "I have never seen Fran work with such intensity and passion as when he was the Secretary of the Army. You would have thought the soldiers were his children or grandchildren." Indeed, doing the right thing for the soldiers and their families became Harvey's obsession, and he was determined to stand firm on their behalf. "In a time of war, we were being advised to decrease the defense budget, and quite frankly, I wasn't about to accept a decrease in an already underresourced army," Harvey said. "Sometimes you've just got to dig your heels in, so I did, and we submitted our budget three and a half months late. I got a reputation for not being a team player."

General Schoomaker said that when Harvey was appointed Secretary of the Army, the expectation was that he would go along with the senior management of the other services and some at the Defense Department who were opposed to increased funding for the Army. When Harvey came on the scene, the service was in the middle of major changes stemming from its long-term involvement in the wars in the Middle East. Although President Bush and Defense Secretary Rumsfeld supported most of the changes that were taking place in the Army and understood the need for a funding increase, other influential players fought hard against it. "The services are always in competition. But we were unbeatable because we didn't just say we needed more money. We approached it by showing the level of readiness we were being asked to maintain and then showing what that readiness would cost. It was a very tangible thing," Schoomaker said. "When they tried to cut $24 billion from the base budget, we could then show them what impact that would have and what it meant in terms of being able to sustain our rotation in Afghanistan and Iraq. These guys were all trying to fight us on the veracity of our facts, but we had the data. It was there."

When the fiscal guidance came down recommending a cut without regard for what that would mean to the troops on the ground, Schoomaker and Harvey had three choices. They could cut personnel, cut force structure, or stand firm and demand that the money be allocated. They chose to stand firm. They refused to submit their budget, and their tactic worked.

Indeed, during Secretary Harvey's brief tenure the Army budget more than doubled from what it had been ten years before. He also sharpened the Army's focus on recruiting. Harvey launched a task force that he also chaired, and that task force came up with a novel idea: Turn all the troops into recruiters.

"In business, everybody knows that the employees themselves are usually the best source of qualified personnel. So we started a program that gave our soldiers a financial reward of a thousand dollars for referring somebody to the force. If he or she referred a new recruit that actually signed up and made it through basic training, that referring soldier would get the reward. We figured nothing's better than a soldier coming home for a leave and seeing his buddies and saying, 'Hey, the Army's a great organization and I'm doing something for the country, and I feel good about myself; you should join too.' It really, really paid dividends. We ended up with a much bigger virtual recruiting force than we really had, although we significantly increased our numbers of actual recruiters too." The result was that in 2006, the Army's active component had its most successful recruiting year ever, bringing in 80,000 new soldiers. Thanks to Harvey and Schoomaker's leadership, the Army was granted the authority to increase its forces permanently to 547,000 by fiscal year 2012.

Harvey is particularly proud of his and Schoomaker's effort to make the Army stronger and more efficient by implementing the Army Business Transformation initiative, a servicewide plan to improve the quality and productivity of the all of the Army's business practices. The initiative was based on corporate methodology called Lean Six Sigma, which is designed to increase responsiveness and cut the waste of both money and time. Harvey and Schoomaker launched the Army Business Transformation initiative in 2005. It is still ongoing and has resulted in significant cost reductions.

There were other notable advancements under Secretary Harvey too. To improve the quality of life for the troops, Harvey redirected $250 million to renovate 20,000 substandard barracks that were home to thousands of soldiers and ordered that the job be completed in its entirety within one year. That mission was accomplished. When he saw troops in Iraq and Afghanistan taking matters into their own hands and outfitting their vehicles with additional armor to try to protect themselves from roadside bombs, Harvey ordered Army engineers immediately to design, test, and qualify the strongest armor additions they could muster. It was done, and Harvey sent the troops in the Middle East more than 14,000 customized armor additions to strengthen their Humvees. To support injured troops, he established the Army Wounded Warrior Program, which helps soldiers rejoin society after an injury and gives them assistance—especially with their medical needs—for at least five years. Under Secretary Harvey's guidance, the Army's casualty reporting, notification, and assistance procedures were revamped totally when it became known that some fallen soldiers' families had been given erroneous information about their loved ones' cause of death and had faced problems with bureaucratic red tape.

In spite of those accomplishments, Harvey was forced to step down from his post in spring 2007. He was pressured by newly appointed Secretary of Defense Robert Gates to resign after allegations of substandard conditions and poor management at the Walter Reed Army Medical Center in Washington, D.C., were made public. However, neither Schoomaker nor Harvey was aware of the problems at Walter Reed. "You can't solve a problem you know nothing about. During my tenure I made dozens of visits to Walter Reed and met with hundreds of wounded warriors and hospital staff. No one—and I mean no one—ever mentioned the temporary outpatient building," Harvey remarked; he said he first learned of the hospital's troubles when he read about them in the newspaper.

As soon as Harvey learned about the issue, the Army staff put together a thirty-four-page action plan to fix the problems, and he directed that the soldiers in the temporary facility be moved into up-to-date facilities at the hospital. "I was asked to resign over the Walter Reed Hospital issue, but the real reason was the budget. It really doesn't bother me if people think otherwise, because the people that count know what the true story is, and the people that count are the Army people," said Harvey. "The bottom line is that the budget went from $98 billion in 2005 to $141 billion for 2009. And today I'm very, very proud of the fact that because General Schoomaker and I stood our ground and refused to compromise, the Army is finally getting the resources it needs to be completely ready for the full spectrum of conflict."

Schoomaker, who retired from the Army a month after Harvey was forced to resign, expressed his deep admiration for Harvey's bold, uncompromising leadership. "He came into a bad situation and ended up making a huge difference. Being a political appointee, they expected him to compromise and take the easy way out, and he didn't. I think he was one of the most effective secretaries we've ever had. We were able to bring the Army through some of the most difficult periods it has ever had to face. Even at the time that we were doing this, we had already been at war longer than we were in World War II. It was very necessary for us to hang for the right reasons for the Army during that period, and we did. And I think that will be Fran's legacy."

Harvey now spends his time serving on a variety of corporate boards. He also keeps in touch with many of the soldiers he met at hospitals and bases during his tenure as Secretary of the Army. "Our nation's greatest treasure is the American soldier, and I was fortunate to have been able to serve them," Harvey said. "The last line of the Warrior Ethos is 'I will never leave a fallen comrade.' On that, I did not compromise. When the newspapers stop printing and the cameras stop rolling, standing on principle is what leaders—true leaders—do. Just as our warriors demonstrate every day in the face of hostile fire and other dangers, they do not wither under pressure, nor do they 'cave,' even when personal costs or their reputation is involved. True leaders must demonstrate through their actions that they will stand up for their principles, that they will rise above outside pressures, that they will make informed and not impulsive decisions, and that they will be held personally accountable for their decisions."

One who also did not compromise his principles in the face of mounting pressure to do otherwise was President Ronald Reagan. In the early months of his presidency in 1981, nearly 13,000 of the country's air traffic controllers went on strike after months of negotiations between their union and the Federal Aviation Agency (FAA). The controllers, who were federal employees, had complained for years about the way the FAA managed them and were demanding better benefits, wages, and working conditions as well as a decrease in hours. The government's stance was simple: It was not going to give more pay in exchange for fewer hours worked. When negotiations between the union and the government hit an impasse, the workers—in violation of federal law—walked off their jobs and went on strike, an act that threatened to shut down the nation's air transportation system.

Robert "Bud" McFarlane (WHF 71–72) was serving as counselor to the State Department at that time; it would be another two years before he became President Reagan's national security advisor. McFarlane recalled that there was a great deal of disagreement in the White House about how to handle the pending strike, with President Reagan standing practically alone against his closest advisors. "There was a cabinet meeting before the strike, and President Reagan said he didn't think we could tolerate a union breaking the law. He said the controllers were acting irresponsibly and putting Americans at risk, and he said he was going to have to fire them all," McFarlane recalled. "Most of his cabinet said, 'Don't do that; it is politically dumb,' and he said, 'I'm going to do it because it's the right thing to do.' And he did it in spite of the political risk and in spite of the question as to whether or not we could put military people into the air traffic control towers fast enough to maintain the system."

Regardless of his cabinet's misgivings, on the day of the walkout President Reagan held a press conference in the White House Rose Garden and issued an uncompromising statement to the controllers, along with an ultimatum: You're breaking the law—get back to work within forty-eight hours or you're fired. More than 11,000 striking workers called President Reagan's bluff, but he did not fold. The president terminated them and barred them from ever working for the FAA again. Although the country's labor unions decried the firings, the majority of the American public supported Reagan's adamant stance and unwillingness to compromise when it came to dealing with lawbreakers.

From President Reagan, McFarlane learned the value of standing firm and refusing to compromise on an issue that critically affected the lives of many Americans. A leader needs to learn when to stand firm and when to practice the art of compromise. As former President Gerald Ford once said, "Compromise is the oil that makes governments go." Another White House Fellow, attorney Nelson Diaz (WHF 77–78), learned that effective leaders also have to be willing to be flexible if they're going to get the job done. A Fellow during the Carter administration, Diaz was only the second person of Puerto Rican ancestry ever to work for the White House, and his principal was Vice President Walter Mondale.

Diaz had worked as an activist on economic development issues for the Latino and African-American communities in Philadelphia before his Fellowship. He recalled that one day he and Mondale were flying to Los Angeles on Air Force Two to plan a birthday party for President Jimmy Carter when they heard a surprising announcement: The president had just signed an arms sale agreement with Saudi Arabia. Mondale did not know Carter was going to consent to such a deal, and he knew it would be extremely unpopular with the Jewish community, of which Mondale was a strong supporter. "The vice president had a choice to either turn the plane around or to continue on the trip," Diaz said. "He consulted with Chief of Staff Hamilton Jordan, who was also on the plane, and we decided not to plan the birthday party but rather to proceed to Los Angeles, which has a large Jewish community. So the focus of the trip changed from a birthday party to holding meetings with Jewish leaders. When we got there, the Jewish leaders were somewhat somber, but the vice president explained the genesis of President Carter's decision to them and asked how we could be more responsive to their concerns. He never gave a hint that he had had no idea the deal was going to happen. He made something positive come out of it. I witnessed his loyalty to the president and his ability to compromise. Having been an activist on the streets, I hadn't learned much about that, but on that trip I learned that sometimes half a loaf is better than no loaf at all."

Diaz would convert that concept into action years later when he was tapped to be general counsel to the Department of Housing and Urban Development by former White House Fellow and HUD Secretary Henry Cisneros (WHF 71–72). Diaz and Cisneros met through the White House Fellows program in the 1970s. Years after finishing his Fellowship, Diaz was working as a judge to reform Philadelphia's court system by ridding it of a seven-year backlog and making changes that resulted in savings of $100 million. When Cisneros, who had been mayor of San Antonio, Texas, was appointed HUD secretary by President Clinton, Cisneros called on his old friend Diaz to serve as general counsel. "I didn't want the job. I didn't want to go work for a friend, and I turned him down three times," Diaz admitted. "But because I trusted Henry and he trusted me and we were both White House Fellows, I ultimately decided to go ahead and take the job. It turned out to be a very successful period."

As General Counsel to HUD, Diaz used litigation settlements to incorporate and implement Cisneros's policies. Diaz arrived at HUD during the most litigious period in the department's history. He resolved twelve major cases that had been pending for a decade and hired as his deputy the lawyer who had brought more suits against HUD than anyone else. "I wanted to demonstrate my willingness to be a listener and to develop a strong trust relationship so we could resolve all those cases," Diaz said. "And I was very aware that I had to use the art of compromise to resolve these very contentious cases. During my time at HUD I also applied what I learned from Vice President Mondale about the need to be loyal to your principal. Compromise and loyalty do go hand in hand. I learned that you must do everything you can to directly and openly engage the individuals with whom you disagree. However, once a decision is made by the leader or a consensus is reached by the management team, whatever the case may be, you need to practice the art of compromise and proceed with the final decision as if it were your own."

Whether you're leading a business or a nonprofit organization, a committee or a board, an athletic team or a family, you must learn when to compromise and when to stand firm. Although it's not possible to resolve every conflict through negotiation and concession, it is feasible in most cases. The tougher decision is when not to compromise, which often puts your livelihood, your reputation, and the organization you lead at risk. Although a leader must stand firm on matters of integrity, there are times when one's core beliefs or principles clearly call for holding out, as President Reagan did with the air traffic controllers. However, many times the issue is not black and white and there is no easy rule of thumb regarding when to act, as was the case with former Army Secretary Harvey's decision to stand firm on the budget he believed was necessary to sustain the war readiness of his soldiers. Ultimately, it comes down to a leader's judgment. The old adage is true: Good judgment comes from experience, and experience comes from bad judgment.

Keep this in mind the next time you have to choose between seeking compromise and holding firm on a critical issue: If you can resolve the matter through give-and-take without sacrificing your core beliefs and integrity, find the middle ground. You'll soon discover what Nelson Diaz and Craig Coy already know: Compromise is the art of making everyone a winner.

CHAPTER 20

LEADERS ARE PROBLEM SOLVERS

When I was a twenty-four-year-old Air Force lieutenant, I was assigned to work as special assistant for General John R. Galvin, Commander of the U.S. Southern Command in the Republic of Panama. I had the honor of serving in that capacity for two years until I was selected to be a White House Fellow in 1988. General Galvin, who went on to become NATO's Supreme Allied Commander, Europe, turned out to be one of the greatest teachers and mentors I've ever known. Throughout my career I have tried to build on the lessons I learned from him, and I've even taken the liberty of borrowing some of his outstanding techniques for shaping future leaders.

General Galvin started teaching me the ways of leadership on my very first assignment. He explained my task to me in his typically friendly manner and then dismissed me to go get it done. Several days later I returned to his office brimming with questions. As I stood on the opposite side of his desk and rattled off a list of inquiries about who, what, when, where, why, and how I ought to go about completing the various challenges I had encountered in the assigned task, I saw the general becoming increasingly agitated. Suddenly he adjusted his reading glasses, stood up, strode around his desk, and looked down at me. He sternly asked, "Lieutenant! How many stars do you have on your shoulder?"

Like a fool I glanced down at my shoulder, looking for stars. "None, sir," I replied sheepishly.

"And how many stars do I have on mine?"

"Four, sir." I felt myself withering under the general's glare.

"Lieutenant, if you want me to do your job, what do I need you for?" General Galvin asked disapprovingly. "You're dismissed."

I turned around and quickly headed for the door with a sinking feeling in my stomach. I was certain that before the day was over I would be shipped off to a military base in Timbuktu and would be forced to admit that I was a dismal failure in my first few days on the job. However, as I was reaching for the doorknob to leave, General Galvin shouted, "Lieutenant Garcia."

I turned around quickly in sharp military fashion, clicking my heels and coming to attention with a loud "Yes, sir." To which General Galvin replied, "Don't bring me problems," he said with conviction. "Bring me *solutions.*"

I spent the next few days hammering out a solution to the general's assignment. When I presented my solution to him, he still wasn't satisfied. He adjusted his glasses, abruptly stood up, strode around his desk, and towered over me again. I braced myself for a sharp barrage of criticism. However, this time General Galvin patiently described exactly what he expected me to do. "Never bring me just one solution. Bring at least three so I know you are actually thinking. Then tell me which one is best and why," he explained. "If you discipline yourself to think of at least three different ways to solve a problem, you will be forced to look at things from a different perspective and you'll never grasp at the first solution that comes to mind."

Later that evening, as I was reflecting on General Galvin's words, I recalled the first book my father ever read to me many years before: *A Message to Garcia* by Elbert Hubbard. The story was set during the Spanish-American War of 1898, and it centered on the story of U.S. Army Lieutenant Andrew Summers Rowan, who was sent on a seemingly impossible mission by President McKinley. The young lieutenant was ordered to deliver a message to General Calixto Garcia, the man in charge of the Cuban insurgents fighting for their country's independence from the Spaniards and to bring back Garcia's response, which would help the United States develop its strategy for facing the Spanish Army. There was a problem, though: No one knew exactly where in Cuba General Garcia and his men were hiding. Rowan was told only that General Garcia was deep in the Cuban jungle.

When given his assignment, the lieutenant asked not a single question and did not request help from anyone. He simply inserted the message in a leather pouch strapped to his chest and set out on his mission, determined to carry it out. Rowan sailed to Cuba aboard a tiny boat, weaving his way among armed Spanish patrol boats and pretending to be a fisherman, until he was able to sneak ashore in the dark. He and his Cuban guide traveled on foot and on horseback, over mountains and deep into the jungle, until at last he found General Garcia and delivered the president's message. However, his mission was only half complete: He still had to return safely with Garcia's response intact.

Miraculously, Rowan completed his assignment and quietly went back to his everyday life. To him, carrying out that mission was his duty, plain and simple. He didn't complain that life wasn't fair. He didn't fret about the seemingly impossible task of getting to Cuba, or slipping past the Spaniards, or climbing the treacherous mountains, or finding one man in a vast unfamiliar jungle whom a lot of dangerous people were looking for too. He just did it, no questions asked.

With the spirit of Lieutenant Rowan on my mind, I made another run at finishing General Galvin's very difficult assignment, but this time it was different. I focused on the solutions, not the problem, and thought about how to tackle it from every conceivable angle. Through that exercise I arrived at three possible resolutions. I then broke them down further and chose the solution that I thought was best, and I prepared an explanation of why I thought it was the best. I presented my solutions to the general, and he was pleased. Mission accomplished.

Looking back, I now realize that General Galvin asked me to bring him solutions not because he didn't know how to solve the problem himself but because by delegating the problem to me, he was trying to teach me the process of developing my own workable solutions. Although the details of General Galvin's first assignment remain classified, I can disclose what I learned as a result of it. I learned that a leader helps the people on his or her team understand how to conceptualize and solve problems for themselves. Great leaders hire, mentor, and develop young leaders who will be good at digging themselves and their organization out of trouble and coach those individuals from day one. Effective leaders resist the temptation to micromanage, and they learn to trust that their people are capable of creating their own solutions.

One former White House Fellow who was renowned for solving problems on a global scale was Julia Vadala Taft (WHF 70–71). Taft was selected as a White House Fellow at age twenty-eight, just one year after earning a master's degree in international relations from the University of Colorado in Boulder. The daughter of an army surgeon, she came to the program a recent divorcee who had been abandoned by her first husband, but with a spirit of adventure and enthusiasm for a lifetime of public service that epitomized the dreams and aspirations for the program of its founders, President Lyndon Johnson and John Gardner.

Few women were selected in the early years of the White House Fellows program, and Taft was the only woman in a class of seventeen. Her fellow classmates Dana Mead, "Burn" Loeffke, Tom O'Brien, and Keith Crisco noted that it must have been like having sixteen brothers, all of whom were very protective of her, especially on the social scene. Taft served her Fellowship year in the Office of the Vice President, where her outgoing personality and abilities were such that she was sought after for management positions in several agencies when her Fellowship year came to a close. She chose the Department of Health, Education, and Welfare because she wanted to help the poor. And in 1974—with the hearty approval of the sixteen big brothers from her White House Fellows class— she married the great-grandson of President William Howard Taft, William Howard Taft IV, who would go on to become the general counsel to both the Department of Health, Education, and Welfare and the Department of Defense; Deputy Secretary of Defense; United States permanent representative to NATO during Operation Desert Storm; and legal advisor to the State Department under Secretary of State Colin Powell.

Beginning in 1975, Julia Taft embarked on a career that would mark her as one of the world's few true experts in caring for and resettling refugees. At the suggestion of HEW Secretary Caspar Weinberger, President Ford plucked her from the senior ranks at HEW to direct the resettlement of refugees from Vietnam, Cambodia, and Laos after the collapse of Saigon. The resettlement program brought 131,000 refugees to the United States in six months. Nothing on such a scale had ever been attempted by this country before. There was no template and no time to plan. The work just had to get done, and Taft directed it all with humor, grace, and a backbone of steel. "Because she was so young—she was only thirty-two at the time—Julia felt comfortable saying, 'I don't have a clue about how to do this, so let's sit down and figure it out,'" said longtime friend and former spokesman for the Defense Department Kenneth Bacon. "People could not say no to Julia."

Taft always said that President Ford's decision to put her in charge of resettling tens of thousands of Vietnamese refugees changed her life. As Bacon noted, "It did more than that. It changed the very complexion and DNA of our nation, and we are a richer nation as a result. At an early age Julia learned lessons that, coupled with her indomitable 'can do' spirit, would bring success in a series of difficult jobs. First, you need coordination when crafting responses to complex emergencies. Second, don't go for the easy solution, go for the right solution. And third, public-private partnerships are almost always better than the government acting alone. She was, after all, a Taft Republican."

After the resettlement was complete, Taft took time to raise her three children with the same values that characterized her life. She insisted that each go on a foreign trip between the junior and senior years in high school to a place where poverty and hunger were endemic so that they all would have a meaningful personal experience in helping others. There was never a time when she did not answer the call for help around the world. Devoted to her husband Will, who in turn supported her life's work with his considerable personal and professional skills, Taft never stopped making friends and important contacts in senior government positions worldwide. Her reputation opened doors, and her friends always answered her calls, doing what they could to respond to the need. Inaction was one of the few crimes she would not forgive.

Taft helped shape the Refugee Act of 1980, which moved the country from an ad hoc resettlement program to the current infrastructure, which includes strong partnerships between the government and private resettlement agencies as well as clear annual goals. Later, as director of the Office of Foreign Disaster Assistance (OFDA) in the Reagan administration, she brought a sense of urgency and efficiency to the post. In December 1987, four strong jolts from an earthquake leveled swaths of towns and cities in Armenia in less than four minutes and left more than 55,000 dead. Ken Bacon recalled, "One day shortly thereafter, a visitor was in Julia's office when she got word that President Reagan had approved aid for the earthquake victims. 'How long will it take to pull it together?' the visitor asked. Without hesitation and with a twinkle in her eye, Julia replied with total confidence, 'The first plane will leave immediately. It's loaded, on the runway, and ready to go. You don't think I'd wait to start until after the president signed the order, do you?'" Taft arrived in the country aboard that military aircraft, carrying only her daughter's pink Strawberry Shortcake sleeping bag because it was the only personal gear she could find on such short notice. The cargo plane otherwise was packed with relief supplies. Chutzpah with charm was one of Taft's trademarks.

Personal courage was another. Her work as the head of the U.S. delegation for earthquake victims in Armenia earned her the Soviet Union's Order of Personal Courage award and a distinguished service award from the Agency for International Development in 1989. On a relief mission to Sarajevo in 1992, she donned a helmet and bulletproof vest and hunkered down in a bathtub when her hotel came under fire.

During her three years at OFDA, Taft and her staff dealt with major flooding in Bangladesh that covered an area almost three times the size of New Jersey and left 25 million homeless, less-publicized floods in the Dominican Republic and India, displaced people in Burundi, a poison gas incident that killed 1,200 in Cameroon, and a locust plague that resulted in widespread famine in the Sahel and Ethiopia. As a result of her work, she was recruited to head InterAction, a coalition of headstrong nongovernmental organizations (NGOs). At first she resisted, saying, "I'm just too disorganized and too bossy for this kind of job." As Kenneth Bacon noted, "It was one of the few times in her life that she was wrong. From 1994 to 1997, she turned InterAction into an important advocacy voice, showing once again that she could herd cats."

In 1997, President Bill Clinton appointed Taft as Assistant Secretary of State for Population, Refugees, and Migration (PRM), a post she held for four years. In 1999, she was named to the additional post of special coordinator for Tibetan issues to promote dialogue between the Dalai Lama and the Chinese government. While serving as the Assistant Secretary of State for PRM, Taft played a key role in protecting the 800,000 refugees driven from Kosovo and in shaping U.S. responses to displacement around the world.

Taft had almost everybody's number and was not afraid to pick up the phone, but because she was a problem solver, people often called her. After leaving the State Department, Mark Malloch Brown, then the Administrator of the United Nations Development Programme, lured her to the

UN, where she served as the director of the UN's Bureau for Crisis Prevention and Recovery, among other things, and formulated and coordinated the plans for the recovery of Afghanistan in 2002.

A close friend of the Dalai Lama and several chairmen of the Joint Chiefs of Staff, Taft was the recipient of awards and accolades from around the world. As White House Fellow classmate Tom O'Brien (WHF 70–71) noted, "In all this, part of Julia's magic was in keeping the focus on solving the problem and getting the job done. Full of marvelous and often hair-raising anecdotes, the point was never about her or what she had done but about the humor she saw in her own experience, the adventure and challenge of doing the right thing, and the enjoyment she found in participating in the truly important events of our time. Julia wanted to share that with everyone she cared about, and she cared about pretty much everyone."

In 2005, Taft learned that she had colon cancer. Determined to beat the disease, she kept up her work and concern for the world's downtrodden and forgotten, even returning to serve as an interim CEO for InterAction. In March 2008, even as she was in the last days of her heroic struggle to beat the cancer, Taft expressed her concerns about others to longtime friend Ken Bacon, who said, "She didn't want to talk about her cancer, although we did a little. She didn't want to talk about her wonderful family and friends, although we did talk about them a little. She wanted to talk about the plight of Iraqi refugees. Specifically, she wanted to discuss the lessons she had learned over the last thirty-three years that could help Iraqi refugees today. She knew that Refugees International and the International Rescue Committee would continue our efforts, but that wasn't enough. She wanted reassurance that we would coordinate with other agencies to bring more pressure on the White House and Congress to protect displaced Iraqis."

Interviewed by the *New York Times* just days after Taft's death, Former White House Fellow and longtime Taft friend Colin Powell was quoted in that newspaper's obituary section on March 18, 2008, as saying that Julia Taft, "was an image of American openness and generosity. Her professional life was committed to people trying to get by on a dollar a day, those who are hungry, without clean water, without medicine, without homes." Taft's obituary in the *Washington Post* on March 19 stated, "It was her ability to bring order to chaos—plus her willingness to get on a plane, helicopter, jeep or riverboat to go almost anywhere that enabled her to make a difference.

Whether in the White House, a refugee camp, or a meeting with government and [nongovernmental organization] officials, she knew how to get people moving."

Julia Vadala Taft was a leader who was an unrepentant and unstoppable problem solver. She never took no for an answer. She fed the hungry, gave refuge to the homeless, and protected the dispossessed—all with energy, ingenuity, and good humor. Most of all, she coordinated the efforts of other problem solvers to increase the odds of success. And as she said each day as she left Will and the children for work with a huge shoulder bag crammed with papers and other reading material and with a huge smile on her face, "Well, I'm off to save the world! We have work to do."

I think Julia Taft was a modern-day Lieutenant Rowan. She instinctively knew what the problem was and focused on finding the best solution. She used every ounce of ingenuity and courage she possessed to get the job done. She always kept a level head and was humble about her incredible achievements. Even when the task was seemingly insurmountable—such as effectively and humanely resettling an abrupt surge of 131,000 refugees— Taft took it on as if it were just another day at the office.

Lieutenant General Edward Rice, Jr. (WHF 90–91), believes he has the key to how she did it. As commander, U.S. Forces Japan, and commander, 5th Air Force, Yokota Air Base, Japan, Rice is the senior U.S. military representative in Japan and the highest-ranking African American in the Air Force. He has held many command positions in his thirty-year career in the military. He not only directed recruiting for the Air Force but also led bomber forces in combat during Operation Enduring Freedom. Additionally, he served as deputy commander for the joint task force that provided disaster relief to those suffering in the aftermath of the 2004 tsunami in Southeast Asia. Rice served his White House Fellowship in the Department of Health and Human Services (HHS), mostly working alongside HHS Chief of Staff Michael Calhoun, whom he classified as a brilliant man with an outstanding ability to get to the bottom of difficulties and resolve them effectively. From Calhoun, Rice learned that preparation is essential to decision making and problem solving.

"Michael Calhoun had exceptional judgment, partly because he was always extremely well prepared. That's a quality I've tried to emulate over the years," Rice said. "I believe the first element for successful problem solving is to have an understanding of the problem. A very successful person once told me that for complex problems, it might take as much as 75 percent of the available time to ensure you have the question right, and if you get the question right, the remaining 25 percent of the time should be sufficient to find the answer. Taking the time to get the question right is very powerful in problem solving. It sounds self-evident, but I see examples every day in which the question is not properly understood and the answer is predictably off the mark."

Rice's problem-solving abilities were put to the test in a major way when he was faced with one of his biggest challenges as a leader: standing up a new flying squadron. "Putting something together of that magnitude from scratch took everything I knew about leadership to get it right. The lesson that comes to mind is that when faced with a huge problem, you have to 'eat the elephant one bite at a time,'" Rice explained. "The scale of the individual activities that must come together to complete the task can appear to be overwhelming at the beginning of the effort, but with a clear vision of the end state and with disciplined planning and execution, it all comes together at the end of the day."

Several years ago I returned from a business trip to find that my assistant had hung a gigantic fifteen-foot-long wooden sign above my office door. The sign says, DON'T BRING ME PROBLEMS. BRING ME SOLUTIONS. I suggest that you post a similar sign and then set about the task of guiding each person on your team toward the goal of becoming a top-notch problem solver. Sure, it takes time and effort to teach problem-solving strategies to your people, but when you experience the payoff, you'll know it was an investment worth making.

CHAPTER 21

LEADERS LEAD BY WALKING AROUND

As senior vice president and general counsel at Catalent Pharma Solutions, Samrat "Sam" Khichi (WHF 04–05) is responsible for the legal department of a massive international organization with nearly $2 billion in sales and around 10,000 employees. Whether he and his staff are dealing with import and export issues, employee law, patent applications or cross-border mergers and acquisitions, Khichi has to be well informed and on top of everything that comes into or goes out of the office. Although some in his position might be tempted to use their desks as the hub from which everything emanates, or "command central," Khichi prefers to get out from behind his and lead by walking around.

Leading by walking around is a skill Khichi first learned as a young lieutenant in the Army. His commanding officers taught him that being out front and being seen by the troops is an indispensable leadership technique in a military organization. Khichi was surprised when that lesson was reinforced strongly during his year as a White House Fellow for Secretary of Housing and Urban Development Alphonso Jackson. "As a White House Fellow I learned that leading by walking around doesn't just have applications in the military. Secretary Jackson stressed the importance of personal interactions and connections at HUD too," Khichi said. "And as I look back though the notes I made after all the face-to-face meetings we had with those incredible leaders during the Fellowship, one of the common takeaways I gained was just this notion of leadership by walking around. The intent is to stay connected with the department in a way that is more meaningful than the way we usually communicate these days. It's beyond e-mail or voice mail; it's outside of exchanging drafts, and it's outside of formal meetings. You must have a way of being seen, of being accessible, and of giving your folks an ability to connect with you quickly and easily."

To achieve that aim, every day before lunch Khichi leaves his desk and starts making his rounds. He walks from one office to another and makes face-to-face contact with each of his twenty team members. He greets them warmly and asks how they are doing and then listens to what they have to say. Khichi repeats the series of personal meetings again each afternoon. "My folks call them 'drive-bys.' It's probably not the perfect name for them because they do end up being more than a few minutes sometimes, depending upon what we end up talking about," Khichi explained. "My team members know that this is their opportunity to raise issues with me and that I'm there to listen. The feedback I've received indicates that they like this way of communicating because it avoids the formality of scheduling appointments or going through e-mails, and I like it because it keeps me connected in real time. The goal is to have two touch points with each employee each day. Do I sometimes only get to have one? Sure, of course, but the goal is to have two. I've found that this technique creates a culture of openness and accessibility and helps my team function more effectively."

Retired four-star admiral of the U.S. Navy Charles "Chuck" Larson (WHF 68–69) also believes in the power of mixing and mingling with one's team. Whether he was serving as superintendent of the U.S. Naval Academy, Commander in Chief of the U.S. Pacific Command, or commanding officer of a nuclear attack submarine, Larson was never one to sit back and wait for his people to come to him. Instead, he engaged in what he calls "walk-around leadership." Whenever someone wanted to brief Larson on an issue happening in his or her space, Larson frequently offered to go meet that person on his or her own turf. He also would pick different sectors of the organization randomly on a regular basis and go there to meet the people and see what they were working on. "On the submarine I was always walking around talking to people on their watch stations, asking them what they were doing or watching maintenance being conducted," Larson said. "As Superintendent of the Naval Academy I made a decision that I was going to have internal relations perfected before I started external relations. Twice a week I would drop in on a class—maybe a leadership or ethics class and then one from another part of the curriculum—and just show up unannounced. Once a week I ate lunch with a random table. I was always out and about and accessible, and people knew they could talk to me because I showed a real interest in them."

Alex Friedman (WHF 98–99), chief financial officer for the Bill & Melinda Gates Foundation, learned the same technique from his White House Fellows mentor, General Charles "Chuck" Krulak. As Commandant of the Marine Corps, Krulak had a habit of dropping by bases without warning. He would stroll casually into the barracks areas unannounced and start talking with the Marines to find out how they were doing. Friedman accompanied Krulak on several of those surprise visits and recalled one particular exchange between Krulak and a Marine at Camp Pendleton in San Diego. Krulak asked the young man how everything was going, and the Marine issued the standard reply: He loved the Marine Corps—it was the best thing ever. Krulak agreed that the Marine Corps was great and then asked the lad if there was anything he *didn't* love about it. The Marine swore he loved absolutely *everything*, but Krulak kept encouraging him to be honest, and finally the man confessed that his knee was hurting and he thought it might have something to do with his right boot. Krulak examined the boot and discovered that the heel was worn out. "General Krulak asked the Marine how many hours a day he spent on his feet, and the Marine replied it was eighteen hours with a full backpack," Friedman said. "Krulak kept talking to the Marine and learned that many of them were having the same problem with their boots, but their commanding officer had been 'too busy' to deal with it."

Krulak went back to the Pentagon and started investigating whether there was a widespread problem with the Marines' footwear and learned that, sure enough, faulty boots had been distributed throughout the corps. Krulak made sure the defective boots were replaced swiftly. "Well, that story got around the Marine Corps in a nanosecond," Friedman said. "You can imagine how impressive that was for an enlisted Marine to have the commandant himself follow up on his problem and fix it and then send him a personal e-mail to make sure everything was resolved. Talk about caring. That sent the message that Krulak actually cared about his people, and you can be sure they didn't forget it. I know I certainly took it to heart."

Another former Fellow, James "Jim" Padilla (WHF 78–79), also knows the value of getting out and mingling with his people. When Padilla was a teenager, he was determined to attend a prestigious Catholic high school in his hometown of Detroit. Tuition was expensive, but Padilla was resolute. The youngster worked at a variety of odd jobs to pay his own way and within a matter of weeks was at the top of his class. An Eagle Scout who would earn the Boy Scouts of America's Distinguished Eagle Scout Award years later, Padilla graduated from the University of Detroit with degrees in chemical engineering and economics. He went to work for Ford Motor Company and was a thirty-two-year-old manager responsible for fuel economy planning when he was selected to be a White House Fellow and assigned to work as a special assistant to Commerce Secretary Juanita Kreps.

Kreps was a wonderful principal for Padilla. She was the first woman ever named a James B. Duke Professor, and she had served as vice president of Duke University. Kreps served on some of the nation's most prestigious boards, including Eastman Kodak, J.C. Penney, R.J. Reynolds, and AT&T, and was the first female director of the New York Stock Exchange. Kreps set a wonderful example for her young White House Fellow, who returned to Ford at the end of his Fellowship year and moved steadily up the ranks. He retired in 2006 after forty years at Ford, where he ultimately became the company's president and chief operating officer.

Padilla's leadership style was one of high visibility among Ford's 300,000 employees: He was rarely at his desk. "You've got to lead from the front," he said. "I had a strong belief that people needed to see their leadership, especially in a diverse operation like Ford. What's happening in the United States has little or no bearing on what's happening in São Paulo, Brazil, or China. So you get out and go meet people. I spent probably half of my time on the road."

One of the trademarks of Padilla's leadership approach was the town hall meetings he hosted frequently with Ford employees around the world. Padilla began each meeting by giving the attendees a ten-minute overview of his thoughts on the current state of the business, and he then opened up the meeting for a question and answer session. Since he had such a strong manufacturing background, Padilla particularly enjoyed visiting the shop floor and engaging with the employees there. No matter where he was in the world, Padilla made sure to spend time with Ford dealers to seek their unique perspectives on the business. "It's so very important that you keep in touch with your constituencies. People should never wonder what the bosses back in the world headquarters are thinking. They should know. So I spent a lot of time working with them so they understood our priorities," Padilla said. "Listen, the action is not in the headquarters. The action is on the ground. Your people should feel comfortable that every decision they make is in sync with the priorities of the organization. By going out there and talking with them and by making sure they understood my perspective, I think that enabled people to take initiative, which was critical to the overriding priorities that we had laid out."

Empowering people to take initiative is what leadership is all about, as Dr. George Ruiz (WHF 06–07) learned by working at Veterans Affairs during his Fellowship year. Truthfully, though, Ruiz already knew a bit about initiative thanks to his dad, a Colombian tire mechanic who often told Ruiz and his little brother Carl, "I do this kind of work every day so you don't have to." Spurred on by his father's words—and at one point during his college days the whizzing noise from a hydraulic drill at the tire repair shop near his apartment—Ruiz graduated from Brown University and Albert Einstein College of Medicine and became a cardiologist specializing in the management of congenital heart defects in adult patients. From his principal, Veterans Affairs Secretary Jim Nicholson, Ruiz saw how important it was to get out from behind the desk and hang out with the team. "One of the lessons I learned early on is what I call the lunchroom rule. I loved it when my secretary would go down and eat with us in the lunchroom," Ruiz said. "I was impressed by that. Whenever I saw him sitting there, I thought, 'You're the man!'"

Ruiz spun that lesson in another direction and came to the conclusion that if he was going to be a leader in the VA during his Fellowship, he would have to emulate his principal and get out from behind his desk. "If you really want to understand something, you need to go to where they make the sausage," he explained. "So I started going around asking stupid questions like 'How do you guys buy things?' I figured they must have an office there that bought the stuff for all of the VA, but everyone kept looking at me like I was crazy. And that was another thing I learned that year—that some of the smartest people I met during my Fellowship asked the simplest questions. It wasn't that they were simple people or that they had simple thought processes. It was because they were able to dissect something down to its most fundamental point and simply ask fundamental questions. It was interesting to me because most medical training is designed to keep you from asking stupid questions."

By going from office to office asking his "stupid question," Ruiz learned that the VA had a decentralized purchasing process that was far from efficient. He wondered how private-sector hospitals with a sharp eye on the bottom line bought their supplies. Ruiz researched and identified the ten largest health care systems in the country and then called their CEOs or other senior executives to find out about their purchasing procedures. The hospital executives told Ruiz how they used group purchasing organizations: contracting agencies that purchase huge quantities of supplies for health care systems. Ruiz became convinced that the VA could save millions by creating its own group purchasing organization. "This idea started to take over my mind, and I got really excited about it. I went and visited VA hospitals, and I visited their purchasing offices, and I talked to all these people down in the bowels of the place about their experiences with purchasing, about why purchasing strategies work or don't work at the VA," Ruiz explained. "I found that it would be difficult to do a group buy under the VA's decentralized system because all the purchasing information was buried in data. The data is there, but it's buried. I wanted to figure out a smart way to put all the data into a usable system, so I asked the secretary to do a large-scale spend analysis. I prepared a presentation that showed how he could save hundreds of millions of dollars if he were to centralize the purchasing system for the VA. He was impressed. He encouraged me to keep working on it, and it ultimately led to the VA doing its first large scale spend analysis, the initial step toward a cost-saving centralized purchasing system."

Sam Khichi, Chuck Larson, Alex Freidman, Jim Padilla, and George Ruiz all learned that the most effective leaders are the ones who are willing to leave their offices and go interact with their teams in a meaningful way. Sure, the view from the C-suite can be exquisite, but the leaders who sequester themselves there quickly become disconnected from their people and in all likelihood won't be allowed to enjoy that magnificent view for very long. If you want to know how best to lead your organization, head down to the lunchroom, the shop floor, or the purchasing office and ask the "stupid questions." Chances are good that your people will be delighted to help you answer them.

CHAPTER 22

LEADERS ARE TRANSFORMATIONAL CHANGE AGENTS

Being in a leadership position is always challenging. Even when profits are up, recruiting is solid, and costs are containable, a leader has to be vigilant and proactive to keep things functioning smoothly. But what happens when a new leader is driven to the scene of an organizational train wreck and expected to get things back on track? When trust is low and tensions are high, what's a leader to do?

Bill Cotter (WHF 65–66) knows the answers to those questions. When he was serving as an assistant to Commerce Secretary John Connor during his Fellowship, one of Cotter's assignments was to find a way to bridge the communication and enthusiasm gaps between career civil servants and political appointees in the Commerce Department. "The civil servants know they will be there way beyond the current administration and are not about to throw themselves wholeheartedly into the latest bright idea from the politically appointed short-termers," Cotter explained. "I realized there were different agendas and time lines for these two groups, but there was also a real mutual respect for common goals. I learned a lot from a series of conversations I had with them, but the essential lesson was that nearly everyone—new and old, highly placed or at the lowest staff level—has some insight to contribute that will make the organization better. A new leader should reach out and have personal conversations with as many individuals, at all levels, as possible and then must keep those conversations going over the years so he or she doesn't lose touch with changing attitudes."

Secretary Connor taught Cotter the value of having weekly staff meetings and creating a climate in which people felt comfortable bringing up issues and challenges. The secretary used the meetings to inform people across divisional lines and to reinforce priorities. "And if there needed to be arbitration or mediation about some conflicts that were developing, the secretary would be there and in a reasoned way try to find something that would work best for the whole and hopefully for each individual department too," Cotter said.

The lessons Cotter learned during his White House Fellows tenure would serve him well when he was tapped to be the president of Colby College in 1979. Colby is a small private liberal arts college in Waterville, Maine, part of a group of elite institutions sometimes referred to as the Little Ivies. However, in spite of its distinguished history and rural charm, there was a major problem on the Colby campus: The fraternities were out of control; in fact, before Cotter arrived, there had been an incident in which drunken fraternity members had thrown furniture, including a piano, out of a frat house on Fraternity Row. There was a fire, and when the fire department came to extinguish it, students disconnected the hoses. Unfortunately, that was not an isolated incident; there were continuous problems. Female students admitted that they were afraid to walk through Fraternity Row because of the verbal—and occasionally physical—abuse they suffered there.

"The faculty was just outraged about this, and many members of the board were outraged too," Cotter explained. "So this was a hot issue that spring before I arrived at Colby, and when I was asked for my opinion of fraternities at an open forum when I first arrived on campus, my answer was, 'Well, I don't know anything about fraternities. I went to a college that didn't have fraternities, and so I need to learn a lot about it before I'd be able to answer your question.'" Cotter swiftly devised a process to determine what to do about the fraternity and sorority system, and for the next two years he carried it out. "The fraternity and sorority system had existed since the 1840s at Colby. Now we had major complaints about sexism, the abuse of alcohol, the low grade-point averages, and the financial and the physical conditions of the houses," Cotter said. "Nobody had made out a series of collegewide expectations, so I said that before we do anything else, we've got to make our expectations clear and then see whether or not the fraternities can live up to what we think would be responsible behavior for members of our community. We worked for about nine months to develop a set of fraternity guidelines. They were approved by all of the chapters as well by the board of trustees and the alumni chapters, so everybody was onboard." After a reasonable amount of time, only a fraction of the fraternities were able to meet the standards, and so Cotter pressed forward, shepherding the stakeholders toward a resolution.

Cotter knew he had his work cut out for him in trying to resolve such an ingrained and controversial problem, but he remembered the lessons he had learned at the Commerce Department. He kept the lines of communication open. He listened to all sides and remembered to get information from everyone concerned, not just the high-level players. He asked the students to make recommendations to the trustees and gave everyone an opportunity to hear about all the alternatives. Finally the day came for the trustees to cast their votes for the best option for dealing with fraternities and sororities on campus, and the result was a testament to Cotter's leadership skill. When the secret ballots were counted, Colby College had voted unanimously to abolish fraternities and sororities at the school and create an entirely new residential life system. The aftermath was peaceful, and the institution moved forward with a renewed spirit of unity. Other colleges, including Amherst, Bowdoin, and Hamilton, soon followed Colby in abolishing fraternities and sororities from their campuses.

"Throughout this process, honest discussion—without turf protection—and complete communication with stakeholders was essential," Cotter said. "I would tell anyone facing the same challenge to be sure that when you start a new position—particularly if you are the CEO—you consult broadly with staff and constituents before making any sweeping changes. And once you have decided on a new initiative, be sure to spend enough time communicating the *reasons* for these changes. Use one-on-one meetings to the maximum extent possible so that those who disagree at least know they were listened to and have heard your side of the argument."

Whereas Cotter recommends one-on-one meetings to promote dialogue and foster an atmosphere of cooperation, George Heilmeier (WHF 70–71) believes in the power of town hall meetings. Heilmeier had been a special assistant to the secretary of defense during his year as a White House Fellow. He remained in government for several more years before returning to the private sector as senior vice president and chief technical officer for Texas Instruments. His next stop was Bellcore (now known as Telcordia Technologies) in 1991, where he served as CEO and faced one of his largest professional challenges.

"At Bellcore I inherited an organization that fought hard to retain its paternalistic, entitlement-oriented, and hierarchal culture," Heilmeier recalled. "While it was no longer possible in American industry, they wanted me to guarantee them job security and annual salary increases regardless of contribution. There was little personal responsibility or accountability. Setbacks were always someone else's fault." Heilmeier knew he would have to clear the air at Bellcore in a hurry; that toxic environment was no place to grow a successful business model. But how would he even begin to solve a problem that large? By thinking about it in a logical way.

During his time in Washington, Heilmeier developed what he calls his "catechism" for managing projects or implementing change. Whenever it was time to launch an initiative or institute a major change, Heilmeier would ask himself the following questions to help organize his thoughts toward the development of a workable plan:

- What are you trying to do? Articulate your objectives without using jargon.

- What is being done today, and what are the limitations of the current practice?

- What is new in your approach, and why do you think it will be successful?

- Who cares? If you're successful, what difference will it make?

- What are the risks and the payoffs?

- How much will it cost? How long will it take?

- What are the midterm and final "exams" to check for success?

At Bellcore, Heilmeier used this "preflight checklist" and then taught it to the people in the company who would be implementing the ensuing changes. Thus, he and his team arrived at a well-conceived plan to rewire

Bellcore for a successful future. Heilmeier also initiated a series of town hall meetings, conducting them twice each week so that everyone eventually would have a chance to meet the new CEO face to face, listen, and be heard. "I always met with my people in their place of work, not mine, no matter what the subject. There were no time limits on the length of the meetings and no cutoffs," Heilmeier said. "The meetings were over when there were no more questions on the topics of *their* choosing. You must listen to your people and get to know them. Anything less is a ticket to frustration and failure for everybody."

Since "frustration and failure" were not on Myron "Mike" Ullman's itinerary, getting to know the people was his first task when he reported for his White House Fellowship. Ullman (WHF 81–82) was the chief business officer at the University of Cincinnati when he was selected for a Fellowship. His assignment was to be an executive assistant to U.S. Trade Representative Ambassador William Brock III and U.S. Trade Representative David MacDonald.

"I didn't know much of anything about trade. I wasn't in commerce, I wasn't a lawyer," Ullman said. "But that assignment gave me an opportunity to use some of the skills I'd already developed at the university. I got extraordinary exposure to all of the other branches of government. Although it was a bit overwhelming at first, I really came to recognize that people are just people and they are just trying to do their jobs. I became less intimidated as I realized that my strengths were complementary to what they were doing in terms of ordering work and making sure that communication lines remained open. Three-quarters of the way through the year, one of my Fellow partners, Tom Shull, went back to West Point to teach, so I went over to the West Wing and was assistant to Chief of Staff Jim Baker and John F. W. Rogers in the Office of Management. So I got a different kind of exposure for the last three months, primarily in the area of management issues and system changes in the White House itself and some of the personnel issues that they were dealing with."

When Ullman completed his Fellowship, he decided to leave the academic world for the retail sector. For twenty years he served in a variety of high-level positions at some of the world's greatest retail companies, including stints as executive vice president of Federated Department Stores, managing director of Wharf Holdings Ltd., Chair and CEO of both R. H. Macy and Company and DFS Group Ltd., and *directeur general* of

Moet Hennessy Louis Vuitton. In every leadership position, Ullman strove to leave each company better than he found it.

His greatest challenge came in 2004 when he was selected to head one of the most enduring American retailers, J.C. Penney. The struggling company nearly had gone bankrupt, and it was up to Ullman to bring about the changes necessary for it to recover and prosper. "Penney's had a great legacy, but it had gotten to a point where the legacy wasn't strong enough to overcome reality. The company had been close to bankruptcy, and they had that turned around by the time I got there. But the legacy issue seemed more important than what had to happen for the next phase," Ullman explained. "The people who were already there were shocked that I didn't come in with a plan, but I knew they were better equipped to talk about the growth opportunities and stumbling blocks than I was. I also knew that we needed to focus on where we wanted to be in five years rather than five months. So we met and discussed those things and got them up on the board."

Ullman guided JCPenney through a process of creating a short, snappy vision statement with the goal of making sure that each of the company's 60,000 employees could understand it. "The vision we came up with is to be the preferred shopping choice for Middle America," he said. "It was very simple, but it said two things pretty clearly: 'Choice' meant we wanted to be number one in that category; and 'Middle America' meant very specifically the price points, the sensibility, and who we're dealing with in terms of diversity." He then helped the organization design a long-range plan with a four-pronged strategy for dealing with customers, merchandise, employees, and performance.

While he was helping establish a clear vision and a long-range plan, Ullman spent time exploring his surroundings and talking to the department heads to get a feel for the company culture. He recalled one conversation in particular that confirmed the need for change at his new company. "There were 1,600 people in the information systems department, and they all got exactly the same percentage raise and exactly the same percentage bonus," Ullman said. "So I asked the person running that department how he could possibly tell me that all 1,600 of those people performed at the same level, and he said they didn't, but he wanted them to think he was fair. I think many middle managers are like that: They think the fairest thing to do is treat everybody the same, and it turns out to be the least fair thing you can do. The people who are performing well above their peers are disadvantaged when they get treated the same as the average, and I would say maybe even more importantly, the people who are not doing well are not helped by being in a role in which they're not contributing as much as they should. They probably should be counseled into some other role or some other setting, but you basically dumb down the team by treating everyone the same. It doesn't mean that it should be based on favoritism. It should be based on what people understand as the yardstick. That's the kind of thing that needed to change if the company was going to have long-term success."

Ullman decided that the best way to change the company's culture was to start the process in smaller groups. He and his human resources director started teaching leadership principles to JCPenney's 500 upper-level managers, breaking them into groups of 30 and creating an atmosphere in which they could participate actively. He then took the same message on the road and presented it to the store managers. As a result, a new language was developed within the company that is understood by all the employees whether they work in a J.C. Penney shoe department in Juneau, Alaska, or in corporate headquarters in Plano, Texas.

The company has flourished under Ullman's skillful leadership. *Fortune* magazine named J.C. Penney one of America's Most Admired Companies in 2007. Despite a progressive neurological disease that probably would have overwhelmed the average person, Ullman has flourished too. In April 2008, the World Retail Congress named him Outstanding Leader of the Year. Being named the world's greatest retail leader doesn't seem to have fazed Ullman, though.

"I take what we're doing very seriously, but I don't take myself very seriously," Ullman said. "I just wanted to do something that made a difference and rebuild the JCPenney team so it will do better when I'm gone. That was my objective. As for this disease, everybody has some kind of adversity to deal with. I just happen to know mine. I've had less and less motor skill, but I'm still able to walk, though it's not pretty to watch. I just convinced myself early on after receiving the diagnosis that if I stayed busy and mentally active, I'd not only do better in terms of my career but also my health. Continuing to work has been healthier for me because I've got a new business family to watch over now, and I can be a mentor to some younger people. It's what they get done that will be the legacy."

Just as Mike Ullman has become an old hand at resuscitating troubled companies, so has Thomas Shull (WHF 81–82). Shull considers himself "an emergency room doctor" of sorts whose job is to stop the bleeding and guide distressed companies toward a complete and lasting recovery. Perhaps Shull was led to a career as a turnaround specialist after seeing his family suffer the loss of its fifty-year-old canning and lumber business, or perhaps it was the focus on problem solving and discipline he was exposed to at West Point and Harvard Business School. Or maybe it was the influence of his White House Fellows principal, Deputy Chief of Staff Dick Darman, who told Shull, "He who controls the process controls the outcome." Whatever the contributing factors may have been, Shull made the best use of all of them, beginning most notably during his Fellowship year when he was selected to help create the Vietnam Veterans Memorial in Washington, D.C.

Many in Washington wanted to steer clear of working on the memorial because there were controversies over nearly every aspect of it. Some, such as Texas billionaire Ross Perot and Senator John McCain, then a private citizen and a Vietnam veteran, were adamantly opposed to its construction and criticized the design as not being heroic or tasteful; others, including Virginia Senator John Warner, were fiercely determined to see it built in honor of the war's fallen heroes. The Memorial Fund had sponsored a national design competition, and an eight-member jury chose a solemn V-shaped black wall created by an unknown Yale architecture student named Maya Lin. Some veterans saw the design of the stark wall engraved with the names of fallen soldiers as an insult. Proponents said the memorial would present a fitting and elegant tribute to those killed in the Vietnam era. Chief of Staff James Baker assigned Shull to represent the White House in meetings with Perot, McCain, Senator Warner, and others, and Shull was instrumental in helping put together the compromise solutions that allowed the memorial to be built.

"No one at the White House wanted to take on the memorial because it was extremely controversial," Shull explained. "Ross Perot was opposed to the original design and did everything he could to try to derail it. Actually, many people were against the memorial, and it sometimes felt as if it were going to die of its own weight. But I shared the vision of the Vietnam Memorial Fund founders that it should move forward, and it did. We kept it afloat while all the necessary compromises were hammered out."

One of those compromises was the design and placement of a statue honoring those who survived the Vietnam War and also the inclusion of a flagpole. Shull discovered that the one who would have to approve the statue and flagpole was J. Carter Brown, Director of the U.S. National Gallery of Art and Chairman of the Fine Arts Commission. Shull had sat next to Brown during one of the White House Fellows' educational luncheons, and the two had enjoyed a nice chat. Shull called Brown to discuss the statue and the flagpole. By the time the conversation was over, Brown agreed with Shull that the two items would not detract from the overall aesthetics of the memorial. Shull asked Brown to put that in writing, and he did.

A few months later, on a Friday afternoon, as the groundbreaking was about to occur, Shull received a call from Jack Wheeler, chairman of the Vietnam Veterans Memorial Fund, asking for help in persuading the Department of Interior, specifically Secretary Watt, to approve the compromise design. He was the last holdout in the approval process. Shull called Bill Horn, a Watt deputy, and told him the White House wanted this done and Watt should approve it. Horn called Watt in Denver, where he was giving a speech, and obtained the green light. Shull then called Jack Fish, an area director of the National Park Service, to ask that the permit for the groundbreaking be issued. On Shull's promise that all approvals had been obtained, Fish agreed to do so. Bob Doubek from the Memorial Fund was waiting inside the Park Service offices to receive the signed permit. Hours later Horn called Shull to inform him that dozens of congressmen at the request of Ross Perot and others opposed to the design had called Watt to try to stop the permit from being issued.

Shull let Horn know that their only recourse would be to seek a cease and desist order from a judge that weekend because groundbreaking would begin on Monday, and it did. "It was a passion of mine to get it done, and I ended up involved in it until the day it was dedicated by President Reagan in 1984," Shull said. "I think the memorial was significant because it crossed a lot of boundaries. As I think back on my White House Fellowship, it's the one thing of which I am most proud."

Shull stayed on in Washington after his Fellowship concluded, serving as deputy executive secretary at the National Security Council and also as military assistant to Robert "Bud" McFarlane (WHF 71–72), President Reagan's assistant for national security affairs. In the mid-1980s, Shull struck out into the private sector and worked as head of strategic planning, recruiting, and organizational development at Sanger-Harris, then a division of Federated Department Stores. His next post was as a senior consultant at McKinsey & Company, where he helped clients in top management positions resolve strategic and organizational issues. In 1992 he became executive vice president of R.H. Macy and Company, launching and managing a turnaround program that created $2 billion in value in only two years and led to the company's successful emergence from bankruptcy. He also led the negotiations that resulted in Macy's merger with Federated Department Stores.

However, it was his role in reviving the iconic luxury retailer Barneys New York in the late 1990s that gained Shull the greatest accolades and cemented his position as one of the country's top turnaround specialists. Barneys, a fixture in New York City since 1923, had filed for Chapter 11 bankruptcy in 1996 and was teetering on the edge of extinction after experiencing a loss of $20 million for the year. Fred Pressman, the company's heart and soul and the son of founder Barney Pressman, had died recently. To make matters worse, the remaining members of the Pressman family were at odds with Barneys' Japanese partner company, Isetan. The bankruptcy and years of financial mismanagement had damaged the company's hip, upscale image. Although Barneys had become insular in regard to changes in the retail marketplace and slow to react to declining revenues, it was clear to Shull that parachuting in with a slash-and-burn cost-cutting strategy would break the spirit of the brand and be counterproductive.

"It's my belief that it's really important to understand the fundamentals of the business going in," Shull said, "and even though cost cutting and that sort of thing is certainly part of a turnaround, it's also really important— particularly in a business like Barneys, which is all about creativity and merchandising—to blend cost cutting and fiscal restraint with the creative aspects. Creativity and fiscal discipline go hand in hand; they're not mortal enemies."

To help Barneys salvage its reputation as a luxury retail destination for chic shoppers, Shull was determined to emerge from the turnaround with the company's strong creative team intact and bolstered. Since nobody knew the culture of Barneys better than did the members of its founding family, Shull recommended that former co-CEOs Gene and Robert Pressman stay on and assume vital roles as merchandising consultants. He encouraged Simon Doonan, Barneys' renowned creative director, to stay with the company too, and he promoted from within to fill other leading merchandising slots. He created generous incentive programs for loyal shoppers and saw to it that employees were trained to provide better customer service. Barneys' culture was retained, optimism was restored, and communication between the team members was enhanced. Next, Shull turned his attention to the store's grave fiscal challenges.

When Shull arrived at Barneys (having being named president and COO and then CEO the next year), the Pressmans and the partner company Isetan were embroiled in a major financial squabble. The Pressmans personally owed Isetan over $600 million, and there was a dispute about the ownership of several Barneys stores in the United States. The parties were at an impasse in trying to find a way to untangle the twisted mess so that everyone could come out a winner. Shull had a plan for reaching a compromise that would save Barneys, but he needed to persuade the Pressmans to give up the lion's share of their equity stake to make it happen. The decision-making process in Shull's contract was that if he could convince just one member of the Pressman family to go along with his idea, that decision would prevail. He did exactly that. The next step was to talk the Japanese company into signing on to the deal.

"The family had been unsuccessful in trying to figure out how to work with Isetan. What we did early on was fly to Japan and reach out to Isetan and treat them with respect. The family hadn't done some of those things," Shull said. "We proposed a debt restructuring transaction to Isetan which we thought was fair, although it was about fifty cents on the dollar of what they had invested. We gave them real estate in New York, Chicago, and Los Angeles as part of a transaction which was valued at about $280 million at that time, plus $25 million in cash, and the Pressmans gave up all but 1.5 percent of their equity stake." Isetan accepted the offer, and Barneys was saved. When Shull left the company just two years after taking the helm, Barneys posted an operating profit of over $18 million.

Shull's artful negotiation skills, which he fine-tuned as a White House Fellow working on the Vietnam Veterans Memorial, made it possible for Barneys not only to recover but to prosper. In the mid-2000s, Shull was responsible for salvaging another long-standing company, Wise Foods, using many of the same principles he applied at Barneys. He says the basics of negotiation are simple. "What I learned in Washington is it's very important to understand what the other side views as success and then try to bridge that gap. To bridge the gap you have to be willing to compromise," Shull explained. "I'm not talking about compromising *principle* but compromising in the best sense of the word. You do what it takes to have all parties feel that they walked away from the situation made whole or at least feeling successful in some way. I try to enter every negotiation with a clear understanding of the other person's perspective so my team and I can provide something of value to them. Turning a company around is really about teamwork. What I do as an outsider coming in is just to fill the leadership void and then work on building a solid team."

Bill Cotter, George Heilmeier, Mike Ullman, and Tom Shull know that a successful change agent must start by developing a clear understanding of the organization's past and present and then lead his or her team toward developing its own vision for the future. By bolstering the team and ridding its path of the obstacles to progress, a leader makes it possible for the team to move forward. As Abraham Maslow said, "You will either step forward into growth or you will step back into safety." The most successful change agent helps his or her team overcome the urge to retreat into the comfort zone and encourages its members to put one foot in front of the other in a steady and optimistic march toward a brighter future.

CHAPTER 23

LEADERS LEAD THROUGH EXPERIENCE AND COMPETENCE, NOT THROUGH TITLE OR POSITION

It takes only a quick glance at John De Luca's curriculum vitae to see why he was selected to be part of the inaugural class of White House Fellows in 1965. His record of scholarly achievements is extraordinary. At the time he applied for the Fellowship, De Luca held a bachelor's degree in political science from UCLA, where he also studied languages and literature. As a Harvard graduate fellow and a Ford fellow, he had earned a master's degree in Soviet studies from Harvard in addition to studying Arabic history, politics, and language. De Luca had lived in the Soviet Union for six months and toured many of that country's greatest cities. He had lived in Rome twice: once for a year as a Fulbright scholar studying Soviet-Arabic relations and a second time on a Scott Fellowship and an Italian Foreign Ministry grant to conduct doctoral research. He had earned a Ph.D. in international relations from UCLA, had become an assistant professor in international relations, and had lectured on U.S. foreign policy and world communism at San Francisco State College. However, when De Luca reported for duty as the White House Fellow assigned to work with National Security Advisor

McGeorge Bundy, the sterling credentials that had opened one prestigious door after another for the young man suddenly meant nothing. He was met with a stone wall: McGeorge Bundy did not want a White House Fellow in his office.

Bundy's attitude was understandable. It was a tumultuous period in Washington. The United States was at war in Vietnam, and in addition, Bundy and his staff at the National Security Council were dealing with a host of other security issues with the Soviet Union, the People's Republic of China, and other potential antagonists. The last thing Bundy needed was some kid hanging around the situation room. He had neither the time nor the inclination to baby-sit John De Luca.

"Bundy had a very legitimate argument. He made the case that it was one thing to have White House Fellows working in the budget or press offices or writing speeches. But none of those positions were as sensitive in terms of national security as this post they were trying to create for me," De Luca explained. "Bundy was an intellectual, a tough guy who had come out of the Kennedy years. He had to deal with Secretary of State Dean Rusk and Defense Secretary Robert McNamara, and they didn't want a guy like me underfoot. But Jack Valenti and Bill Moyers argued that if this White House Fellows program was to succeed, then right off the bat there should be no area off limits."

So Bundy relented, but only to a point. He told the Fellows program and its cheerleaders, Valenti and Moyers, that De Luca could work in his office on a trial basis. However, he would be given assignments—complex, demanding assignments—just like everybody else, and he would be allowed to stay only if he could pull his own weight and do the work. De Luca accepted the challenge without hesitation. He knew that he was being watched at all times, but he kept his head down and completed his assignments, which mostly dealt with the war in Vietnam. It wasn't long before De Luca's coworkers began to send more work his way as word spread around the office that the young White House Fellow could handle the difficult tasks they were assigning him. Eventually De Luca realized that he had passed muster, and he was included in practically everything at the National Security Council. "But it was under the strictest confidentiality," said De Luca. "I couldn't even tell the other Fellows what I was doing."

Bundy impressed on De Luca the importance of recognizing the unique and valuable roles of each member of the White House team. He counseled his White House Fellow never to elevate the function of the National Security Council at the expense of other departments, because he expected everyone on his staff to respect and uphold the roles played by all the department secretaries. "That was a big lesson for me right from the start," De Luca remarked. "Just because I was there at the White House and just because I could call a general and have something done didn't mean that I had a superior position. To be effective I would have to enlist others. I would have to become part of a network in which they would respect what I was saying on an independent basis rather than on a chain-of-command basis. That was very important. In fact, it forged for me the rest of my entire career."

The National Security Council offered a hands-on learning environment for De Luca, and one instance in particular tested his collaboration skills in a profound and meaningful way. In normal circumstances, the Vietnamese not only were able to grow enough rice to feed themselves but typically had enough left over for export. However, the war put a damper on the country's agriculture system, and the Vietnamese were running out of rice. "This loomed as a great crisis. Senior staff at the National Security Council was called upon to get rice to Vietnam," De Luca explained. "I was enlisted in the effort to use rice surpluses, which required U.S. Department of Agriculture cooperation, Defense Department merchant ship carriers, military protection of the ports, and sufficient trucking capabilities. Time was of the essence, and success was only accomplished through a collegial network that understood the gravity of the situation."

The lesson of building a collegial network was reinforced when Walt Rostow became national security advisor midway through De Luca's Fellowship. Like Bundy, Rostow was a holdover from the Kennedy White House, an eminent scholar who had written highly regarded books on economics and political theory. Rostow was a consensus builder and a diplomat. He would not tolerate staffers who threw their weight around. He encouraged his team to form personal ties with their counterparts around the world and also with the media. He dramatically expanded De Luca's role beyond Vietnam and allowed him to deal with issues connected to the Vatican, Europe, and Indonesia.

De Luca saw how foreign policy formulation flowed and how it passed through the National Security Council and touched all the other departments in the course of its development, along with how it took a coordinated effort to create, polish, and submit policy for the presidential imprint. It was a consensus-building process that put him in contact with people across the federal government spectrum, and it reinforced the lesson he had learned from Bundy: He would have to earn the right to lead.

"Leadership doesn't mean the occupation of a title. A title does not automatically confer power upon you. You have to earn it. And boy, I learned that from dealing with the people in the federal government," De Luca said. "Remember, we were at war, and I was put on the Vietnam coordinating committee, and you had to know your stuff, especially a guy like me, a White House Fellow. If I wanted to be effective, I had to get to know all the different departments and all the different people who would work with me. I was constantly on the go to find out what so and so was thinking or to go over to the State Department and spend some time there in meetings they were having. I learned to always bring something that they needed, always bring some way to help them expedite their roles. That was something I learned from Walt Rostow's personality and his style."

At the end of De Luca's Fellowship, he stayed on in Washington for a few more months to serve as Senator Frank Church's special assistant on international issues, and then he and his wife, Jo, returned to San Francisco with their baby daughter, Gina. At that time, the San Francisco mayor's race was in full swing and one of the candidates, a prominent antitrust attorney named Joe Alioto, asked De Luca to advise him on how to appeal to Russian-American voters. De Luca accepted the challenge. Alioto was elected, and in a surprise move he chose De Luca to be his deputy mayor, a new position Alioto created to help him run the city.

"And one of the very first things he wanted was to go to Washington to meet Lyndon Johnson, because we needed waivers for the city, and he wanted to meet Bundy, who was then head of the Ford Foundation, so we could get monies for our police," De Luca said. "It could only have been the invisible hand of destiny that would bring me to such a place as that, and so rapidly." The lesson De Luca had learned as a White House Fellow suddenly came back to him as he realized that on its own the title of deputy mayor of San Francisco probably would have been insufficient to get him into the White House and the Ford Foundation. However, because he had earned respect through his diligence and hard work in Washington, he and Mayor Alioto were granted access to Johnson and Bundy. Their requests were approved.

Running a city is always a challenge, but that was especially true of San Francisco in the late 1960s. A serial murderer nicknamed the Zodiac Killer was terrorizing area residents. Racial turmoil was prevalent. There was a simultaneous strike of the police and fire departments and a string of random killings known as the Zebra murders committed by a group of radical Black Muslims. Student protests were common, and there was citywide unrest when Dr. Martin Luther King, Jr., and Robert Kennedy were assassinated. The pressure was intense. De Luca often slept at city hall and was rarely home on weekends. To make matters worse, Alioto was embroiled in civil suits both as a plaintiff and as a defendant and was indicted by a federal grand jury on bribery charges stemming from his earlier work as an antitrust attorney. Responsibility for the day-to-day running of the city fell to De Luca. For nearly eight years he worked tirelessly at that post, not just putting out the proverbial fires that seemed to flare up daily but also moving the city forward.

"Our office and staff had to win public, media, and departmental support through the rational marshaling of facts and benefits in order to achieve several important victories during that time," De Luca explained. "The Market Street $22 million bond vote, approval of the Transamerica Building, the Embarcadero Financial Center, the Performing Arts Center, the route for Highway 280, and the list goes on and on—none of this could have gone forward had we not demonstrated sufficient management skills to keep the city safe in the midst of all the turmoil."

At the end of his term as deputy mayor, De Luca took his career in an entirely different direction when he accepted an offer to head the San Francisco–based Wine Institute, an organization that represents the interests of over 1,100 wineries and wine-related businesses at the state, federal, and international levels. The troubled institute was in desperate need of a strong and talented leader. Membership had dropped by half because of a conflict over dues. The organization's finances were a mess. If De Luca could not turn things around in a hurry, the Wine Institute would go bust. Again, he called on lessons learned during his White House Fellows years to rescue the failing organization.

"I remembered that authority did not automatically confer executive power and results," De Luca said. "I exercised a balanced collegial style and made a strong case for unity of purpose and effort." Under De Luca's thirty-year leadership, the Wine Institute—and the California wine industry—flourished. He was able to lure back nearly all those who had abandoned ship before his arrival, and it was at his insistence that research was conducted to look into the health benefits of wine consumption. He pushed for a code of advertising standards that prohibits the use of celebrities in advertising as a way to cut down on underage drinking. De Luca created an export office that greatly expanded American wine exports. When it gave De Luca its 2004 Lifetime Achievement Award, *Wine Enthusiast* called him "a quiet but effective ambassador for wine" and praised his ability to keep "a low profile, opting for the role of diplomatic insider."[42]

"I have not shied away from the responsibilities entrusted to me in the forty years since my White House Fellows experience, but the emphasis on creating a network of colleagues and leading through the commanding heights of expertise and not title of office has brought gratifying personal and professional rewards to me," De Luca said. "You are accepted based upon your own knowledge and your own ability to help rather than anything that emanates just from the office itself."

The ability to help undoubtedly was what caused Arthur "Gene" Dewey (WHF 68–69) to be propelled from his post as an assistant to a high-ranking military officer into a White House Fellowship at the U.S. Agency for International Development (USAID). A graduate of West Point and Princeton, Dewey already had done a tour in Vietnam and had completed Commander General Staff School before being sent to the Pentagon, where he ended up as an aide to four-star General Frank Besson, Jr. "General Besson was an extraordinary person. He was about fifteen years ahead of the rest of the Army," Dewey said. "It was such a privilege to work closely with someone like that because he just cut through the bureaucracy in a way which ultimately prepared me for the White House Fellows program. I think that's the key to getting things done in the government. You have to know how to get over or through or around the bureaucracy to get things done."

Dewey wanted to create a game plan for his Fellowship year, but without knowing what the job would entail, it was difficult to come up with a detailed plan. Instead, he decided to take a general approach and

---

[42] Steve Heimoff, "John De Luca, a Quiet but Effective Ambassador for Wine," *Wine Enthusiast*, December 15, 2004, p. 56.

be as operational as possible by always being on the lookout for a problem or set of problems to solve. Dewey's principal at USAID, Bill Gaud, was happy to give him a chance to solve a problem and sent him to Nigeria to find out how the agency's relief effort there was panning out. USAID was spending a great deal of money supporting those caught up in the Nigerian–Biafran war, and Gaud questioned whether all the supplies were getting through.

Dewey traveled to the war-torn region and found that the Nigerian Air Force was shooting down relief planes during the night airlifts, and so he hatched a plan to get food in by using a combination of sealift and riverboats. He returned to USAID with his news and his recommendation and promptly was sent to brief Clyde Ferguson, President Nixon's newly appointed special representative for Nigeria–Biafra at the State Department. "So I mentioned my idea to Ferguson when I briefed him, and he said, 'Listen, come and work with me for a couple of weeks. I'd like to launch this scheme,'" Dewey said. "It was called the Cross River Scheme at the time. When it floundered and came close to failing, it was known as the Dewey Scheme. It just got so intense that it was mutually decided with Gaud that I would stick with Ferguson at the State Department until the end of the Fellowship year."

With no previous experience coordinating large-scale relief efforts, Dewey set about the task of making the project safer and more efficient. One of the first entries on his to-do list was to determine how many Biafrans there actually were so that he could send in a sufficient amount of food and supplies each night. He learned about a man from the Centers for Disease Control who had a reputation for using statistics to come up with innovative ways of solving problems. He and Dewey created a formula that was based in part on the numbers of smallpox vaccinations that were administered in the region before the war. They came up with a figure of just over 3 million people, and that was the number Dewey used in planning and executing the relief effort. "That was a rather novel technique," Dewey said. "I'd never run into this approach before where you wheel out all the disciplines that you can imagine that might have some bearing on the problem."

As the efforts to bring relief to the people of Biafra continued, Dewey became more involved in the diplomacy required to set up a formal, enduring procedure—based on the Cross River Scheme—for getting food and other supplies to the Biafrans. The Nigerians agreed with the procedures Dewey and Ferguson proposed, but the Biafran leader, Governor Ojukwu, refused to accept it even though the plan clearly was designed to benefit his people. Ferguson gave up and returned to the United States, while a dejected Dewey departed for one of the bases used as a stop for the relief supplies. He collapsed on the beach, heartbroken for the people of Biafra.

The next day, Dewey was summoned to meet with a Catholic bishop on the island. He did not want to see the bishop, fearing that the man would side with the Biafran leader and waste everyone's time criticizing the American efforts to provide aid. Unfortunately, that was exactly what happened. The bishop reeled off a litany of complaints about how the United States was not doing enough to help the Biafrans and how everyone always sided with Nigeria. In despair, Dewey confronted the bishop with the truth: Ojukwu was the one holding up the agreement while the innocent people of Biafra paid the ultimate price for his stubbornness. Dewey explained the entire Cross River proposal to the bishop, whose attitude gradually began to soften. The conversation closed with the bishop promising that when Ojukwu came to confession later that week, he would have a talk with him and get him to change his mind.

"I remember thinking, 'So much for that. That will be the day when the bishop raises this issue with Ojukwu.' So I went back to Washington," Dewey said. "But incredibly, I received a call a couple of days later from the Biafran office in New York saying that General Ojukwu had accepted the Cross River proposal. That was quite an eye-opener for me because we had all these plans and formulas for how to persuade Ojukwu to accept the proposal, and it ended up taking something totally different to reach him."

At the conclusion of Dewey's Fellowship, he returned to the military, where he completed a second tour in Vietnam. At the end of that tour, he was recruited to be director of the White House Fellows program during the Nixon administration. He later was appointed Deputy Assistant Secretary of State for Refugee Programs by President Ronald Reagan. Dewey says that the greatest leadership lesson he learned from his White House Fellowship was the necessity of being prepared and becoming an expert. His title as a White House Fellow meant virtually nothing as he designed and tried to execute the Cross River plan in Nigeria. What counted was his expertise and his attitude. "I learned that you don't go into a job without preparation and the right mindset. You have to be able to put your mind to developing the strategy for reaching your objectives," Dewey said. "You can't be dependent upon a lot of advisors giving you a blueprint. You've got to be able to visualize and formulate that framework yourself and then inspire other people to join in, to embrace it and become enthusiastic about it."

For more than four decades, the White House Fellows program has given hundreds of young Americans the tools, experiences, and mentors necessary for them to become confident, well-prepared problems solvers and leaders. In return, the Fellows have brought Lyndon Johnson's and John Gardner's vision to life by using their leadership skills to make the world a better place. Full, zestful, and knowledgeable participation in a free society—that was Lyndon Johnson's dream, and creating the White House Fellows program was his way of making that dream a reality. The program was his gift to the young people of America, and the priceless value of that gift is not lost on any of us who were fortunate enough to have received it.

I think John De Luca spoke for all the former Fellows when he said, "That incredible year with the White House Fellows set in motion everything good that followed. For me, that year is still alive and ongoing, not some sort of ancient history that has ossified. It's like I never left the program. It's been a rolling, evergreen experience for me. I've been blessed by it. Yes, blessed is the right word."

PART III

BECOMING A WHITE HOUSE FELLOW

CHAPTER 24

BECOMING A FELLOW

*In founding the White House Fellows program, [President Johnson]
hoped to provide our nation's finest young men and women with an
opportunity to know and understand the responsibilities and the challenges of public service.*

—LADY BIRD JOHNSON

PLOTTING THE COURSE TO FELLOWSHIP

When designing the selection process for the White House Fellows program, Tom Carr and the Commission made sure the road to the White
House was not a cakewalk. A run-of-the-mill application and interview
process wouldn't do, and so they worked up a series of hazards designed to
intimidate and eliminate applicants. Carr, who had gained a profound
understanding of leadership models from his studies at The Citadel, his
combat tours in Korea, and his participation in high-level federal management internships, sought advice on how to select the best of the best
from experts at the Rhodes Scholarships, the College Entrance Examination Board, the U.S. Naval Academy, the Peace Corps, and Exxon, to name
a few. At University of North Carolina President Bill Friday's urging, Carr
became a member of the John and Mary R. Markle Foundation's selection
committee, where he discovered an effective technique for conducting the
final selection of Fellows. Through his association with the Markle Foundation, Carr said, "I learned that a weekend selection meeting enhanced by
the presence of the committee members' wives can be a powerful tool, so
we incorporated that idea into our own White House Fellows plan." That

old-fashioned approach to selecting the Fellows was certainly a function of the times and could be classified as quaint today. Although the commissioners' spouses no longer play an official role in the selection process, every year since the program's inception the final selection of the White House Fellows has been done during an intense three-day weekend retreat.

But first things first. The process of becoming a White House Fellow begins as most things related to government do—with filling out a form. However, this is no ordinary form. Tom Veblen (WHF 65–66) called the White House Fellows paperwork "the mother of all application forms" and said that simply looking at the packet told him that becoming a Fellow would be arduous.

"What, the commission wanted to know, had I been doing with my life? To paraphrase, they requested that I provide—completely and accurately—the particulars of my existence, including the exact time and address for every place I'd lived and the name, address, and telephone number of every individual who had influenced my life, or so it seemed," Veblen recalled. "They wanted details on my education and honors and my extracurricular activities. They required essays on the sources of my enthusiasms as well as the particulars of my hopes, dreams, and aspirations. Then, to smoke out the reality of all this, I was to give the name, title, address, and telephone number of five persons—no relatives, please—who would not only vouch for me but also write a letter and complete an exhaustive form detailing their views on my character, competence, and potential."

Despite the grueling application, Veblen, who at that time was a young corporate vice president of Cargill Inc., buckled down, filled out the form, and sent it in. He thought it might be fun to test President Johnson's claim that the White House Fellowship selection was a nonpartisan contest in light of the fact that he was a conservative Goldwater supporter.

Little did he know that he had played straight into LBJ's hands.

THE APPLICATION

The first step in applying for a White House Fellowship is to conduct a serious gut check. This is not an application for the fainthearted or for those with a short attention span. It contains an extensive series of questions and requirements designed to assess the applicant's level of achievement, leadership potential, and commitment to public service. It also lays the foundation for a thorough FBI background investigation and security clearance if one is accepted for a Fellowship. Completing the application package is an undertaking that requires great attention to detail, and so it's wise to start the application well before the February 1 deadline.

Although a sample application is included in the Appendix, the actual application, which becomes available each September, must be completed online at www.whitehouse.gov/fellows. It can also be downloaded at www.whitehouse.gov/fellows/about/pdf/ApplicationGuide.pdf. Detailed instructions are included for each of the three parts: the Administrative Data section, the Qualification Narratives, and the Letters of Recommendation. The instructions must be followed to the letter or the application will wind up on the reject pile of those who can't follow directions.

Although it's listed as the application's final section, the Letters of Recommendation are the smartest place to start, since success there hinges on the schedules and whims of other busy people. A minimum of three letters is required, but candidates may submit up to five. Among other things, references are asked to provide "candid and specific responses" regarding the applicant's strengths, weaknesses, creativity, integrity, writing and public speaking abilities, and leadership skills. References also are asked to imagine what they expect the applicant will be doing two decades from now. Obviously, the most compelling recommendation letters are those written by people familiar enough with the aspiring Fellow to answer the questions with authority, and so references should be solicited only from those who can provide well-rounded, in-depth commentary on a candidate's achievements across the spectrum. Recommendations from prominent individuals who seem to have only a shallow knowledge of the applicant won't do.

The second part of the application—the ten Qualification Narratives—starts off simply enough by asking for details about education, professional experience, and volunteer activities; this is tedious but not a mind bender. However, questions 6 through 10—the essay questions—can create some anxiety, especially for those for whom writing is a chore. Take question 8, for example. What other program requires its applicants to write a 500-word "Memorandum for the President" outlining and advocating a specific policy proposal? Indeed, many successful applicants do that frequently when they're Fellows. Take Betsy Roe (WHF 91–92), who during her year at the White House Office of Domestic Policy wrote fifteen one-page decision memorandums to President George H. W. Bush through her principal Roger Porter (WHF 74–75). Porter served his Fellowship year as executive secretary of President Ford's Economic Policy Board, writing hundreds of memorandums on agenda items for the daily cabinet-level meetings. Another question asks candidates to describe—in 300 words or less—their life's ambition! Clear and concise responses and essays free of spelling and grammatical errors are expected of all candidates who want to work as a White House Fellow at the highest levels of the executive branch.

Last but not least is the Administrative Data section. This is the standard nuts-and-bolts part of the packet, with spaces for name, address, citizenship, and date of birth. There are also questions about military service, misconduct, and criminal history as well as inquiries about federal debt and child support delinquency. This section is completed online, and the Qualification Narratives are uploaded immediately afterward. The Letters of Recommendation are mailed separately by their writers.

NARROWING THE FIELD: THE REGIONAL FINALS

Applications that meet the deadline are processed at the White House Fellows Office, where the staff ensures that the applicants meet the program's prerequisites, to which there are no exceptions: They must be U.S. citizens, not be civilian employees of the federal government, have earned at least an undergraduate degree, and be well established in their professions. There are no longer any age restrictions, but the program was designed to provide hands-on government experience to Fellows early in their careers, and the selection process generally adheres to that aim. Each complete application is read by at least three former Fellows, including at least one in the same professional field as the applicant. Those readers score each application, with high marks for those who hold the most promise on the basis of early professional achievement, demonstrated leadership, commitment to public service, and evidence of being able to work well with others. Approximately 120 regional finalists are chosen for further scrutiny. Those candidates are invited to an interview at one of ten regional panels held each March and April in cities across the nation. The regional panels are made up of distinguished citizens from each city, and to protect them from lobbying attempts, their names are kept confidential until the day the regional finalists arrive for their day and a half of interviews.

Regional finalists are expected to submit a narrative biography, a photograph, and the paperwork necessary to launch the FBI background investigation. Tom Carr recalled that in the program's early years, the background check was called a "full field investigation" and was carried out by experts from the Civil Service Commission (CSC), who visited or phoned dozens of each candidate's associates. The CSC prepared a report on each applicant that was hundreds of pages long, and it was Carr's job to summarize those reports one by one, distilling each into a brief memo that contained only the key points. The President's Commission would use that document as an aid in selecting the Fellows. After the program's first few years, the FBI took over responsibility for the background checks because many White House assignments require high-level security clearances. Candidates who have been named regional finalists should let those close to them know that they can expect a call or visit from a federal agent.

Levi Strauss CEO Robert D. Haas (WHF 68–69) wanted to keep his candidacy a secret until he knew whether he'd been accepted to the program, and so he didn't tell his business partners that he had applied. One afternoon while on a business trip, Haas received a frantic call from his panic-stricken partners. They had just been paid an unexpected visit by two FBI agents asking questions about Haas's character, associations, and activities. Exactly what, the partners demanded to know, had he done to warrant an inquiry by the FBI?

My background check for the White House Fellows program turned out to be much more than I bargained for. Because my late father had been the personal physician to Panamanian general and dictator Manuel Noriega, I was required to undergo a grueling four-hour polygraph examination. The FBI wanted to be absolutely certain that I was not a Panamanian operative trying to infiltrate the highest reaches of the American government. Of course, the test revealed that I was a loyal American whose sole motivation was to serve my country, not sabotage it. Nevertheless, the polygraph exam was a nerve-racking experience that I sincerely hoped was a once-in-a-lifetime event for me.

Regional finalists spend one and a half days being questioned by distinguished panelists, who review their applications with them to get a general feel for their grace under fire as well as their overall suitability for the White House Fellows program. Former program director Jocelyn White saw many Fellows come and go during her time at the helm from 2001 to

2005, and she knows exactly what kind of person the interviewers are seeking. "A good Fellow is 'low maintenance.' There's a lot to be said by that," White explained. "We're looking for people who are self-starters, who get along, who are not going to get in fights in their placement, who are mature enough to find their way and do well, who don't need their hand held every minute, and who aren't likely to be miserable for the wrong reasons."

In preparing for these interviews, regional finalists should develop a clear, coherent statement about why they should be selected to be a White House Fellow and both a thirty-second and a three-minute elevator pitch. Furthermore, they should be fully prepared to discuss not only their professions, achievements, and aspirations but also their understanding of and opinions about current national and world events. On the basis of the results of the regional interviews, the field will be narrowed to approximately thirty to thirty-four national finalists, whose names are announced in April.

AN INSIDE LOOK AT SELECTION WEEKEND: THE NATIONAL FINALS

Those selected as national finalists are flown in early June to the Washington, D.C., area for a three-day interview process called Selection Weekend even though it's sometimes held during the week. For many years this retreat was held at Airlie Center, a lush estate outside Washington, but since 1996 it has taken place in Annapolis, Maryland, where the finalists are subjected to two and a half days of highly competitive interviews conducted by the President's Commission on White House Fellowships. The commissioners divide into panels, with each panel conducting formal individual interviews of each finalist. The Commission members also hold informal discussions and group interviews with the candidates at scheduled coffee breaks, meals, and social hours during which the candidates are always on display and constantly being watched and judged. Tom Johnson, who served on the President's Commission and helped select several classes of Fellows, said, "This selection process is more intense than that for the White House itself."[43] The weekend culminates in an intense closed-door deliberation during which the commissioners select the coming year's White House Fellows.

---

[43] Richard L. Williams, "Highest, Hardest Achievement for 15 High Achievers," *Smithsonian*, August 1978, pp. 38–47.

As former Fellows and later as members of the President's Commission, Dana Mead (WHF 70–71) and Roger Porter (WHF 74–75) have experienced Selection Weekend on both sides of the interview table. Mead and Porter helped select Fellows for twenty-five and twenty-four years, respectively, and their distinguished service has helped sustain the program for decades. To begin the final selection process, Porter gives each finalist's application close to an hour of his undivided attention, during which he searches for evidence of the three characteristics he believes are essential to a successful Fellowship. "First is the ability to write and to think clearly. People who write clearly are generally also people who think clearly," Porter explained. "White House Fellows have a very high threshold that they need to clear, and I want to be sure that when they are put in a high-level assignment, they are going to be able to fulfill it. Second, I look for their capacity to work well with others. Do they have an abrasive personality or a collaborative personality? That's essential to know because most of the work that goes on at the top of organizations, whether it's governmental or nongovernmental, involves people working very collaboratively with others. Someone may be brilliant, but if they don't have the capacity to work well with others, then their ability to contribute will be greatly diminished. The final thing I look for is whether or not they have their ego under control. Are they focused on the success of the organization, or are they focused on more personal measures of success?"

Mead said that since he wanted to hit the ground running each June, he also began his assessment by studying every finalist's application carefully and making notes that he could use during the actual interview and deliberations. He took a dim view of candidates who submitted sloppy paperwork that contained misspelled words and those who failed to follow the instructions on the application, both of which indicated a lack of attention to detail. Candidates who oversold themselves on their applications also caught Mead's eye, and not in a good way. He also paid a "huge amount of attention" to the reference letters, which he felt disclosed more about the candidates than did their own essays, though he read those carefully too. From this preliminary paperwork exercise, Mead would begin to rank the candidates in order, with one colossal caveat: He knew he might be dead wrong. "I've always been mindful of the fact that you could get very surprised by meeting the individual and find that he or she wasn't like that application at all," he explained. "You always had to keep an open mind."

Once Mead actually met the candidate, he would try to imagine that person as a top-flight leader in his or her own field. "If this person is a fire-fighter," he said, "could he lead a big department? If he's a lawyer, could he be a Supreme Court nominee or the head of a huge white shoe law firm?" This was a helpful exercise for Mead because he believed that the most important consideration in selecting a White House Fellow was *competence*: the simple ability to do the work at the highest level of the executive branch of government. Aptitude was a primary concern for Mead because he and the other commissioners knew—and still know—that the program's continued existence hinges on the success of each individual Fellow. The commissioners, Mead said, are going to pick only people they know will succeed, because "your reception in a department or in a staff job at the White House is really only as good as the last Fellow that was in that job. That's an important consideration, and I weighted it heavily."

Next, Mead looked for candidates who displayed the psychological resiliency to handle high-level work. The questions he and other commissioners asked during the interviews were designed to find out just how far a candidate could be pushed before he or she went over the edge. During a Selection Weekend in the late 1970s, *Smithsonian* magazine writer Richard L. Williams was allowed to sit in on some interviews, and he recorded this exchange between an unnamed commissioner and a Fellowship finalist:

Q: What makes you angry?
A: Who says I'm angry? I'm not angry.

Q: What I'm trying to get at is, What makes you tick?
A: Well, I'm not ticking either. But I get what you mean. . . .

Q: Assume you're at work on the job. Your assignment, right now, is to draft a speech the President has to make before a Jewish group, defending the plane sales to the Arabs. How do you go about it?
A: Um. Well, I start by swallowing hard. And then. . . .[44]

---

[44] Richard L. Williams, "Highest, Hardest Achievement for 15 High Achievers," *Smithsonian* August 1978, pp. 38–47.

The goal with questioning like that, Mead said, is to smoke out candidates with fragile personalities and, conversely, to detect those with towering egos. Neither would be able to function effectively in a fast-paced office full of high-performing, aggressive bureaucrats. Demanding candidates who issued declarations such as "I wouldn't work for So and So if you paid me" or "Don't send me over to that idiot at the Department of Such and Such" instantly were counted as "knockouts" by Mead and the other commissioners. Whether the candidate was down for the count or a home run hitter, at the end of each interview Mead would ask himself this question: Is that someone I'd like to work with?

DELIBERATIONS

Once the last interviews are done and the candidates have departed, the commissioners meet for deliberations that according to Mead generally last five hours or more. "It can be a very exhausting process," Mead said. "It takes time, and people take it very seriously." Throughout Selection Weekend, the commissioners typically have shared their opinions and reservations about individual candidates, and that speeds the decision-making process. For example, if a commissioner has identified a perceived shortcoming in a candidate or has a gut feeling about a candidate one way or another, he or she will share that insight with another interviewer, who will use it as a springboard when he or she interviews the candidate later. Therefore, by the time deliberations roll around, it is unlikely that there is any key facet of a candidate that at least one commissioner has not explored. During their deliberations, the commissioners discuss whether each candidate fits the description of the ideal Fellow as described by White House Fellows Director Janet Eissenstat in a White House Fellows newsletter from July 2006:

> The Fellows who go on to make their mark in the world are focused and passionate about their work, yet they retain an intellectual curiosity about the broader world around them. They are flexible and responsive to challenges and change. These Fellows demonstrate a personal and professional maturity that manifests itself in the ability to have intelligent discussions marked by intellectual honesty and a deep respect for their fellow man. Importantly, they are also results-oriented and take responsibility seriously. They are humble and recognize that in order to be a truly successful leader, you must remain connected to your core values. No

matter how often positions and titles change, or how fiercely the pressures from the world encroach upon their personal lives, it is their ability to deal with ideas and issues with honesty, integrity and courage that matters most. The Fellows and prospective Fellows who embody these traits are truly worthy examples for all Americans to emulate and wonderful sources of inspiration for us all.

After considering all these factors, within a short time and frequently without much dispute, the commissioners usually are able to come together and pare down the original group of finalists to eight to ten new Fellows who are on virtually everyone's list. It's the remainder of the Fellowship slots that are the most challenging to fill. There are usually strong opinions—both pro and con—about the remaining candidates, and the commissioners spend considerable time debating and making their way toward a decision on each one; that helps explains the wide variation in the numbers of Fellows each year. The Commission recommends between eleven and nineteen new Fellows to the president each year, although the actual number within those parameters varies with the commission members' assessment of the quality of the pool in a specific year. The commissioners tend to stop deliberations once consensus (or near consensus) becomes difficult to achieve, the rationale being that if there's so much uncertainty about whether the remaining candidates would make good Fellows, that's too much doubt for comfort.

Three days after returning home from Selection Weekend, the finalists receive a phone call and e-mail with the news they've been waiting for: whether they are one of the eleven to nineteen new Fellows who will be spending the upcoming year in the nation's capital, rubbing elbows with America's leaders and power brokers in all sectors of the nation's life.

WELCOMING DIVERSITY

The White House Fellowship program is part of the federal government, and so it is an equal opportunity employer and selection cannot be influenced by race, color, creed, religion, sex, age, national origin, sexual orientation, or disability. In its early years, the program would accept only applicants between the ages of twenty-three and thirty-five, but that limit was abolished at the threat of an age discrimination lawsuit. When considering their final selections, Dana Mead said that the commissioners "never discussed how many African-American candidates we had, or how many women, or military personnel or lawyers we had, or what geography was represented. People may have been *thinking* about it, but we never explicitly discussed it. We just let that fall out, and we counted the bodies after the battle." Roger Porter concurred, saying, "It was something that happened. I was on the Commission with John Gardner, and he emphasized over and over again in our deliberations that there were no quotas for anything—males, females, regional, ethnic group—anything. We're looking for excellence, and there's plenty of excellence out there to find. I never took into consideration people's demographics, and inevitably, we ended up with a very diverse class." The overall makeup of the program's alumni clearly demonstrates that the Fellows are a fair reflection of the American population.

However, that was not the case the first year, when Lady Bird Johnson lamented the fact that not a single woman was selected. Indeed, at least one extremely capable young woman who applied that year was not chosen. By the time the first class of Fellows was selected, North Carolina native Mary Elizabeth Hanford had graduated from Duke University, done postgraduate work at Oxford, and earned a master's degree in education and a law degree from Harvard. Even though she didn't make the final cut—she was selected as an alternate—Tom Carr remembers Hanford well. He acknowledged that her regional panel "may have reflected a prevalent regional view of the role of women and their opportunities at that time. But probably there were no women the first year because I did a lousy job of getting the word out. I plead guilty, but I guarantee we worked our tails off to remedy the problem!"

Carr also notes that Mary Elizabeth Hanford—later known as Senator Elizabeth Dole—managed to have a stellar career in public service despite not being selected to be a White House Fellow. Dole joined President Ronald Reagan's cabinet as Secretary of Transportation, the first woman to hold that position. She then was sworn in by President George H. W. Bush as the nation's twentieth Secretary of Labor in January 1989. Dole left President Bush's cabinet in 1991 to become only the second woman since founder Clara Barton to serve as President of the American Red Cross, an organization larger than many Fortune 500 companies. In January 1999, she concluded her service at the Red Cross and sought the Republican presidential nomination. Despite not being selected in that first class of White House Fellows, Elizabeth Dole has had a remarkable public service career, winning 54 percent of the vote in November 2002 to serve the people of North Carolina in the United

States Senate, until she was recently defeated in the November 2008 elections. The next year Jane Cahill Pfeiffer (WHF 66–67) was selected as the first woman in the program, and in 1978 when NBC picked her as its chair of the board, the *Los Angeles Times* called her "perhaps the most powerful woman in America."

One person who did make it into the inaugural class was Ronald Lee (WHF 65–66), who was not only the first African-American Fellow but also the program's first military officer. Lee was from Springfield, Massachusetts, and had been nominated by Congressman Foster Furcolo for an appointment to the U.S. Military Academy. He graduated from West Point in 1954, the first African-American graduate from any of the New England states and only the twenty-fifth African-American graduate in the 152-year history of West Point. He earned a master's degree in business, spoke Vietnamese and French, and was an airborne ranger who served in combat as an operations advisor to the 9th Vietnamese Division.

His initial preference was to work as a special assistant to Secretary of Defense Robert McNamara, which he thought would be a boost to his military career. However, Lee recalled that "McNamara during our interview said, 'How would you react if I asked you to call in a three- or four-star general and chew him out?' and I said, 'I'd love it, but they wouldn't,' and McNamara said, 'The more important question is how far would your career advance after that occurred?' Well, obviously that would be the end of my military career. 'Exactly, and that is why the Defense Department is not the right place for you.'"

Tom Carr remembers that "Ron Lee was an incredibly promising young man, and when the Defense Department fell through, I sent him over to see President Johnson's chief of staff Jack Valenti to see what he could do." Ron Lee went to see Valenti, and after a few brief moments he told Lee to follow him right into the Oval Office. "President Johnson was very gracious and asked me who in his administration I'd like to work for, and I said Larry O'Brien," Lee recalled. "He asked me why I chose O'Brien, and I said it was because I felt that the Great Society legislation—the things that were going to make people in the United States more equal and bring the country together—was the most important thing that was going on." And then President Johnson said, 'That's exactly right, young fella; that's what I consider to be my legacy to the United States—the entire body of legislation that we're passing.'"

Larry O'Brien was an advisor to President Johnson and was also his special assistant for congressional relations. He was a powerful force in Democratic politics, and in the 1950s he had been the organizational genius behind John F. Kennedy's two successful U.S. Senate races in Massachusetts and then his 1960 national campaign for the presidency. In 1964, he ran Lyndon Johnson's winning campaign against Senator Barry Goldwater, a landslide victory. He is credited for being the architect of the Great Society legislation, and everyone in and around Washington—and many points beyond—was aware of his influence. Johnson had been planning to reward O'Brien with the position of Postmaster General. "President Johnson picked up the phone, pressed a button, and said 'Lar, get down here.'" O'Brien entered the room and saw Lee, and he immediately broke into a grin and said, "Hey, Ronnie! How are you doing?" The stunned president listened while Lee and O'Brien explained that they had known each other for twenty years, since the time O'Brien had worked as a congressional aide for Congressman Furcolo, who had appointed Lee to the U.S. Military Academy. "You got me, young feller," the president replied. "I like that." And thus began a friendship between a young new White House Fellow and the President of the United States.

Lee was assigned to work with O'Brien and accompanied him to his new position as U.S. Postmaster General, where Lee would be put in charge of reenergizing the U.S. Postal System and transforming it into a public corporation. He did such an exemplary job that O'Brien asked him to stay on at the end of his Fellowship year, but there was a hitch: Lee still had an obligation to the Army. When deciding whether Lee could accept the Fellowship, the general counsel for the Department of Defense had determined that he would have to pay the Army back two years for the privilege of spending one year in a Fellowship. "O'Brien said that if the commander-in-chief wanted me to stay, it could be worked out," Lee said. "The president said he wanted me to stay because this was not a good time to be bringing others up to speed on all of the things O'Brien and I had started at the Post Office Department, so he called the Secretary of Defense to find out why I should not be released."

The president was given a long list of reasons. As a West Point grad with ranger and counterinsurgency training and a person fluent in foreign languages including Vietnamese, Lee was simply too valuable an asset to the Army. At a time when doctors' tours were being extended and eighteen-year-olds were being drafted to fight in Vietnam, there was absolutely no way a volunteer officer could be released for political reasons. If he was released and the president's antagonists caught wind of it, it would be devastating to the White House and the Pentagon. However, the president was determined that Lee remain in his administration, and he instructed the Department of Defense to make it work.

"The result was that as of September 1, 1966, I became the commanding officer and all the troops of a one-person Army unit designated the U.S. Army Element: United States Post Office Department. I do not know all of the players at the White House, Postal Service, Pentagon, Civil Service Commission, White House Fellows hierarchy, and maybe even the Justice Department, who took part in that determination," Lee said. "The good news was that I was permitted to stay and work on the reorganization plans and start making significant changes. The bad news was that I was still a major in the Army, unbeknownst to everyone at the Postal Service, and drawing $11,000 per year in a $27,000 job. That was a lot of money in those days. The cabinet secretaries made only $35,000, and members of Congress $25,000. After one year in that job, I went to Larry and told him that I was so poor that I had to either start making the salary assigned to the position or return to the active Army. Larry appealed to the president, who called the Defense Department and requested my release. As required by Army regulations, an efficiency report had to be submitted. The Postmaster General of the United States was the rating officer and the president of the United States was the endorser, and I was released from the Army in June 1967, but with no retroactive pay differential!"

Lee later would become Assistant Postmaster General under President Richard Nixon and one of the highest-paid African Americans in government service. O'Brien later would become chairman of the Democratic National Committee and Commissioner of the National Basketball Association.

MILITARY FELLOWS: PROMOTING UNDERSTANDING

Although civilian federal government employees have always been prohibited from applying to the Fellows program, uniformed military applicants have been welcomed, and many won Fellowships in the program's first three years. In fact, some commissioners thought they won too many. At a President's Commission meeting in May 1968, the commissioners decided to prohibit applications from *all* government employees, effectively barring active-duty military personnel from competing for White House Fellowships in the coming year.

Charles R. "Chuck" Larson (WHF 68–69) said that as the Fellow assigned as naval aide to President Nixon, he worked to get military personnel accepted back into the program. "My rationale was that one of the great values of the program was the interaction between classmates with very diverse backgrounds," Larson explained. "Some of our class had never had any association with the military, and as a naval officer I learned to appreciate those who served in such areas as the Peace Corps and the Sierra Club. My Fellowship exposed me to things I never would have learned in the military. It broadened my horizon and influenced my thinking. The end result was that Nixon put the military back in after an absence of only one year. The military personnel that followed, like Colin Powell, would never have had the chance had the decision stood." Chuck did pretty well himself, rising to become a four-star admiral in the Navy. He served as Commander-in-Chief-of the U.S. Pacific Command and Superintendent of the U.S. Naval Academy.

However, servicemen and servicewomen were not the only ones who benefited from military inclusion in the White House Fellowships. Before becoming a Fellow, Mimi Ghez (WHF 00–01) directed a national grassroots campaign against domestic violence. When it came time to choose her assignment, she decided to do something totally unexpected and asked to be assigned to the Department of Defense. Ghez said she never had met a serviceman or servicewoman until the day of her regional fellowship interview, when another applicant—an Army special forces officer—defied her stereotypical view of soldiers when he revealed that he'd hung a picture of Helen Keller in his daughter's room so that she could be inspired by a true leader. "It was my first inkling that warriors come in all forms and that many of them want peace as much as I do," Ghez explained. "It surprised me like crazy."

During her Fellowship year at the Pentagon, the young peace activist visited a Marine Corps boot camp, flew in a B-52 bomber, and ducked below the sea's surface in a ballistic missile submarine. When she heard another member of her Fellowship class describe himself as "a soldier, a father, and a Christian," she was deeply moved. When her Fellowship ended, Ghez helped establish an advocacy group that supports the families of servicemen and servicewomen stationed in Iraq. "[My Fellowship] experiences gave me a whole new respect for people who serve, and I take those experiences with me," Ghez said.

CHAPTER 25

FELLOWS AT WORK

The White House Fellowship is clearly the best fellowship in America, and it's probably the best fellowship in the world. I don't think that's an exaggeration at all. I mean, think about what we did. We got to work at the highest levels of government for a year. We got to choose where we traveled and who we met with. We had lunch with the most important people in the country three times a week, and we could ask them anything we wanted. There's nothing like it in the world—nothing.

—Assistant Secretary of State
Daniel Sullivan (WHF 02–03)

JOB PLACEMENT

The reality of selection barely sets in before the newly minted Fellows are back on the hot seat again, this time for Placement Week in July. The Fellows spend Placement Week shuttling around Washington, D.C., for a series of interviews. They are jockeying for job assignments while the White House staff and cabinet officers, or "principals," are competing for their choice of Fellows.

In the days leading up to Placement Week, the Fellowship Office gives every principal who wants a White House Fellow a book containing each Fellow's full application packet, photograph, and biography. The principals are asked to indicate which Fellow or Fellows they'd most like to work with in the coming year. At the same time, the Fellows are asked for their work site preferences. On the basis of everyone's wishes, the Fellowship Office schedules six to eight interviews for each Fellow. These interviews are crucial not only to the success of the Fellowship year but also to the years beyond. Consider Doris Meissner (WHF 73–-74). Although she was not a lawyer, Meissner always had been interested in legal issues. When it came time to indicate where she'd like to work in her Fellowship year, she chose the Department of Justice under Attorney General Elliott Richardson. The White House Fellows office scheduled her interview and sent her to see Richardson on the appointed day.

"When I got to my interview with Elliott Richardson, he asked me why I wanted to come to the Justice Department since I wasn't a lawyer," Meissner recalled. "So I said what only a thirty-year-old would be bold enough to say. I looked him straight in the eye and said, 'Because justice is too important to be left to lawyers alone.' The minute I said that I saw this look come across his face that told me I was going to get that job, because he understood that answer and was intrigued by it and my brashness." Meissner was right: She got the job, focused her attention on immigration, and at the conclusion of her Fellowship year continued her work in Washington in a variety of agencies and departments until 1986, when she left to join the Carnegie Endowment. Meissner would return to Washington in 1993 when President Bill Clinton chose her to serve as Commissioner of the Immigration and Naturalization Service, a post she filled for seven years. "I trace an enormous amount back to the White House Fellows experience because that brought me into government at a level with a vantage point that is so unique. I never would have been in those places had it not been for the Fellowship in the first place," Meissner said. Most Fellows agree that the Fellowship placement interviews are among the most critical meetings of their lives.

After the interviews, the Program Director must do the federal government equivalent of what Diane Yu (WHF 86–87) calls "computer dating": matching a willing Fellow with a willing department, agency, or White House office. Then he or she announces each Fellow's new job assignment, which begins on September 1 and ends on August 31 of the next year. Fellows all earn a standard salary that coincides with federal pay grade GS-14, step 3. In 2008, that amount was $103,565. After receiving their job assignments, the exhausted Fellows return home and prepare for their move to Washington, D.C., and the start of what promises to be a remarkable year of learning and leadership.

NOW YOU'RE INVOLVED . . .

Howard Zucker (WHF 01–02) had graduated from George Washington University's School of Medicine at the ripe old age of twenty-two and gone on to earn his J.D. from Fordham and his Master of Laws from Columbia. He had been around the block a time or two by the time he was named a White House Fellow under President George W. Bush, but Zucker still was awed to find himself riding through the streets of Washington in a government car across from his new principal, Department of Health and Human Services Secretary Tommy Thompson, and he was pleased when Thompson struck up a conversation by asking what he would most like to get out of his Fellowship year.

"I want to get involved in health care policy and understand how it works," the eager young physician replied.

"How involved?" Thompson asked.

"Completely involved."

"Totally involved?

"Yes, totally, completely involved."

Thompson gathered up the tall stack of files piled beside him and plunked them down on Zucker's lap. "Summarize these by tomorrow morning," he said. "Now you're involved."

There are as many ways to craft a Fellowship year as there are Fellows. However, most Fellows, like Zucker, want to become entirely immersed in projects important to their principals. After the terrorist attacks on September 11, 2001, Thompson sent Zucker to work with Congress on the response to the anthrax crisis. "If I thought something was important, he would let me work on it," Zucker recalled. "He gave me complete freedom. Any meeting I wanted to sit in on, anything I wanted to do . . . it was just the most unbelievable experience."

WHERE IN THE WORLD IS MARSH CARTER?

Although most Fellows carry out the bulk of their duties at their desks in Washington, many have the chance to travel to meetings or events either with their principal or on behalf of him or her. One jet-setting Fellow was Marshall "Marsh" Carter (WHF 75–76). A Fellow at the U.S. Agency for International Development (USAID), Carter was part of a team that laid out an electronic surveillance system in the Sinai desert after a peace agreement between Israel and Egypt brokered by Henry Kissinger. Then, only a week after he returned to Washington from his desert mission, a massive earthquake struck Guatemala, killing 23,000 people and injuring 76,000. "This was an opportunity for my principal, Dan Parker, to demonstrate the value of U-2 photography in disaster relief, so he got permission from President Ford to have a U-2 photograph the whole country," Carter recalled. "I went out to California to Beale Air Force Base and brought 800 pounds of U-2 photography back to Washington, and then we got some more of these light tables and photo interpreters, and we went to Guatemala. The earthquake was so big that the central government didn't know the extent of it in the countryside. So that technique worked very well." Next, Carter was off to the western African nation of Mali for yet another project, this time to extend the application of technology to basic developmental problems, which was cutting-edge stuff in 1975.

SLEEPLESS IN URUGUAY

One Fellow whose work earned nearly as many frequent-flier miles as Carter's was Diane Yu (WHF 86–87), who called her work assignment under U.S. Trade Representative Clayton Yeutter a "unique, never-to-be-equaled experience." In only her third week on the job, Yu found herself on Air Force Three with the country's top multilateral trade experts, jetting to the largest successful trade round to date, the Uruguay Round of trade talks under the General Agreement on Tariffs and Trade, now known as the World Trade Organization.

Yu spent "a week characterized by tantrums and teamwork, 'deep throat' intrigue and side deals, confrontation and conflict, cold weather and sleepless nights." Her specific role there was one she invented and offered to do: serving as the note taker for all the one-on-one meetings— six or seven each day—that Secretary Yeutter, who headed the U.S. delegation, conducted with the trade ministers from other nations. Since he was the head of the U.S. delegation and the chief negotiator, it was important for other members of the American contingent to know what he was doing. The problem was that Yu couldn't take notes at the meetings for fear that it would inhibit frank dialogue. Instead, she had to memorize the conversations, including who said what. "It was the most challenging written assignment I'd ever had," Yu recalled. "When the meeting broke, I'd race to the computer, which I had only learned to use the week before, and furiously type up what I could remember from the meeting and then distribute the notes around to the entire delegation. In that way, the other U.S. negotiators were informed immediately of progress and any significant developments that had surfaced in Clayton's meetings." After the Uruguay trip, Yu also went on trade missions and attended meetings in Switzerland, France, and Canada during her Fellowship year.

PERSUASION IN PARIS
Another Fellow who kept his bags packed and his passport handy was Dr. Gilbert S. Omenn (WHF 73–74), who, through his assignment to the Atomic Energy Commission, played a major role in protecting the world from nuclear catastrophe. Omenn, a physician who recently served as president of the National Academy for the Advancement of Science (NAAS) and currently serves as a professor of internal medicine, human genetics, and public health at the University of Michigan, entered the AEC offices during the 1973 Arab oil embargo, in which the members of OPEC, as well as Egypt and Syria, suspended oil shipments to countries that were providing support to Israel during its conflict with Syria and Egypt. At the Atomic Energy Commission, Omenn coauthored a report that served as a foundation for U.S. energy policy and also participated in talks that promoted nuclear nonproliferation. The French government had announced that it would provide nuclear materials to Pakistan, and the AEC chairperson, Dixy Lee Ray, arranged talks in Washington between herself and the French energy minister. It was during those talks that the French official marveled at Ray's poodle, Jacques, and expressed his desire to get one for his daughter. Ray sent one of Jacques' puppies to the minister and then sent Omenn on a diplomatic mission to Paris to follow up and persuade France to withdraw its pledge of nuclear support to Pakistan. The minister was amenable, and the offer to Pakistan was rescinded.

FROM FELLOWSHIP TO SENATE CONFIRMATION
Because of his travel opportunities and access to high-ranking government officials—including the president—Daniel Sullivan (WHF 02–03) classified his Fellowship year as being "off the charts." Rather than serving as an assistant to a cabinet official or a White House staff member, Sullivan, who had graduated from Harvard and Georgetown universities and had served in the Marine Corps, was given a senior post on the National

Security Council staff, serving as director for international trade. His principal was National Security Advisor Condoleezza Rice, who went on to become Secretary of State in 2005. During Sullivan's Fellowship year, he traveled the world with U.S. Trade Representative Robert Zoellick, a wonderful mentor who never missed an opportunity to pass on a valuable leadership lesson. He also participated in meetings with President Bush, twice briefing the president on economic trade policy. He was asked to stay on in his position at the end of his Fellowship year. He did so for another two years until he was recalled to active duty by the Marines and sent to Iraq to work on the staff of General John Abizaid, Commander of the U.S. Central Command. Shortly after returning from his tour of duty in 2006, Sullivan was nominated by the president and confirmed by the Senate for his new position as assistant secretary of state for economic, energy, and business affairs.

"The White House Fellowship is clearly the best fellowship in America, and it's probably the best fellowship in the world," Sullivan said.

DINNER WITH A KING ON AIR FORCE ONE

Another Fellow whose travels led him to a one-of-a-kind experience is Frederick Benson (WHF 73–74). Benson, while assigned by White House Chief of Staff Alexander Haig to monitor energy policy activities during the waning months of the Nixon administration, was sent to hand-deliver important documents to the president in Key Biscayne, Florida. Benson ended up flying back to Washington on Air Force One with the president and his entourage, which included Nixon's Irish setter, King Timahoe. The president was in his private quarters, and the rest of the staff had gone back to the press section of the plane, leaving the dog and Benson, who was sitting in a front-row seat with a table over his lap, eating a steak dinner.

"I was feeding every other bite of my steak to King Timahoe, and we were having a good time when I felt someone's presence, and here was President Nixon standing over me with his arms folded, tapping his foot and smiling. And I couldn't stand up! I'm a military guy and I've got this table I couldn't get out from underneath, and I didn't know what to do—I was just sitting there. And he said to me, 'Are you enjoying your steak?' and the first thing I could think of to say was, 'Not half as much as your dog is,' and he just looked at me and rocked back and forth on his feet and turned around and went back in his private quarters without another word, and he never came back out for the duration of the trip. Later, the press guys told me that you don't speak to the president like that—it was too informal. That was a pretty heady day."

ALL THE COMFORTS OF HOME

The record for the most work-related travel in one Fellowship year probably belongs to Karen Galatz (WHF 85–86), who was assigned to work with Secretary of State George Shultz. Galatz traveled to thirty countries during ten trips abroad with Secretary Shultz and State Department staffers. Some of the trips were in preparation for the historic 1985 Geneva Summit between President Reagan and Soviet leader Mikhail Gorbachev, in which the two leaders began the dialogue that ultimately would lead to the end of the Cold War.

"The airplane was a combination of office and home. We would be gone for ten days, and there were fax machines and computers and typewriters and briefing books, and everybody was piled in together—journalists, the secretary's security detail and staff, and Mrs. Shultz," Galatz recalled. "It really was quite remarkable. We were in Europe over Easter, and when we got back on the plane, there were little Easter candies for everybody. We celebrated Mrs. Shultz's birthday with cake and song aboard the plane. We worked hard but also had fun. One time, I beat somebody in Trivial Pursuit because just as the plane was landing, I was asked a sports question about a golf course. I quickly claimed I had a partner, none other than the Secretary, who of course knew the name of the golf course. On these trips, you were sitting next to the experts in all aspects of international relations, and listening to them was a graduate-level course in diplomacy."

JUST ANOTHER DAY AT THE OFFICE

Some Fellows say it was the day-to-day workings of the federal government that left the biggest impression on them, and they got an insider's view of all the action with no jet-setting required. Every day, down every corridor in Washington, there is the potential for history to be made, and since 1965 there has been a Fellow nearby to witness it. Don Furtado (WHF 67–68) was working in the White House when Martin Luther King, Jr., was assassinated, and he watched troops setting up firing positions on the lawn below his office window as smoke rose over the city. He recalled the indelible image of a concerned President Johnson standing in shirtsleeves in a West Wing hallway, reading news reports of the unfolding crisis as they rolled off the clacking teletype machines. Furtado also was there the day the president shocked the country—including his own senior staff—with the abrupt announcement that he would not run for reelection.

At the end of his Fellowship year, Furtado left Washington with a new outlook on government and the people who serve. "I was sometimes surprised by the extent to which decisions were made by the president because it was simply the 'right thing' to do, sometimes despite substantial pressure to do otherwise," Furtado explained. "I came away from my year as a White House Fellow, plus two other forays into the federal government, with great respect for the integrity and abilities of many of the senior civil servants with whom I dealt, an opinion that obviously differs greatly from the typical public perception."

Another Fellow who witnessed—and even participated in—history in the making was Roger Porter (WHF 74–75). A former Rhodes Scholar, Porter was handpicked by Vice President Gerald Ford to serve as one of his assistants. The two had hit it off during their face-to-face interview—so much so, in fact, that Ford asked Porter to come to Washington early and start work before the Fellowship year began. Porter received permission from the White House Fellows director to work outside the normal parameters of the program, and a week later he was packed and ready to head to the nation's capital.

"I left Cambridge the morning of August 8 in my car loaded with my belongings to drive down to Washington. I was on the Massachusetts Turnpike when I heard the news that President Nixon was going to address the nation that night at nine o'clock. I always expected that he would announce his resignation," Porter said. "So I arrived that evening and watched the resignation speech on television, and the next morning I went to the White House. As I was going up the elevator into the old Executive Office Building, the elevator doors opened and there was Vice President Ford and a couple of Secret Service agents on their way to Ford's last meeting with President Nixon. He said, 'Oh, I see you finally made it.' I was sent to his offices, where I received my first assignment in government, which was to make myself useful."

Porter was proofreading a document for one of the vice president's staff members when a messenger arrived. "You must be the luckiest person I've ever met," the man told Porter. "Come with me." Moments later, Porter was ushered into a room where he was introduced to Donald Rumsfeld, Dick Cheney, William Scranton, Rogers Morton, and Jack Marsh: the transition team that would advise Gerald Ford as he assumed his new duties as president of the United States. "I was announced to them as their secretary," Porter recalled. "I spent my first sixteen days as a White House Fellow working with the transition team and preparing the report that would instruct President Ford on how to organize his White House."

After the transition, Porter served as executive secretary of the President's Economic Policy Board, a cabinet-level entity that met daily in the White House and once a week with the president. At the end of his Fellowship year, he accepted President Ford's request that he stay on for the duration of his term. Porter returned to the White House during the Reagan administration, serving almost five years in the Office of Policy Development. He later spent four years as assistant for economic and domestic policy for President George H. W. Bush.

A FLY ON PRESIDENT REAGAN'S WALL

One of my White House Fellows classmates, Jonathan George (WHF 88–89), is one of the most humble people I have ever known. A descendant of Quanah Parker, the last chief of the Quahadi Comanche Indian tribe, George preserves his rich Native American culture through strong ties with his family. His mother's job as a counselor for the Bureau of Indian Affairs required many moves during his childhood, and George attended sixteen public schools in ten states as a youngster. He is now a U.S. Air Force brigadier general and a Deputy Administrator for the National Nuclear Security Administration, and though his achievements might justify a bit of swagger, he evinces instead a calm, deeply professional, and modest demeanor. I was not surprised to learn that one of his greatest memories from our Fellowship year was of sitting quietly in the Oval Office—a fly on the wall—watching the nation's most powerful men sip scotch and discuss the news of the day.

George's principal, Agriculture Secretary Richard Lyng, was an old friend of President Reagan's, having served as the Director of Agriculture in California when Reagan was governor. On Fridays after their work was done at the state capitol, they often would drive over to a city called Hangtown outside

Sacramento to have a drink and talk about the issues. The tradition continued in Washington. Several times each month, Lyng and Reagan pals such as Commerce Secretary William Verity, Jr., Chief of Staff Ken Duberstein, and Treasury Secretary James Baker, among others, would get together in the early evening to watch the *MacNeil/Lehrer News Hour* together in the Oval Office. Secretary Lyng brought George along for a few of these gatherings, and although George did not participate, he felt honored to be there.

"After a hard day in the mines, they would sit together and see what was being reported on *MacNeil/Lehrer* and talk about it for almost two hours," George explained. "They were a like-minded, focused group of men who were comfortable with each other and had known each other for years. They talked about the issues. It wasn't a sarcastic thing. There wasn't any posturing going on or pretentious actions; it was just exactly what I thought the inner circles of the powerful in Washington would be like. I just sat in the back of the room and kept my mouth shut. I was humbled and grateful, and it wasn't lost on me what a rare opportunity that was."

SOME ENCHANTED EVENING

Another Fellow whose time in Washington was full of rare opportunities was Travis Matheson (WHF 07–08). The young state trooper not only rode mountain bikes with President Bush nearly every weekend during his Fellowship but also got to attend one of the grandest White House events of the year. His principal, Secretary of Transportation Mary Peters, invited him to escort her to a lavish state dinner honoring French president Nicolas Sarkozy. "I am sure much of the beauty and elegance of the event was lost on my lack of social sophistication, but I will say I was stunned by the way everything was presented," Matheson recalled. "Each table had a beautiful arrangement of brilliant pink, orange, and red roses in the center. The silver, china, and glassware were also beautiful with gold trim and images of the White House on the plates. And the service was amazing. It seemed like if you even glanced at your wine or water glass, it was instantly filled!" Secretary Peters went out of her way to ensure that Matheson felt included and at ease as she took him around to introduce him to First Lady Laura Bush, Vice President Dick Cheney, and other distinguished guests.

More than anything else, Matheson was thrilled by the warm welcome he received from the president. "President Bush remembered me from the bike rides," Matheson said. "He even remembered that I was a state trooper from Washington State and introduced me to President Sarkozy as such. I was very proud and honored."

After a dazzling meal and speeches by both presidents, the guests were treated to after-dinner entertainment: a "fireside chat" between General Washington and General Lafayette. The U.S. Army Chorus sang a stirring rendition of "The Battle Hymn of the Republic," and the U.S. Marine Band played waltzes in the Grand Foyer. At 10 p.m. the guests were escorted out of the White House through the West Wing, and Matheson's big night came to an end. "My 'chariot' dropped me off at the Metro station, and I was soon on my way home to my wife and kids as the best-dressed fellow on the Metro," Matheson said. "It was truly a magical evening."

AN ACTION-PACKED WEEK

When Reverend Dr. Suzan "Sujay" Johnson Cook (WHF 93–94) thinks back on her Fellowship year, she quickly recalls not one enchanted evening but one exhilarating *week* in particular. Cook is an ordained Baptist pastor, speaker, and author who in 1983 was the first African-American woman in the 200-year history of the American Baptist Churches USA to be elected a senior pastor. At the time of her Fellowship, she was pastor of the Mariners' Temple Baptist Church in Manhattan. Cook was assigned to work with Carol Rasco, President Clinton's chief domestic policy advisor.

"I'll never forget my third day on the job," she said. "The cabinet was meeting downstairs in the Roosevelt Room, and when President Clinton walked in, Carol introduced me to him. Then the president walked me over to meet the other cabinet members, including the new drug czar, Lee Brown, who had been the New York police commissioner. So the president said, 'Lee, this is our new White House Fellow.' And Lee said, 'Well this is my *pastor!*' He attended my church, so I already had a connection. It was phenomenal."

Cook obviously made a strong impression on the president, because before that first week was done he sent her on a very special mission: to attend the National Baptist Convention that was being held in New York. "Historically the convention does not have women at leadership levels. It's not a written rule, but it had never happened, so there was sort of a closed door policy. I was a colleague, but I was also a woman, so I had obviously not been invited," Cook said. "Well, President Clinton sent me to be the

White House representative to that convention. I would never have gotten in otherwise, and when I got there, they were like, 'Okay, President Clinton sent you. Would you like to make some remarks?' This was all in my first action-packed week."

In the final week of her Fellowship, Cook returned to the Roosevelt Room to sit in on her last cabinet meeting. At that meeting, former White House Fellow Henry Cisneros, who was serving as secretary of housing and urban development, made her an offer she couldn't refuse when he asked her to work for him as HUD's faith liaison. Cook accepted and over the next two years worked with HUD to develop its faith initiative. Then, in 1996, President Clinton appointed Cook to his advisory panel, the President's Initiative on Race. She has authored several popular inspirational books since that time.

HOW ABOUT HOT DOGS?

Although it's true that presidents are always looking for sharp Fellows like Dr. Cook to help further their political initiatives, at least one Fellow was singled out by a commander-in-chief in need of personal advice. Caro Luhrs (WHF 68–69) was the first physician ever selected for a White House Fellowship. When she learned that she was being assigned to the Department of Agriculture, she thought a terrible mistake must have been made because she didn't know the first thing about growing crops; she was from the city and had never set foot on a farm. However, it turned out to be the perfect placement for Luhrs, who quickly discovered that there was much more to the Department of Agriculture than corn and soybeans. It had all kinds of interesting things for a doctor to get involved with: it handled food programs, poultry and meat inspections, disease prevention, and much more.

Once she got her bearings, Luhrs dived in and quickly established herself as a go-to person in the department on issues of human health. In fact, she caught President Nixon's attention at a cabinet committee meeting in which the participants were discussing hunger and proper nutrition in the United States. It was March 17, 1969, and the room was full of experts, cabinet members, and staff, including Daniel Patrick Moynihan, who was serving as Nixon's counselor for urban affairs. Moynihan was sporting a verdant green tie and gigantic green boutonniere in honor of Saint Patrick. "It is a long time to remember back," Luhrs said. "If it had not been

St. Patrick's Day and if Pat Moynihan hadn't been dressed like a great, cheery leprechaun, I would not be so absolutely certain about the date." Luhrs recalled that as she entered the room, the president pointed out that she was the first woman in his presidency to participate in a meeting in the cabinet room. Throughout that discussion Luhrs was called on repeatedly for advice, so frequently, in fact, that she kept hoping there might be some other physician in the room with her name. She showed incredible grace under pressure, and her responses so impressed the president that on June 16, 1969, at an afternoon reception in the State Dining Room of the White House, he said:

> A few weeks ago we were considering, in the Cabinet Committee on Urban Affairs, the problem of hunger in America. It was a very big meeting. All of the members of the Committee were there and there were staff members and experts completely surrounding the members of the Committee and filling the room to its capacity.
>
> During the long discussion, which took about three hours, one of the major problems which had to be considered was the problem of nutrition, the problem of proper diet, to what extent that contributed to the general problem not only of the poor but of all Americans insofar as their health was concerned.
>
> I noted that participating in the conversation on several occasions, not simply voluntarily but because she was often called upon by the Secretary of Agriculture and the Secretary of Health, Education, and Welfare, was a woman who was sitting immediately back of the Secretary of Agriculture, a young woman, obviously very intelligent and obviously the one in that room who knew more about nutrition than all the people in government and all the others in the back. She was one of the White House Fellows, a graduate of the Harvard Medical School.
>
> And afterward I spoke to her and I found that in this particular area there is a need in the medical profession for far more emphasis than we presently have. So my perspective was broadened as a result of having her participate in that meeting. She made a contribution that might not have been made had not she been in Washington at that time serving in that year's program. That is an idea of what all of the Fellows can contribute in their various fields, not perhaps as dramatically as she did but certainly in every way.

Luhrs was flattered by the president's kind words. "He made a big fuss over me, which was very nice," she recalled. "And in a subsequent cabinet meeting I was sitting behind him, and everybody was talking about pesticides, and the next thing I know, he's reaching behind his chair and he's passing me a note. It said, 'I'm on a cholesterol diet. How about hot dogs?' He wanted to know if I thought it was okay for him to eat them because he knew I was looking into the proper amount of fat in hot dogs. So I had this little note from the president, and I thought, Jeepers, this is a long story and I don't have any paper with me, so afterwards I went up to President Nixon and answered his question with some nutritional advice on hot dogs, and I kept his note for posterity's sake."

Immediately after leaving her Fellowship at the Department of Agriculture, Luhrs was asked to serve on Pillsbury's board of directors, which was a major step not only for her but for women in general, because in the 1960s it was virtually unheard of for women to serve on major corporate boards in the United States. Luhrs also served on the boards of her alma mater, Swarthmore College, and the Uniformed Services University of the Health Sciences. "All these opportunities naturally led to other opportunities for me to contribute to society," Luhrs said. "As I look back, I give the White House Fellows program the credit for being the 'grandfather' of it all. For me, the program worked just as it was designed to work, and I am very grateful to have had that experience."

DOUBLE TROUBLE

It is not unusual for Fellows to get together regularly during their Fellowship year and talk about their victories large and small, commiserate about difficult assignments, or talk about what they might do if *they* ran the show in Washington. Classmates William Cotter and Harold Richman (WHF 65–66) were assigned to two different departments for their Fellowship year—Commerce and Labor, respectively—but they still spent time together comparing notes about their departments' strengths and in some cases their challenges.

After a few months, one startling thing became clear to them: If Labor and Commerce were merged into one department, the nation would be better served. A combined department would be more efficient and eliminate a lot of redundant red tape. "We wrote this little paper outlining our plan. Bill gave one to his principal, and I gave one to my principal, Labor Secretary Willard Wirtz," Richman said. "We timed it so that it was close to the end of our Fellowship so our whole year wouldn't be destroyed as a result of it. I was supposed to have lunch with Wirtz in his office, which was going to be an end-of-the-year lunch, and I didn't hear from him, so I went to see him. He had the paper in his hand and he threw it down on the table, and he said in this really aggravated voice, 'So you want to put an end to this department, do you?' I said yes, and I went over with him what the reasons were, and he just smiled and said it was a great idea. The fact that we got such support was amazing to me."

And so, on January 10, 1967, President Lyndon Johnson took the podium for his State of the Union Address, and in one section of his speech to the nation he declared:

> I have come tonight to propose that we establish a new department—a Department of Business and Labor.
>
> By combining the Department of Commerce with the Department of Labor and other related agencies, I think we can create a more economical, efficient, and streamlined instrument that will better serve a growing nation.
>
> This is our goal throughout the entire Federal Government. Every program will be thoroughly evaluated. Grant-in-aid programs will be improved and simplified as desired by many of our local administrators and our Governors.[45]

Soon afterward, President Johnson announced that he would not seek reelection. He became a lame duck, losing the political clout it would have taken to orchestrate such a massive overhaul, and the historic proposed merger was all but forgotten. Nonetheless, two former White House Fellows will always remember how close they came to turning a bright Fellowship idea into a lasting legacy.

CHECK YOUR EGO AT THE DOOR

Before becoming senior medical correspondent for CNN, Dr. Sanjay Gupta (WHF 97–98) was—and still is—a practicing neurosurgeon. Gupta's Fellowship assignment was as an assistant to First Lady Hillary Clinton, and he recalls that there was no room for ego in the Office of

---

[45] http://www.lbjlib.utexas.edu/johnson/archives.hom/speeches.hom/680117.asp.

the First Lady: If he was asked to make copies to speed the completion of a project, he did it. "There were days when I would simply just run faxes back and forth. There was no job too small," Gupta said. "But on the same day that you'd be running a fax from one office to the next, you'd get a call from the First Lady's office specifically to come sit down and talk to the First Lady about a project that she was working on. It might be an asthma initiative in an urban setting, or it might be domestic violence in South America, so you'd sit down and talk to her, and all of a sudden you become a person who is helping guide that office."

BUILDING A BETTER PENTAGON, ONE MEMO AT A TIME

Most Fellows, like Gupta, do a fine job on their Fellowships from day one, but occasionally even the most well-meaning Fellow misses the mark. That was the case for Alexander S. Friedman (WHF 98–99), a Clinton administration Fellow assigned to the Pentagon under Secretary of Defense William Cohen. Friedman, who went on to become the chief financial officer for the Bill & Melinda Gates Foundation, said his sincere attempt to "do something positive" during the early days of his assignment backfired badly.

"I interviewed all the [service] secretaries through the Joint Chiefs and tried to get at the things they thought were going right around the building. I wanted to find out how the Pentagon worked and what wasn't working," Friedman explained. "So I wrote this long memo after a couple of months of analysis about what I thought were some of the low points and some ways to improve the Pentagon. Well, you can imagine how *that* went over. The secretary was like, 'Keep this guy away from me—I don't want him sending me any memos.'"

Shortly after Friedman completed his deeply unappreciated memo, an imposing figure strode into his office. It was General Charles "Chuck" Krulak, commandant of the Marine Corps.

"I read your memo," Krulak growled.

"Oh," Friedman gulped. "Did you hate it too?"

Krulak shook his head. "I've been saying the same things for years. The difference is I've got four stars on my shoulder," he said. "You've got to know what you're talking about before you write these memos."

Friedman looked the general in the eye and declared, "I'm up for it, sir. What do I do?"

Krulak took the gutsy young upstart under his wing and turned what surely would have been a dismal year as the loneliest guy in the Pentagon into a whirlwind experience that Friedman will treasure forever.

One of the best perks of his year in Washington? "I became [Krulak's] banker, and we talk to this day," Friedman said. "The Fellowship was really a great experience, and I made a lifelong friend."

OVAL OFFICE KUDOS

In spite of a few clumsy but earnest mistakes like Friedman's, White House Fellows have contributed more than anyone imagined was possible. Their efforts have been lauded by every president they've served. For example, President Richard Nixon said of the program, "At the time it was developed . . . it was generally thought that those who would be selected as Fellows from around the country would have an opportunity to broaden their perspective . . . what we found is that the presence of the White House Fellows in the departments has broadened *our* perspective."[46]

Then there was this from President Ronald Reagan: "I'm the fifth president to preside over this program and like my predecessors I value it highly—as a vehicle for developing new leadership for the nation, as a source of fresh talent for the executive branch, and as a symbol of the kind of achievement we want to encourage and reward."[47]

At a White House ceremony celebrating the program's thirtieth anniversary, President Bill Clinton said, "The White House Fellows program is one of the few things in this intensely partisan town that we have managed to make truly bipartisan. It has thrived . . . and if I could turn it into a virus, I would put it into a shot and give it to everybody who is now working in Washington, D.C."[48] President Clinton also had high praise for the program at John Gardner's memorial service, where he said, "I have been the primary beneficiary for eight years of the White House Fellows Program. It has had an enormous impact on what we did and the way it was done."[49]

---

[46] http://www.presidency.ucsb.edu/ws/print.php?pid=2103.

[47] Fortieth Anniversary DVD on the White House Fellowship.

[48] http://www.clintonfoundation.org/legacy/062295-president-names-white-house-fellows .htm.

[49] President Bill Clinton, remarks at memorial service for John Gardner, April 2002.

Naturally, the first to sing the Fellows' praises was their founding father, Lyndon Baines Johnson, who declared at a White House ceremony in 1967 that "two years ago when we established the program, we thought that its main benefits would be educational, serving chiefly the Fellows themselves. Today we are not so sure who really gains the most, the Fellows or the government they serve."[50]

---

[50] Stephen P. Strickland, *The President's Commission on White House Fellows during the Administration of President Lyndon B. Johnson, November 1963—January 1969, Administrative History*, Volume 1, November 1, 1968.

CHAPTER 26

THE EDUCATION PROGRAM

I was surprised and thrilled to find that Washington is full of people who love what they do and who do it for the loftiest of reasons.
—WIRELESS GENERATION CEO AND COFOUNDER
LARRY BERGER (WHF 94–95)

EARNING A PH.D. IN LEADERSHIP

Throughout the Fellowship year, there are approximately seventy-five luncheon meetings, or seminars, at the White House Fellowship offices at 712 Jackson Place, NW, across the street from the White House. The meetings are with high-level leaders in both the public and the private sectors, including the President as well as members of the media, CEOs of Fortune 500 companies, and other influential people. These off-the-record meetings are designed to augment the Fellows' job experience by giving them an opportunity not only to listen but to engage in spirited, candid discussions with many of the nation's leading figures. Although the slate varies each year and has included current and former presidents, cabinet officers, bankers, generals and admirals, Supreme Court justices, artists, scholars, journalists, members of Congress, entrepreneurs, and leaders of all stripes, the meetings are always highly anticipated by the Fellows. They are the equivalent of a Ph.D. in leadership. Many Fellows confess that these meetings are among the most enjoyable and meaningful activities in the entire Fellowship year.

In a letter to friends and associates describing his Fellowship experience, Tom Veblen (WHF 65–66) told of the people he'd met in seminar sessions who "have gone out of their way to detail their jobs, their problems, and most helpful of all, their personal views on what makes government tick." Then Veblen began dropping a series of names that certainly must have impressed the folks back home. He wrote that he and his class recently had met and talked at length with President Johnson, the Surgeon General, the Chair of the Federal Communications Commission, the secretaries of Commerce and Labor, the head of the Peace Corps, the Mayor of Atlanta, and several more high-level leaders—and he had been a Fellow for only three months!

A CANDID CONVERSATION

Since the meetings are totally off the record to encourage free discussion, some Fellows take the opportunity to ask questions they'd never dream of raising in public. Out of curiosity, Walt Humann (WHF 66–67) asked a standard question of all the elected officials he met in sessions during his Fellowship year: Why are you a Democrat or a Republican? The standard answer usually had something to do with philosophical reasons or party-line virtues. "But when they were candid, and many surprisingly were candid, the answer was always the same—expediency," Humann said. "Governor Nelson Rockefeller said it best when he said, 'I ran as a Republican because I could never get a [expletive] nomination from the Democrats.' As a result, my leadership style has been to remain fiercely independent, work 'both sides of the aisle,' and thereby never have people withhold support for my projects because they think I might be using my leadership position to springboard into a political office."

MEETING THE PRESS

Julissa Marenco (WHF 07–08) was the general manager of Telemundo WZDC-25 in Washington, D.C., that area's leading Spanish-language station. Marenco managed a hefty staff and a multi-million-dollar budget at WZDC-25, but she's a broadcast journalist first and foremost. Therefore, when she learned that her class would be attending a live broadcast of *Meet the Press* after which she would have a chance to meet her hero, show host and NBC News Washington Bureau Chief Tim Russert, she was blown away. "As a broadcaster, I have had a profound respect for Mr. Russert from afar for many years," Marenco said. "During the Fellowship selection process, I remember being asked which three individuals I would have dinner with if I could choose anyone. Tim Russert was at the top of my list." On Sunday, February 24, 2008, Marenco and her classmates entered the legendary *Meet the Press* set at WRC 4 Studio A in Washington, D.C., and watched Russert deftly question Ralph Nader about his role in the 2000 presidential election. For the second half of the show, Russert was joined for a roundtable discussion by a group of esteemed journalists that included Doris Kearns Goodwin (WHF 67–68).

"Immediately after the taping, Mr. Russert joined our class for a group picture by the famous *Meet the Press* backdrop," Marenco recalled. "He then came over to speak with us for a 'few moments.' Forty-five minutes later, he was still fielding our questions and you could visibly see his excitement as he described the never-ending primaries and his anticipation at the upcoming presidential elections." Marenco said Russert shared stories about his family, especially his father, 'Big Russ,' and his son, Luke. "Fatherhood was his greatest joy. He told us about the day Luke got a tattoo. He was furious until he found out it was a tribute to him and his father—their shared initials 'TJR.' When Luke explained that he always wanted his father and grandfather on his side, Mr. Russert's anger gave way to emotion and pride." Tragically, Marenco's class would be the final group of Fellows to join Russert on his set. Less than four months after hosting the White House Fellows with such warmth and generosity, Russert collapsed and suffered a fatal heart attack while recording voiceovers for an upcoming segment of *Meet the Press*.

OFF THE RECORD WITH THE PRESIDENT

Every class of Fellows meets with the sitting president as part of its education program. Some have that opportunity more than once. President George W. Bush met at least twice with each class during his tenure. Founding director Tom Carr estimated that during the Johnson administration, the Fellows met with the president up to five times each year as well as having meetings with the First Lady in the family quarters and lunch with the Vice President at his home. "The most striking sessions tended to be those in the evening with the president alone in the White House mess," Carr recalled. "These were usually held late in the evening, and they were long, featuring monologues and sometimes tortured accounts of the day's or week's activities. The comments were fueled by the Diet Dr. Pepper the president sipped as he agonized before his very sympathetic audience."

During those intimate meetings, the Fellows may ask the president anything they want, and they often are surprised at the candor of his responses. Since the Fellows respect the confidentiality of these meetings, we are not privy to exactly what is said there, but certainly the Fellows take away rare insight into the thoughts of our nation's chief executive. Many apply the lessons they learned there to their post-Fellowship lives.

Jack Valenti, who served as special assistant to President Johnson and functioned as his de facto chief of staff, was among the most loyal and enthusiastic supporters of the White House Fellows program until his death in 2007, and he thoroughly enjoyed watching the Fellows' reactions to President Johnson's arrival for a casual chat. "The door would come bursting open, and this six-foot-four figure, Lyndon Johnson, would descend on these astonished, unsuspecting White House Fellows. You can imagine—young people suddenly are sitting down at a table with the President of the United States! 'Exhilarating' is an inadequate word to fit the description."[51]

Westley "Wes" Moore (WHF 06–07) and his class experienced that exhilaration twice: They had two substantial meetings with President George W. Bush, who was a great supporter of the program. President Bush was alone when he met with the Fellows; unlike most presidents, he left all staff members outside the door. Moore said that when President Bush arrived to meet with his class, he entered the room with no introduction and sat down, putting his feet up on the table. He invited the Fellows to ask whatever questions they liked and made certain that each Fellow had at least one chance to speak with him directly. "The first real impression that you get from him is just how normal he really is. There are really no airs about him," Moore explained.

---

[51] Jack J. Valenti, White House Fellowship Fortieth Anniversary Gala Celebration, Washington, D.C., 2005. Valenti invited every class of Fellows while he was head of the Motion Picture of America Association to its private theater in Washington, D.C., to view a new film. Valenti's abiding support led the program to name a yearly award after him: the Jack Valenti Friend of the Fellows Award for a non-Fellow who has shown dedicated service and support for the program.

"One thing I found very interesting is that a lot of elected officials or people in appointed positions generally seem to like the softer questions more than the direct questions. President Bush was the opposite. He was much more comfortable with direct questions and gave very matter-of-fact answers. It was really more like a conversation. And no matter what your political persuasion is, no matter what people think about the policies or the person, it was an incredible feeling to be there. I'm the first member of my family to be born in this country—my grandfather was Jamaican, and my grandmother was Cuban—and I'm sitting in the Oval Office for two hours talking with the President. What an unbelievable feeling."

The President let them know about his admiration for the White House Fellows program and then gave them a hint about why he was happy to spend so much time with them: "We expect a lot out of you," he once told a group of Fellows during a meeting in the Oval Office. "We expect you to go back to your units, or your businesses, or your universities, or perhaps government agencies and lead, to set high standards, to set a good example, and to serve something greater than yourself. That's what the Fellows program is all about."

A FAMILY AFFAIR

The Fellows are not the only ones who benefit from the program's educational offerings. Many of them bring spouses to Washington, and founding director Tom Carr recalled that as he was designing the program, his wife, Haskell, expressed concern about the impact the program might have on the Fellows' families, particularly the spouses. "Haskell's fear was that the Fellows would spend long days surrounded by opportunities for achievement and personal growth, while the wives—they were all wives back then—sat at home and took care of kids," Carr explained. "She vowed not to let that happen. At the very beginning of the program we invited wives to as many education sessions as possible."

The spouses would tour agencies and meet with speakers at sites throughout the city, and occasionally the Fellows and their spouses would be invited to attend exclusive White House ceremonies, dinners, and parties. Those arrangements were made in large part with help from White House Social Secretary Bess Abell, whose job it was to decide which White House events Fellows could be invited to. "I remember once calling Bess, at the behest of the Fellows, to see if they could attend one more event they had gotten wind of," former director Steve Strickland said. "I apologized to Bess for asking, given that the Fellows had just been at the White House the previous week. 'Don't apologize for pushing, Steve,' Bess said. 'Don't forget, if there had been a White House Fellows program in Lyndon Johnson's early years, he would have been a Fellow, and he would have been the first in line asking the White House if the Fellows could come more often!' I hope all the Fellows from the first four classes know what a good friend and ally—what a good godmother—they had in Bess Abell."

The spouses of today's White House Fellows occasionally are invited to attend White House functions such as dinners, receptions, and parties, and they also are included in educational meetings now and then. However, their level of participation is not as intense as it was in the early days, perhaps because many spouses, now both wives *and* husbands, tend to have opportunities for enrichment through their own jobs, not to mention busy calendars!

FELLOWS AROUND THE WORLD

Another highly anticipated component of the Fellowship education program is travel, during which the Fellows see firsthand the impact of U.S. domestic and foreign policy at home and abroad. At the beginning of their year in Washington, the Fellows discuss where they would like to travel and what they hope to study at each destination, and the class then votes on which trips to suggest to the Director, who makes the final decision about where the class will go. Fellows have witnessed the fall of the Berlin Wall and studied the effects of nuclear policy in Pakistan and India. They've traveled to Botswana to learn about strategies to address AIDS/HIV, and they've studied border and customs issues on the ground in Miami. From the USSR to the Panama Canal to the Middle East to meet with both Israeli and Palestinian leaders, the Fellows have traversed the globe and returned home with an enriched sense of the common humanity of the world and the challenges that face its diverse peoples and governments.

When their trip to Russia was canceled because of President Carter's boycott of the 1980 Winter Olympic Games in Moscow, Marsha "Marty" Evans (WHF 79–80) and her class promptly recalibrated. It was shortly after the Camp David Accords, and so they scheduled a trip to Egypt and Israel. Upon their arrival in Cairo, the class asked to meet President Anwar

Sadat, and to their amazement, permission was granted, though only for a brief, cursory encounter.

"They prepped us for a photo opportunity, and we weren't supposed to talk to him. We were supposed to just be really nice, smile in the photo, and get on with it," Evans recalled. "But President Sadat decided he actually wanted to meet with us, and we spent two and a half hours sitting with him in his villa on the Nile discussing the Middle East peace process. One of my classmates asked him where he got the strength to go on each day when the problems are so huge, and he talked about how his strength came from his village and his heritage. It was one of the most moving soliloquies I had ever heard, and my takeaway was that even world leaders at the height of tense periods and extreme difficulty still have humanity. As a class, most of us have singled that out as one of the most amazing experiences of our lives." Evans's classmate, Mari Aponte (WHF 79–80) remembered that "President Sadat told us about a letter from President Carter on the importance of putting the peace process in motion. He said he thought about it and thought about it and finally wrote back, 'Dear Jimmy, Be Bold.'"

A BITTER CUP OF TEA

Although Evans and Aponte were buoyed by their policy study trip, one group of White House Fellows was haunted by theirs. While the world watched in horror as protesters were brutally beaten in Beijing's Tiananmen Square in 1989, that year's White House Fellows felt especially close to the drama. The intrepid class had just returned from a tour of Asia, including stops in China. In Shanghai they had shared tea and frank conversation with a quiet elderly dissident who, in spite of having been a political prisoner for years under Mao, still was protesting the communist regime's ongoing violations of human rights. As the editor of a rebel newspaper that had been banned and closed down repeatedly, the soft-spoken, courageous old man continued to defy the government, and his quiet bravery made a lasting impression on the Fellows.

"After we flew home, we were enthralled along with the rest of the world at the breathtaking courage of the Tiananmen protesters and saddened—but not surprised—by the ruthlessness of the crackdown," said John Shephard, Jr. (WHF 88–89). "We feared for the old dissident and wondered about his fate. We never found out what happened to him, but there's no doubt that even with all the economic success that China has achieved in the two decades since, there is still a long way to go on basic human rights for all China's citizens. I also have no doubt that the undying courage of unsung heroes like the old dissident, along with the unstoppable force of information technology, will ultimately bring it about."

FROM COLD WAR TO WARMER RELATIONS

Thanks to the Cold War and the ensuing sweeping changes in the Soviet Bloc, many classes chose the former Soviet Union as the focus of their policy study trip. Even though George Heilmeier (WHF 70–71) was a world away from his work assignment at the Pentagon, where his focus was on military affairs in the Soviet Union, his mind was always on his job. He remembers scanning the Russian skyline for antennas the entire time he was in Russia, taking note whenever he saw one. "I would do a 'back of the envelope' calculation to determine on what frequencies they were operating and ask myself if these sites might be places where they were doing special work. That was more or less my special interest, because I knew that when I went back, Secretary of Defense Mel Laird at his Monday morning meeting would say, 'George, I want you to tell us about what you saw when you went to the Soviet Union and what kind of discussions you had.' So I more or less tried to assimilate what I was seeing and hearing in a way that might be of interest to the folks in the Pentagon."

Former Secretary of State Colin Powell (WHF 72–73) wrote that being on the ground in Russia gave him a perspective he could not have obtained any other way. "I began to get a visceral feel for this country, one that comes from touching, feeling, and smelling a place rather than only hearing or reading about it. What I sensed was the common humanity of all people, including these Russians who were then supposed to be our mortal enemy. The people I met on the train, passed in Red Square, and rubbed elbows with at the GUM department store were not political ideologues. They were the Soviet equivalent of my own family—a mother buying groceries for supper, a tired father headed home after a hard day at the ministry mailroom, kids thinking more about the soccer prospects of Moscow against Kiev than about spreading Marxism globally."[52]

---

[52] Colin L. Powell with Joseph E. Persico, *My American Journey* (New York: Random House), p. 171.

PEELING BACK THE LAYERS IN AFRICA

After leaving his White House Fellowship, Henry Cisneros (WHF 71–72) went on to become the four-term Mayor of San Antonio, the first Hispanic-American mayor of a major U.S. city. He was appointed Secretary of the U.S. Department of Housing and Urban Development by President Clinton, the first Fellow to become a cabinet secretary. A class trip to Japan would set the stage for Cisneros to score a major coup for his city years later when, after nearly two decades of building on connections established in Japan as a White House Fellow, he and a group of dedicated local leaders persuaded Toyota to open a plant in San Antonio. Cisneros credits another policy study trip—this one to Africa—with giving him the understanding he needed to make San Antonio a stronger, more efficient place during his terms as mayor. In Africa, Cisneros saw for the first time how all the layers of societal infrastructure—agriculture, electricity, ports, water systems, roads, and more—come together. "It is too complex to see in a modern industrial society, but seeing it where the layers were pulled back as they were in Africa was the key for me. When I became mayor, that was the stuff of my work, and I ended up championing things that were not normal issues for a minority because I had had that experience in Africa."

Another of Cisneros's classmates was strongly impressed by that trip to Africa too. In one east African village, Deanell Tacha (WHF 71–72) and her classmates hiked past mud and grass huts where children played outside in the dust. Suddenly, a little girl with a dazzling smile reached out and handed Tacha a small clay doll she had made. "She gave it to me as proudly as any child would give a treasured gift," Tacha recalled. "I intended to take it home, but when I got back to my hotel that night, my preoccupation with Western sanitation drove me to wash the little doll in the sink before I packed it in my suitcase. Well, it was not clay at all—just dried mud. Horrified, I watched the little doll wash down the drain. I remember crying most of the night about my extraordinary self-preoccupation, mourning a lost connection caused by my silly worries. I wish I could find that little girl today. I can still see her face and still feel my desolation when her precious gift was lost forever down the drain. For me, it has been a symbolic reminder of the trivial things that divide us."

THE CLEAN PLATE CLUB

However, it was not all tears for Tacha during her class's international trips; her mischievous classmates made certain of that. In State Department briefings and at embassies throughout their travels, the Fellows were warned that in some countries you are expected to eat whatever you are served, for to refuse it would be an insult to the host. With those words still fresh in their ears, the Fellows attended a lavish formal dinner party in South Vietnam with some of the country's highest-ranking military and government officials. They were seated at tables of eight, with four Fellows and four Vietnamese officials at each table, and Tacha was the only woman at her table. "The first course arrived. It was a clear broth soup with what appeared to be a raw bird's head, beak and all, as the centerpiece of the soup. My memory is that even the eyeball of the little bird peered back at me. I looked at my soup, saw the bird's head, and began chatting animatedly with my Vietnamese neighbors. When I next looked back into my soup bowl, there were *four* bird's heads. Somehow my colleagues had managed to pass their bird's heads under the table and plunk them into my soup while I was talking! I do not think I ate my soup that night, but there was a lot of giggling going on around the table—so much for adapting to cultural norms!"

APPENDIX

INSTRUCTIONS
FOR QUESTIONS 1-10

The following questions should be answered in a single multi-page document, comprised of a new page or pages for each question. Your name and question number should appear in the upper right hand corner of each page. Do not include the questions with your answers. Even though you are answering ten questions, you will upload only one document.

1. PROFESSIONAL AND EDUCATIONAL COMBINED SUMMARY

On a separate sheet of paper, under the heading "Professional/Educational Summary", please provide a chronological listing of every position you have held, beginning with the most recent. Include dates, employers and/or schools attended. Account for all periods of unemployment. Please limit your response to one page; details can be furnished in response to later questions.

Example:

11/98 to present Senior VP, Acme, Inc.
9/96 to 11/98 Sales Director, Acme, Inc.
6/96 to 9/96 Unemployed/Job Search
8/94 to 6/96 MBA student, Big Univ.
6/94 to 8/94 Service Project in Peru
9/90 to 6/94 Student, Small College

2. EDUCATIONAL BACKGROUND

On a separate sheet of paper, type the heading "Educational Background" and include the following information:

1) Under the heading "School Attended" list all schools attended with degree or diploma earned, name of school, location, and dates attended.

2) Under the heading "Activities" list all of the major extracurricular activities in which you participated. Briefly explain each one and list the level of your participation, including any offices held, and the length of your membership. List major awards or recognitions received.

3. PROFESSIONAL EXPERIENCE

On a separate sheet of paper, type the heading "Professional Experience" and provide details about your employment history. Begin with your current position and account for all periods of employment and unemployment. Do not substitute a resume. You may use as many sheets of paper as required. Employer's contact information not necessary for jobs held over seven (7) years ago. Use the following as a guide:

Dates of employment
Exact job title
Employer
Employer's address and phone number
Nature of the business
Number of workers you supervised

For your current position, please provide a brief narrative description of the work you performed, not to exceed 200 words. You may also describe previous work accomplishments, but do not exceed 100 words for each description.

4. VOLUNTARY ACTIVITIES

On a separate sheet of paper, type the heading "Voluntary Activities" and list the major civic and social activities (not related to your job) in which you have participated. Use the following as a guide:

Name of organization
City and State
Purpose or objective of the organization
Size of organization
Your level of participation
Dates of your participation
Awards or recognition you received

5. PROFESSIONAL ACTIVITIES

On a separate sheet of paper, type the heading "Professional Activities" and list the major business and professional activities in which you have participated. Use the following as a guide:

Name of the organization
City and State
Purpose or objective of the organization
Size of organization
Your level of participation
Dates of your participation
Awards or recognitions you received

Figure 1. White House Fellowship Application.

6. MOST SIGNIFICANT PROFESSIONAL ACHIEVEMENT

On a separate sheet of paper, type the heading "Professional Achievement" and describe what you consider to be your most significant contribution within your professional field. Please limit your narrative to 200 words.

7. MOST SIGNIFICANT COMMUNITY SERVICE CONTRIBUTION

On a separate sheet of paper, type the heading "Community Service Contribution" and describe what you consider to be your most significant contribution to your community. Please limit your narrative to 200 words.

8. MEMORANDUM FOR THE PRESIDENT

On a separate sheet of paper, type the heading "Memorandum for the President" and write a memorandum for the President making a specific policy proposal. Explain why you think it is important, what issues it raises, and why you think the President should support your proposal. Please limit your memo to 500 words.

9. LIFETIME GOALS

On a separate sheet of paper, type the heading "Lifetime Goals" and describe your life's ambition, what you hope to accomplish or achieve, and what position you hope to attain. Please limit your narrative to 300 words.

10. WHY I WANT TO BE A WHITE HOUSE FELLOW

On a separate sheet of paper, type the heading "Why I Want to Be a White House Fellow" and describe your motivation for applying for this fellowship, what you consider to be your major strengths and qualifications for the program, and what benefits you feel are likely to result from your participation. Please limit your narrative to 300 words.

Figure 1. (*continued*)

LETTERS OF RECOMMENDATION

Please reproduce the Candidate Evaluation form that is part of this application and give it to a minimum of 3 and a maximum of 5 people who know you well. Recommenders should have a direct knowledge of your qualifications and character. At least one of your recommenders should have professional competence in your field, at least one should have knowledge of your major community or civic activities, at least one should have knowledge of your business or professional accomplishments, and at least one should be your current supervisor, if applicable.

Letters of recommendation must be submitted by mail. Use of an express mail service is strongly urged. Each recommender should seal the letter in an envelope, sign his or her name across the seal, and mail it to:

THE PRESIDENT'S COMMISSION
ON WHITE HOUSE FELLOWSHIPS
c/o Sheila Coates
1900 E Street, NW, Room B431
Washington, DC 20415
Phone for express mail: (202) 606-2575

Letters of recommendation must be postmarked by February 1, 2009 to be eligible for consideration

White House Fellowship Application
CANDIDATE EVALUATION

To: _____
INDIVIDUAL COMPLETING EVALUATION

From: The President's Commission on White House Fellowships

Subject:_____
APPLICANT'S NAME

Thank you for taking the time to write a recommendation for the White House Fellowship applicant named above. A letter incorporating candid and specific responses to the questions below will help the President's Commission select the next class of White House Fellows, 11 to 19 individuals from across the Nation who will come to Washington to work for one year as paid, full-time special assistants to Cabinet officers and senior White House officials.

Your letter must be submitted via mail. Full instructions for mailing the recommendation will be provided by the applicant. **The application deadline is February 1.**

1. How long and in what connection have you known the applicant?

2. What are the applicant's major strengths? Please relate an occasion in which these strengths were demonstrated.

3. What are the applicant's major weaknesses?

4. What impact has the applicant had within his/her professional field?

5. What impact has he/she had in the community, outside of the applicant's professional realm?

6. What has the candidate done that you consider creative?

7. How would you describe this candidate's writing ability?

8. How would you describe this candidate's intellectual ability?

9. How would you describe this candidate's public speaking ability?

10. How would you describe this candidate's personal integrity?

11. How would you describe this candidate's consensus building, negotiating and leadership skills?

12. What do you expect this candidate to be doing in 15 to 20 years?

Figure 2.   White House Fellowship Candidate Evaluation.

ACKNOWLEDGMENTS

My work life as an entrepreneur, investment banker, board member, and author can get downright chaotic sometimes. But no matter how far I've traveled or how crazy my day has been, there's one particular image I can conjure at will that always has a way of grounding me and bringing me back to what matters most to me. It's an image of my family—the people I love more than anything else in life. There's my beautiful wife Cristina who edited and improved my early drafts and supported me every step of the way. Her grace, wit, and wisdom never cease to delight and inspire me. For that, and so much more, this book is dedicated to her.

Then there are my four precious children—Olivia, Sterling, step-daughter Amparo, and my youngest, Paloma—who are the center of my universe and the reason I get up every morning. I am so proud to know each of these amazing young people, and I'm incredibly honored to be their Dad.

Special thanks to my mother, Marilyn McCarthy Garcia, whose commitment to education, not only to mine but also to the hundreds of other children she taught in her 22-year career as a seventh grade science teacher in the public schools, has inspired me to never stop learning and expanding my world view. Mom helped select the title for this book, and, along with her best friend, James "Spike" Lay, they cheered me on every step of the way, just as they always do. My gratitude for my mother is immeasurable, just as it is for my late father, Dr. Carlos A. Garcia, who served in the 1970s as the Republic of Panama's surgeon general. My father taught me what it means to serve others honorably and to be a true leader.

And although they too have been gone for many years, the images of my grandparents Estanislado and Virginia Garcia in Panama, and

"Dr. Mac" and Suzy McCarthy in Daytona Beach, Florida, will never fade from my memory. Neither will I ever abandon the exceptional set of values they passed on to me and my siblings—Ginger, Colleen, and Brian—whose steadfast support and encouragement makes them three of my greatest allies in life.

The newest additions to my family portrait are my in-laws in Quito, Ecuador—Dr. Alberto Avila, his wife Susi, Alberto's mother Laurita, and the rest of the Avila clan: Beto and Isabel, Dario and Fernanda, and Gaby, who have been as welcoming and supportive of me as if I were a natural-born member of the family.

I also want to acknowledge the debt to my close friends George Burden, Mark Hageman, Mike Ramos, and Robert Staples for their great counsel and constant encouragement.

By having all these incredible people in my life, I have been richly blessed.

I could not have completed this ambitious project without a first-rate team. Pamela Suarez worked on every aspect of the book, especially researching, fact-checking, and editing—she made every single page of this book better. My highly capable longtime assistant, Angela Murcia, conducted advance research and set up over two hundred interviews, ensuring that I had everything I needed to make the most of each one in the shortest time possible. She also made certain that all the interviewees filled out their written questionnaires in a timely manner. And Ginger Wilmot skillfully transcribed the audio files from the LBJ tapes and prepared transcripts of all those interviews, sometimes under incredibly tight deadlines. These three extraordinary women kept the project moving forward and did it with extraordinary patience, professionalism, and good humor.

I must also recognize one of my mentors, retired Major General Bernard Loeffke, a former White House Fellow who is currently serving as a medical missionary for the poor in troubled hotspots around the world such as Sudan, Afghanistan, and Somalia. Twenty years ago, "Burn" helped me prepare for the White House Fellows selection process, and it was he who encouraged me to write this book four years ago. He has had a big impact on my life, and he is a true American original.

Jack LeCuyer, Executive Director of the White House Fellows Foundation and Association (WHFFA), applied his outstanding fact-checking, editing, and proofreading skills to each chapter and was an invaluable resource to me as I brought all the elements of this book together. Diane Yu, former president of the WHFFA, is responsible for securing the project's initial approval, and went on to pave the way for all the interviews that would follow. She also encouraged me to think beyond the 35 high-profile people I had originally selected for inclusion in the project and to invite the entire alumni network to participate.

Also helpful in supporting the project was Myrna Blyth, recent chair of the President's Commission on White House Fellows and former publisher and managing director of the *Ladies' Home Journal* and *More Magazine*. Janet Eissenstat was the Director of the President's Commission on White House Fellowships during the time I was writing this book, and she provided a great deal of support and was kind enough to link me with recent Fellows who had interesting stories to tell. Other former directors who assisted me were Tom Carr, Stephen Strickland, Hudson Drake, David Miller, Arthur Dewey, Bernard Loeffke, Landis Jones, Marcy Head, Jackie Blumenthal, Jocelyn White, and Brooke Shearer.

Many people who were connected with the program in its early years offered priceless perspectives and support as I stitched together the history of the White House Fellows. Tom Johnson helped me gain extraordinary access to the LBJ Library and its collection of historic documents and tapes. Bill Moyers, David Rockefeller, Bill Friday, and former Secretary of Labor Willard Wirtz were more than charitable in sharing their unique insights into how the program came together and how it functioned early on. Because of their long tenures on the White House Fellows Commission, Dana Mead, Roger Porter, and Fred Benson offered a treasure trove of anecdotes and details about how the program's selection process has evolved over the years. And Doris Kearns Goodwin, whose White House Fellowship set the stage for her to become one of Lyndon Johnson's most trusted confidantes, took time from her busy schedule as a Pulitzer Prize–winning writer, historian, news analyst, and Boston Red Sox fan to generously share her one-of-a-kind perceptions of LBJ.

Several White House Fellows are recognized nationally for their scholarship on leadership, and their ideas have found their way into the pages you read. Tom Cronin is the author, coauthor, or editor of 12 books on American government and politics, and countless articles and scholarly papers on leadership. He is the McHugh Professor of American Institutions and Leadership at Colorado College and the President Emeritus of Whitman College (1993–2005). Earl Walker is a professor of management and leadership at The Citadel, and founding dean of the School of Business Administration. He retired as an Army colonel in 1993 after 26 years of service and 18 years of teaching leadership courses at the U.S. Military Academy at West Point. Earl has authored innumerable books, articles, and papers on leadership over his long career of action and reflection. I am deeply indebted to Tom and Earl for their help and guidance.

My friends Raymond Arroyo, Tom Carr, and Pablo Schneider each read the manuscript and provided helpful comments and editorial assistance. Many former White House Fellows also read and critiqued various drafts of the manuscript, and the book is infinitely better as a result. Many thanks to Karen Galatz, Nancy Kelley, Mitchell Reiss, John Shephard, Diane Yu, and Kinney Zalesne.

I want to express my deepest thanks to Ivy Latimer, a former executive of McGraw-Hill and a member of the PRIMER network of Latino business leaders, who introduced me to my publisher. To my editor, Knox Houston, and my attorney, Ken Browning, who both supported me with expert guidance and superb counsel throughout this process, I send my kindest regards and sincere thanks. And as always, I am eternally grateful for the support of my longtime business partner, Camilo Salomon, who is one of the smartest, hardest-working, and most honest men I know. Many thanks also to our new partners—Martin Cabrera, Robert Aguilar, and Robert Libertini—thank you for your belief in us.

I also want to acknowledge the encouragement I've received from all my close friends at PRIMER, The Executive Committee (TEC, now Vistage), and the Young Presidents Organization (YPO)—especially from my forum members—and from all the exceptional friends I've made through my service to the U.S. Air Force Academy, Aetna, and the board of directors of Winn Dixie Stores.

To all those who have offered to fan out across the country and help promote this book and its leadership lessons—Myrna Blyth, Carolyn Chin, Clay Christensen, Shelby Coffey, Cesar Conde, Bill Drummond, Jami Floyd, Doris Kearns Goodwin, Sanjay Gupta, Jeff Hall, Walt Humann, Tom Johnson, Matt Miller, James Muller, David Neuman, Roger Porter, Sharon Richie Melvan, Rick Stamberger, Susan Stautberg, Diane Yu, and Kinney Zalesne—I thank you for applying your energy and dedication to this project and to the continuity of the White House Fellows program. As usual, the White House Fellows network has proven to be a powerful force!

Of course, I thank all of the White House Fellows who participated in the project with such generosity and zeal. Engaging in a dialogue about leadership with these outstanding individuals was one of the most enlightening, entertaining, and moving experiences of my life. I deeply regret that I could only include stories from half of them in this book. It is my sincere desire to use the many remaining lessons in a future volume.

And finally, I want to thank God for filling my life with opportunities, challenges, and an abundance of love; and for giving me the gift of His grace so that I may face each new day with hope and a peaceful spirit.

INDEX

ABOUT THE AUTHOR

Charles P. Garcia is the bestselling author of *A Message from Garcia*. His personal story is as dynamic and inspiring as his books. Whether he's serving as a key advisor to some of the world's most important business, military, and political leaders, founding his own highly successful company, surfing a towering wave off the Hawaiian coast, or racing his Dodge Viper, he does it with a refreshing blend of gusto, style, and down-to-earth approachability.

Since graduating from the U.S. Air Force Academy and earning a master's degree in public administration from the University of Oklahoma as well as a law degree from Columbia Law School, Garcia has made a mark in business, government, the military, and education—and as a role model to the Hispanic community. In 1997, at the age of 36, he founded a global business that was ranked eighth on the *Inc 500* list of fastest-growing privately held companies in the country. *Hispanic Business* identified Garcia as one of the 100 most influential Hispanics in the United States, and Univision Television selected him for their series *Orgullo Hispano* (Hispanic Pride), which spotlights Hispanics who have made an exceptional impact on the culture and life of American society.

In 1988 at age 27, Garcia was selected as one of 14 White House Fellows that year. He later received two more presidential appointments: the first was to serve on a national education commission, and the next was to serve as chairman of the U.S. Air Force Academy Board of Visitors, which oversees all operations at the military academy. Additionally, the governor of Florida appointed him to serve as the only Hispanic member of the state's Board of Education. Garcia has worked in three presidential administrations and has advised a Cabinet secretary, a governor, and a former NATO Supreme Allied Commander on diverse issues ranging from education, drug interdiction, Latin American politics, counterinsurgency training, and more. A highly decorated military officer, Garcia was tapped to be the behind-the-desk military analyst for Telemundo during the Iraq War and has appeared as a commentator on *Crossfire*, Fox News, CNN, CBS, Univision, CNN en Español, and *The Cristina Show*.

Garcia has attended corporate governance courses at Harvard Business School, the Wharton School, Columbia Business School, and Northwestern University's Kellogg School of Management. He currently serves on two Fortune 500 company boards—the board of directors of the Winn Dixie Stores, Inc. and an advisory board of Aetna—and has become a highly sought-after speaker, presenting talks on leadership at Fortune 500 companies, professional associations, government agencies, and other organizations worldwide. By using anecdotes to illustrate character-building lessons learned throughout his lifetime—from his childhood growing up in Latin America to his thrilling years in Washington, D.C., working alongside the world's most respected leaders, to launching his own successful global firm from an empty broom closet—Garcia shares inspiring stories of leadership, public service, entrepreneurship, and family life that motivate and energize audiences in powerful ways. His deep sense of peace, his commitment to public service, and his infectious zest for life have inspired thousands of people around the world—his trademark takeaways can change your life or transform your organization.

For more information about him, go to www.charlespgarcia.com.

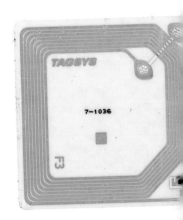